Understanding Government Contract Law

Understanding Government Contract Law

Terrence M. O'Connor

MANAGEMENTCONCEPTS

ƒƒƒ
MANAGEMENTCONCEPTS

8230 Leesburg Pike, Suite 800

Vienna, Virginia 22182

Phone: 703.790.9595

Fax: 703.790.1371

www.managementconcepts.com

Printed in the United States of America

Library of Congress Cataloging-in-Publication Data

O'Connor, Terrence M.

Understanding government contract law / Terrence M. O'Connor. -- 1st ed.

    p. cm.

 Includes index.

 ISBN-13: 978-1-56726-187-5

 ISBN-10: 1-56726-187-6

 1. Public contracts--United States. 2. Government purchasing--Law and legislation--United States. I. Title.

KF850.O26 2007

346.7302'9--dc22

                    2006035995

ABOUT THE AUTHOR

Terrence M. O'Connor has practiced government contract law for over 35 years. He graduated from Notre Dame Law School in 1970. He then studied urban and regional planning, receiving a master's degree in regional planning from the University of North Carolina at Chapel Hill in 1972. He began practicing law as a federal attorney at the National Capital Planning Commission in Washington, D.C., and later moved to the Appalachian Regional Commission.

After 15 years as a federal government attorney, he went into private practice, focusing on litigation and teaching. In 1991, he received a master of laws (government procurement law) degree from the George Washington University Law Center.

He has tried more than 70 criminal jury cases and more than 20 civil/non-jury administrative hearings, including government contract claims before the U.S. Court of Federal Claims and various Boards of Contract Appeals, including the ASBCA, GSBCA, DOTBCA, AGBCA, IBCA, and VABCA. He has also argued claim appeals before the U.S. Court of Appeals for the Federal Circuit. Mr. O'Connor has also litigated government contract protests before the Government Accountability Office (GAO) and the U.S. Federal District Court.

DEDICATIONS

This book is dedicated to those who have been wonderful influences in life:

To Carol, as always the love of my life

To Kathleen, Maura, and Tate, as always the loves of my life

To my mom, who has been the best coach I have ever known

To the guys at Notre Dame who made law school enjoyable:
Joe Leahy, John Plumb, Bob Greene, Mike Kelleher, Jim Kirker,
John Klein, Terry Hanratty, and Joe Theismann

To the lawyers who taught me the trade:
Bob McCloskey, Ray Gallagher, and the late Dan Shear; and

To the non-lawyers who have been such a big help with getting this
book published: Myra Strauss and Ben Nussbaum—and to Jack Knowles
who first broached the idea of this book and who continued to
encourage my work on it.

TABLE OF CONTENTS

PREFACE

As a lawyer trying to write a government contracts book for non-lawyers, I ran into the dilemma of having to decide which master to serve: the lawyers or the non-lawyers. I decided to go with the non-lawyers, since there are already a number of fine law books for government contract lawyers.

In focusing on the non-lawyers, my goal was to make the book as readable as possible. So, in writing this book I did some things lawyers would not do. For example, instead of putting legal citations in the text or at the bottom of the page, I made them endnotes in the hopes that the text would flow better. In the same vein, on several occasions I've taken literary liberty with direct quotations from legal decisions in the hopes of making the quotations more readable. For example, I have deleted legal citations within the quotations because they tend to slow down the reading of the quotation. And if the quotation I used had itself a quotation from another judge's opinion, I deleted the internal quotation marks, again to try to make the quotation more readable.

Part I

The Parties

How's this for an impossible job description:

> "Contracting officers are responsible for ensuring performance of all necessary actions for effective contracting, ensuring compliance with the terms of the contract, and safeguarding the interests of the United States in its contractual relationships."

In all the law dealing with contracting officers, this is the best summary of the contracting officer's job. It's at FAR 1.602-2. From this quote, it's clear that a contracting officer is supposed to be a protector of the government's interests—an advocate for the government in the same way lawyers are to be advocates solely for their clients.

But then this same FAR section goes on to throw the contracting officer a curve, or perhaps a U-turn. In "safeguarding the interests of the United States," the contracting officer, according to FAR 1.602-2(b), is supposed to:

> "Ensure that contractors receive impartial, fair, and equitable treatment."

So, a contracting officer is supposed to be a judge trying to treat a contractor fairly and reasonably. But whose side is the contracting officer on—on the government's, as a sheriff protecting the government's interests, or on neither the government's nor the contractor's, as a judge?

Unfortunately, FAR has no answer. Having created this tension between the contracting officer as a guardian of the interests of the government and the contracting officer as a judge, FAR does not say much about **how** the contracting officer is supposed to do this job. There is really no instruction manual for contracting officers describing how to do the job FAR gives them.

And if there is no instruction manual for one party to the government contract—the contracting officer—how can the other party—the contractor—anticipate what the contracting officer is supposed to do?

Part I starts by looking at all aspects of the contracting officer's job.

In Chapter 1, we look at the contracting officer as a judge. In this role, contracting officers must follow two basic rules: they must be fair and reasonable, and they must make decisions that are independent—made without pressure from their lawyers, their bosses, or their auditors.

In Chapter 2, we look at the other job the contracting officer has—safeguarding the interests of the government. We look at how a contracting officer protects the taxpayers and the U.S. Treasury.

In Chapter 3, we look at one of the downsides of the contracting officer's job—the contracting officer as defendant. An unfortunate and rare role a contracting officer might play is that of a defendant in a lawsuit by a contractor or by a member of the public injured during a contract.

In Chapter 4, we look at the flip side—the uncertain, evolving law regarding the contracting officer as a plaintiff. One part of this role is bounty hunting. Because members of the public can turn into whistle-blowers and share in any fraud recovery they lead the government to, perhaps a contracting officer can earn one of these lucrative recoveries as well. We also look at whether a contracting officer can sue members of the public for acts like defamation of character.

In Chapter 5, we look at the government contractor and the most common problems a contractor finds: making sure the government employee involved has authority to do the deal (because a deal made with unauthorized government employees typically ends in no contract with the government); avoiding promising to provide one set of personnel and then switching to another set after the contract has been won; and avoiding getting involved in fraud.

Chapter 1

The Contracting Officer as Judge

CONTENTS

A ccording to FAR 1.602-2(b), a contracting officer is supposed to

> "Ensure that contractors receive impartial, fair, and equitable treatment."

This FAR provision adds black robes to the contracting officer's wardrobe. It makes the contracting officer a judge. A judge's decisions should be fair and reasonable, and they should be reached independently—without bias or pressure from someone else.

So in this role, the contracting officer is not supposed to narrowly advocate for the government: he should not be driven by saving the government time or money or by making the process easier on the government. All decisions a contracting officer makes—those in the solicitation process and those in the contract administration process—have to be, first, fair and reasonable. So in the first section of this chapter, we look at what this vague phrase means in day-to-day procurement.

We look at the contracting officer's being fair and reasonable from three perspectives. First, we discuss general rules for how a contracting officer can be fair and reasonable. We next look specifically at what it means to be fair and reasonable in the solicitation process and, finally, in the contract administration process.

In addition to being fair and reasonable, a contracting officer should reach decisions independently. Just as judges should not be pressured into making decisions that are not truly their own, the decisions of a contracting officer should be his own opinions. So in the second section of this chapter, we look at what makes a contracting officer an independent decision-maker.

A "FAIR AND REASONABLE" JUDGE

The requirement in FAR 1.602-2(b) that a contracting officer must "ensure that contractors receive impartial, fair, and equitable treatment" is too vague to be of any real help in the day-to-day life of a contracting officer. So it's not surprising that there is little law on what this FAR provision means.

Fortunately, laws passed by Congress (statutes) and decisions handed down by courts (case law) give the contracting officer a lot more guidance. One federal law gives the Government Accountability Office (GAO) the right to review decisions a contracting officer makes in the solicitation process.[1] GAO's test of the contracting officer's actions is rationality or reasonableness. Good examples of what *fair and reasonable* means come from GAO decisions.

Other federal laws make courts the judge of whether a contracting officer's decision is reasonable.[2] In legalese, courts ask whether a contracting officer's decision was "arbitrary and capricious." So, good examples of what *fair and reasonable* means come from court decisions dealing with the "arbitrary and capricious" test. What does this almost-clichéd phrase "arbitrary and capricious" mean? It means that a contracting officer must use a reasonable way (process) to reach a reasonable decision (substance).

In determining whether a contracting officer's decision is arbitrary and capricious, precedent says that the contracting officer must consider "relevant data and provide a coherent and reasonable explanation of" the decision.[3]

But when you think about it, making a contracting officer act reasonably can be both a blessing and a curse. It's a blessing because it acknowledges that in procurement there is not **only one** decision that is the right decision. Courts use the phrase "zone of reasonableness" to show this.

For example, if you are buying a car to use in a carpool, buying an SUV, a minivan, or a six-passenger sedan would all be reasonable. It would be unreasonable to buy a sports car or a bus. If a contracting officer chose a six-passenger sedan for a carpool vehicle, a judge who herself would have chosen an SUV would have a hard time finding the contracting officer's decision unreasonable. So, because a contracting officer simply has to make a reasonable decision to be right, the test of reasonableness is a blessing.

In a sense, the reasonableness test makes judges leave their personal preferences at home. That's the way the founding fathers wanted it. Under the theory of separation of government power, Congress (the legislative branch of government) has told judges (the judicial branch) to let the procurement people (the executive branch) do their job. Courts generally defer to an executive branch decision, even if the particular judge might not agree with it and might prefer a different decision, as long as the contracting officer's decision is "reasonable."

> "If the court finds a reasonable basis for the agency's action, the court should stay its hand even though it might, as an original proposition, have reached a different conclusion as to the proper administration and application of the procurement regulations."[4]

So it's a blessing that a court won't force a contracting officer to follow a judge's personal belief. But "reasonable" is also a curse. First, it seems too vague to work with as a practical matter. Aren't we **all** reasonable? Or at least, aren't **we** reasonable? (It's the other person who isn't reasonable.) Isn't it hard for everybody to agree on what is reasonable and what is not? Second, people always have a reason for doing something, so isn't everything, therefore, automatically reasonable? It's at this point that the apparently redundant word *good* has to be added to *reason.*

But although there might be gray areas allowing reasonable people to disagree, some decisions are clearly unreasonable, whether the decision is made in the solicitation process or in the administration process.

Three Simple Rules for Always Being Fair and Reasonable

Decisions of courts, boards, and GAO show three good rules for reasonable decisions:

Rule 1: To be reasonable, the contracting officer's decision must be in writing.

One of the surest ways for a contracting officer to be found "unreasonable" is to make an important decision and have nothing in writing to explain it.

> "[GAO] is able to assess the reasonableness of an agency's source selection process only where adequate documentation of that process exists. Without such documentation, we cannot be certain that the agency action was not arbitrary."[5]

> The DLA sent out Requests for Quotations (RFQ) for sheet metal. The low bidder lost the best value award, protested, and won. There was no documentation showing that the contracting officer had performed any kind of analysis comparing the vendors with respect to which vendor was the best value.[6]

Without documentation, a contracting officer's decision is unreasonable.

Rule 2: To be reasonable, the contracting officer's written decision must show that the contracting officer actually thought about the decision instead of making a thought-less, knee-jerk decision.

One judge made this point nicely when he said, "Procurement officials must use judgment . . . ; they cannot act as 'automatons.'"[7]

> A construction contractor asked the government to allow it to substitute "in the public interest," as allowed by a contract clause, an item not in the specification. The contracting officer refused to even consider alternatives, insisting on the contractor's following the specification. A court concluded that the contracting officer's decision to reject the substitution without considering the alternatives the contractor had presented was arbitrary and capricious.[8]

Rule 3: To be reasonable, the contracting officer's written, thoughtful decision must follow the rules for making a decision.

FAR often gives good advice here. For example, a contracting officer's decision on who won a contract should follow the rules in FAR 15.308:

> "The source selection decision shall be documented, and the documentation shall include the rationale for any business judgments and tradeoffs made or relied on by the SSA [Source Selection Authority], including benefits associated with additional costs."

A contracting officer's documentation on a contract award has to compare the pros and cons of the offers.

The Department of Veterans Affairs issued a best value solicitation for prescription glasses. Classic scored 180 and Opti-Lite scored 170. The award memorandum that the contracting officer prepared concluded that Classic should get the contract because it had the highest combined total score. GAO sustained Opti-Lite's protest. The contracting officer's documentation had to include the rationale for any trade-offs made, including the benefits associated with additional costs. "It is improper to rely, as the agency did here, on a purely mathematical price/technical trade-off methodology. Because there was no qualitative assessment of the technical differences between the two proposals, the award was improper. Without this assessment, there was no way to determine whether Classic's technical superiority justified the cost premium involved."[9]

In addition to these general rules, there are specific rules for being reasonable in each of the two phases of government contracting—the contract solicitation phase and the contract administration phase.

Being Fair and Reasonable in Awarding a Contract

The contracting officer must carry out every step in the solicitation process reasonably. So from the start of the solicitation process (drafting the solicitation, getting it out on the street, receiving bids or offers, evaluating them) to the end of the solicitation process (choosing the winner and deciding whether the winner is responsible), the contracting officer must be fair and reasonable.

For example, if a losing vendor challenges the contracting officer's use of a firm fixed-price contract instead of a cost reimbursement contract, or the use of a negotiated procurement as opposed to a sealed bid process, the test of the contracting officer's choice is "how reasonable was that choice?"

Although the solicitation process has many steps, four steps bring the most vendor complaints. One is *competition*—was it full and open? The second is *discussions*—were the discussions the contracting officer had with those in the competitive range of a negotiated procurement "meaningful"? The third is *evaluation*—did the contracting officer or evaluation panel fairly evaluate proposals? The fourth is the *award*—did the contracting officer fairly pick the winning contractor?

We will look more closely at these four problem areas in the solicitation process. In doing so, we will look at the decisions of GAO and the courts to determine whether the contracting officer's decision was reasonable.

Competition

"Full and open competition" is the law, specifically, the Competition in Contracting Act (CICA).[10] This law is carefully monitored by GAO and the Court of Federal Claims (CFC), which review how a contracting officer carries out CICA.

One of the most common examples of competitions not being fair and reasonable is a sole source procurement. In such a procurement, the contracting officer concludes that only one source can provide what the government needs, so the contracting officer does not do full and open competition.

To be fair and reasonable, a contracting officer's sole-source justification must make sense and must have the proper paperwork behind it.

Bad documentation and bad logic can sink a contracting officer's sole source justification.

The Defense Supply Center Columbus (DSCC) announced that it intended to buy metal tubing on the sole-source basis from the original equipment manufacturer (OEM), Specialized Metals, because that company was the only responsible source for the tubing. But the user agency had trouble establishing exactly what the piping was used for. DSCC said the piping was used for "certifying welders" and for other purposes, but the user agency didn't know what those uses might be. There were also problems with the paperwork backing up the sole-source decision. The contracting officer used a justification and approval (J&A) form that was pre-printed, so all the contracting officer could do was to check various boxes. GAO said the contracting officer's documentation was unreasonable: the J&A was "inadequate consisting of only a check mark entered on statements on a pre-existing form. There is no explanation or justification to support the check mark entered. . . . DSCC is essentially accepting at face value the requiring activity's assertion that this particular product is the only one that will meet their needs. . . . there also appears to be unquestioning acceptance by DSCC, the requiring activities, or both, of the OEM's apparent insistence that its product is unique in ways that are essential to its function but cannot be revealed." GAO sustained the protest.[11]

Perhaps the most important part of the decision is the criticism that GAO had for the contracting officer in this case. GAO said there was no indication that the "contracting officer ever questioned why the item was needed or when information could be obtained from the OEM." As GAO put it not too subtly:

> "The DSCC is requiring absolute adherence to unknown parameters which may or may not be necessary to satisfy the government's actual need." It concluded that contracting officers "cannot take a docile approach and remain in the sole source situation when they could reasonably take steps to enhance competition. The agency cannot blindly rely on statements to justify a blanket rejection of any alternative part submitted without the OEM's technical data."[12]

A contracting officer can **significantly** limit competition, especially when human safety is involved.

When procurements for a unique agency requirement involve human safety, such as building security at the Pentagon, the government clearly has the right to set high security requirements, regardless of whether some, or even many vendors are excluded because they can't meet the high requirement.

The government needed security services at the Pentagon and other DOD facilities in the Washington, D.C., area. Its Request for Proposals (RFP) set security requirements and standards much more strenuous than those of the existing contract. These higher standards were required by the events of 9/11. One of the requirements was that the winning contractor would have to have an interim secret facility clearance **prior** to the closing date of the RFP. DoD was concerned about the lengthy process involved in getting clearances and the possibility that the potential winner of the contract would ultimately not get the clearance. Although these requirements were high, the agency still received 16 offers. A protest about how limited the contracting officer had made competition was denied. GAO held that an agency has broad discretion in deciding what its needs are. And the agency has even more discretion when human safety is involved. "Where a requirement relates to national defense or human safety, as here, an agency has the discretion to define solicitation requirements to achieve not just reasonable results, but the highest level of reliability and effectiveness. . . ."
Allied Protection Services Inc., B-297,825, March 23, 2006.

Fair Discussions, Meaningful Discussions

One of the more difficult, and protestable, jobs a contracting officer has in the solicitation process is making sure that the discussions with vendors in the competitive range are fair and reasonable. In other words, are these discussions "meaningful"?

In plain English, FAR says a contracting officer's job here has a "must," a "must not," and a "maybe."

FAR 15.306(d)(3) gives the legalese for the "must" and the "maybe."

> "At a minimum, the contracting officer must . . . indicate to, or discuss with, each offeror still being considered for award, deficiencies, significant weaknesses, and adverse past performance information to which the offeror has not yet had an opportunity to respond. The contracting officer also is encouraged to discuss other aspects of the offeror's proposal that could, in the opinion of the contracting officer, be altered or explained to enhance materially the proposal's potential for award. However, the contracting officer is not required to discuss every area where the proposal could be improved. The scope and extent of discussions are a matter of contracting officer judgment."

The "must." At a minimum, a contracting officer must discuss "deficiencies, significant weaknesses, and adverse past performance information to which the offeror has not yet had an opportunity to respond."

The "maybe." The contracting officer "is encouraged to discuss other aspects of the offeror's proposal that could, in the opinion of the contracting officer, be altered or explained to enhance materially the proposal's potential for award. However, the contracting officer is not required to discuss every area where the proposal could be improved. The scope and extent of discussions are a matter of contracting officer judgment."

The "must not." FAR 15.306(e) describes what a contracting officer can't do. A contracting officer must not, for example, favor one offeror over another, reveal "an offeror's technical solution, including unique technology, innovative and unique uses of commercial items, or any information that would compromise an offeror's intellectual property to another offeror;" or reveal "an offeror's price without that offeror's permission."

It's the "maybe" that gives a contracting officer the most problems. FAR gives contracting officers a lot of discretion or freedom in deciding how to carry out discussions with those in the competitive range. But this broad discretion is not unlimited. At some point, a contracting officer can abuse this discretion.

Good examples of a contracting officer's not having meaningful discussions with offerors come from GAO decisions. GAO sees "meaningful discussions" as being slightly different from the FAR requirement but certainly consistent with FAR's emphasis on fairness: discussions can't be misleading or inadequate:

> "It is a fundamental precept of negotiated procurements that discussions, when conducted, must be meaningful; that is, discussions may not mislead offerors and must identify deficiencies and significant weaknesses in each offeror's proposal that could reasonably be addressed in a manner to materially enhance the offeror's potential for receiving award."[13]

So, in GAO terms, misleading discussions or inadequate discussions violate the requirement that the contracting officer have "meaningful discussions" with offerors in the competitive range of a negotiated procurement. By conducting misleading or inadequate discussions, a contracting officer would be unreasonable.

Before looking more closely at what makes discussions misleading or inadequate, some general rules apply.

According to GAO, a contracting officer **is not required:**

- To advise an offeror of a minor weakness that is not considered significant, even where the weakness subsequently becomes a determinative factor in choosing between two closely ranked proposals.[14]
- To disclose deficiencies still remaining in the offeror's proposals or to conduct successive rounds of discussions until omissions are corrected.[15]

But a contracting officer **is required:**

- To tell an offeror that its proposal would have to be fundamentally altered to be acceptable.[16]
- To say more than simply that an offeror has to "review [proposed labor hours] and revise if necessary" when those hours were substantially less than the government estimate and to discuss disparity of prices from the undisclosed government estimate.[17]

Misleading discussions

GAO has described how a contracting officer can have misleading discussions:

> "An agency may not, through its questions or silence, lead an offeror into responding in a manner that fails to address the agency's actual concerns; may not misinform the offeror concerning a problem with its proposal; and may not misinform the offeror about the government's requirements."[18]

Here's a great description of what GAO considered misleading discussions:

> "The protester was encouraged to reduce its price during discussions and, after it did so, its price in its best and final offer was evaluated as so 'unrealistically low [as to] evidence a lack of understanding. . . .' In [this case] not only had the agency failed to inform the protester that its pricing was already viewed as unrealistically low, but the agency had advised the protester that its pricing was rather high and encouraged the firm to review its proposal for additional savings."[19]

Inadequate discussions

The second test of fair and reasonable discussions is how adequate the discussions were. A contracting officer has to "point out weaknesses that, unless corrected, would prevent an offeror from having a reasonable chance for award."[20]

Discussion of proposed personnel

When discussing personnel proposed by an offeror, the contracting officer need not discuss the experience, or lack thereof, of all proposed personnel as long as he gives the offeror a chance to discuss the experience of key personnel.

A Treasury Department solicitation for financial crimes investigative services made key personnel the second most important technical factor. The government asked Base Technologies, Inc., about only BTI's key personnel and not all personnel BTI had proposed. GAO denied the protest: "Here, even assuming that the agency did not reasonably apprise BTI during discussions that its proposal would be downgraded if the proposed personnel did not have law enforcement or extensive years of experience, this weakness related only to BTI's ability to achieve a maximum score under this subfactor, and did not prevent BTI from having a reasonable chance for award. Thus, discussions were not required to be conducted with BTI on this point."[21]

What would constitute inadequate discussions of personnel? Another GAO decision gives two examples:

"Instruction to offerors to 'review [proposed labor hours] and revise if necessary' did not constitute meaningful discussions of a deficiency that the proposed hours were substantially less than government estimate where the agency's evaluation and discussions did not provide for offerors to explain deviations from the undisclosed government estimate; . . . and it was unreasonable for an agency not to hold discussions on disparity between proposals and an undisclosed government estimate."[22]

Discussion of price

FAR gives a contracting officer more advice on how much the contracting officer can say during price discussions. According to FAR 13.306(e)(3), the contracting officer may tell one or all offerors how the government developed its own price estimate:

"The contracting officer may inform an offeror that its price is considered by the Government to be too high, or too low, and reveal the results of the analysis supporting that conclusion. It is also permissible, at the Government's discretion, to indicate to all offerors the cost or price that the Government's price analysis, market research, and other reviews have identified as reasonable."

GAO also says that the issue is not whether a price is too high but rather whether it is unreasonable:

"With regard to the adequacy of discussions of price, an agency generally does not have an obligation to tell an offeror that its price is high, relative to other offers, unless the government believes the price is unreasonable."[23]

One easy but unacceptable solution to this dilemma is to be vague, not precise—to tell an offeror with a high price a vague cliché like "sharpen your pencil." But at some point, a vague discussion of price becomes an inadequate discussion of price.

After Creative Information Technology, Inc., (CITI) submitted an initial offer of over $110 million, with the prices of other offerors ranging from a low of $15 million to a high of $167 million, all the agency told CITI was that its proposed price was "overstated . . . please review your revised price/cost proposal." CITI revised its offer down to approximately $89 million. The next highest price was $38 million, with the lowest being $10 million. The independent government cost estimate (IGCE) was $13,062,405.60. GAO said that "agencies must impart sufficient information to afford offerors a fair and reasonable opportunity to identify and correct deficiencies, excesses or mistakes in their proposals. . . . CITI could not be reasonably expected to have understood the true nature and magnitude of the agency's concern with its proposal based upon the information provided by the Army during its discussions with CITI, thus rendering those discussions essentially meaningless."[24]

Fair Evaluation of Proposals

"Fair and reasonable" is also the rule for evaluating proposals.

GAO spells out exactly how it decides whether the evaluation of a proposal by the contracting officer is fair and reasonable:

> "We will not reevaluate [proposals] but instead will examine the agency's evaluation to ensure that it was reasonable and consistent with the solicitation's stated evaluation factors and applicable statutes and regulations."[25]

Notice that this standard assumes that there **is** documentation. Such documentation is often called the *supporting record*. In a previous section, we discussed how the lack of documentation often shows that the contracting officer has not been fair and reasonable.

Notice also what GAO will **not** do during its review: reevaluate proposals. It will not reevaluate proposals because evaluating the proposal is the agency's job. Instead, it takes the agency's evaluation and asks three questions.

Question 1. Did the scoring system used by evaluators and the final evaluation itself pass "the laugh test?" Are both the process and the result of the process reasonable on their face?

Although a contracting officer generally has the right to decide how to evaluate the proposals of offerors, the evaluation must be "reasonable." An evaluation process that considers a contractor's past performance on irrelevant contracts is unreasonable.

An Air Force solicitation promised offerors that the Air Force would review their "relevant" present and recent past performance. United Paradyne Corporation (UPC) lost the contract and protested to GAO arguing that the evaluation process was unreasonable and won. The Air Force's scoring system was flawed. It considered **all** of an offeror's prior contracts, including those that were not relevant. For example, the Air Force rated one of UPC's contracts 0 out of a maximum score of 60 for relevance; this score of zero was used to calculate an average score for past performance. To GAO, the Air Force's past performance scoring process "was unreasonable because it had the effect of penalizing offerors with relevant experience such as UPC . . . for their non-relevant experience. . . . In UPC's case, for example, the protester's performance on the predecessor contract to the effort solicited here, for which it had received a relevance score of 60 of 60, was given the same weight in the computation of its past performance score as its performance on" the irrelevant contract for which it had received 0 out of 60 points.[26]

It is also unreasonable to not evaluate all price elements.

A GSA solicitation for repairs and alterations to government buildings told offerors it would evaluate only the mark-up rates for contractor overhead, general and administrative costs, bonds, insurance, other indirect costs, profits, and other fees that the offeror would use for pricing the projects. Other cost-price factors like the number of labor hours proposed and the cost of materials would not be evaluated. GAO found that the solicitation violated FAR's requirement that cost or price to the government be evaluated in all procurements. "Considering only mark-up rates fails to represent the agency's best estimate of the likely relative cost to the government of the proposals competing for umbrella contracts."[27]

An unreasonable way of carrying out a reasonable evaluation process is to score the best offer as the worst one and the worst one as the best.

> "In a best value evaluation looking for the best building for the government to lease, and using a scoring system in which the better proposal was to get more points, an agency evaluated what clearly was the highest quality building and gave it a low score but gave a high score to a clearly inferior building."[28]

On its face, such a backward scoring system was laughable, or in the polite prose of GAO, not reasonable.

Question 2. Did the contracting officer actually use only the evaluation factors she said she would?

To be reasonable, contracting officers must follow the rules they set for a solicitation. GAO says that:

> "An agency may not induce offerors to prepare and submit proposals based on one premise, then make source selection decisions based on another. Accordingly, once offerors are informed of the evaluation criteria against which proposals will be evaluated, the agency must adhere to the stated criteria or inform all offerors of all significant changes."[29]

A solicitation said that the contracting officer would evaluate proposals on a pass/fail basis. But in the actual evaluation, the government awarded additional points based on how well proposals met the requirements.[30]

Question 3. Did the evaluators follow the law, statutes, and regulations?

There should be no need to explain this question. It's unreasonable for evaluators to not follow the law, including FAR regulations applicable to the evaluation process. See the example on the previous page about the GSA solicitation for repairs and alterations to government buildings.

Generally (because there can always be exceptions), answering these three questions makes an evaluation of solicitations reasonable.

Fair and Reasonable Award Decision

We've already mentioned several ways the contracting officer's award decision can be unreasonable, like a "paper-less" decision and a knee-jerk decision. These unreasonable actions are often found in the award process. And in best value decisions, there's a third way—an improper trade-off decision.

Mechanical decision-making process

Anytime the contracting officer makes a knee-jerk, literally "thought-less" decision, the contracting officer is in trouble. One of the biggest mistakes contracting officers can make is failing to show that they have thought out a decision.

So thought is essential. In a best value procurement, a contracting officer has to decide which offer is the best deal for the government. This assumes the contracting officer thinks about it. A contracting officer who simply says, "A proposal that scores 95 is higher than a proposal that scored 90," is not thinking. It might be true, but no thinking was involved in the decision. A 95 and a 90 might be considered technically equal. This decision-making process is too mechanical.

The Department of Veterans Affairs issued a solicitation for prescription glasses. Classic Optical Laboratories Inc. submitted the top-rated technical proposal and the second lowest price. When the scores were added, Classic scored 180 and Opti-Lite scored 170. The contracting officer gave Classic the contract because it had the highest combined total score. GAO said this was unreasonable. . . . "The [contracting officer's] decision was based on a purely mechanical application of the numerical scores for the technical factors and price. . . . The contracting officer's [decision] provided only the total technical and price scores for the proposals evaluated and in each instance stated that the total score for technical and price would determine the final ranking of vendors and award."[31]

No documentation

FAR 15.308 clearly describes what the paperwork on an award decision should look like:

> "The source selection decision shall be documented, and the documentation shall include the rationale for any business judgments and trade-offs made or relied on by the SSA, including benefits associated with additional costs."

Details really show the reasonableness of a decision. When the contracting officer explains why a vendor is "the best value," she must say why. Contrary to the cliché, in procurement there's no "devil in the details." If there are no details, the contracting officer may well lose a protest.

> The USDA Forest Service scored proposals on the basis of a maximum possible 160 points. The higher-priced proposal scored 134, while Shumaker Trucking and Excavating Contractors, Inc., scored 93. GAO said the Forest Service's decision document was inadequate. One paragraph simply pointed out the large point spread between the scores of the technical proposals of the two competitors. A second paragraph gave the contracting officer's opinion that the additional cost "is justified based on the superior scoring on past performance and technical approach." That was it. To GAO, this wasn't enough. The agency had focused on the higher technical score "without discussing what, if anything, the spread between the technical scores actually signified. The record contains no evidence that the agency compared the advantages of the awardee's proposal to those of Shumaker's proposal, or considered why any advantages of the awardee's proposal were worth the approximately $400,000 higher price. In this case, the Forest Service's trade-off was inadequate because its mechanical comparison of the offerors' point scores was not a valid substitute for a qualitative assessment of the technical differences between the offerors . . . .[32]

Unreasonable trade-offs

It's OK for the government to pay more money for a better value as long as the solicitation warns vendors that the government intends to do that. The tough question is this: How much more is too much more? At some point, it's unreasonable for the contracting officer to pay more. But where is that point?

GAO decisions vary, so we will describe only a few. One factor bearing on the issue is the role price was supposed to play in the award decision. FAR 15.101-1(b)(2) says that the government must tell offerors how important price will be, compared to the technical factors, in the award decision:

> "The solicitation shall state whether all evaluation factors other than cost or price, when combined, are significantly more important than, approximately equal to, or significantly less important than cost or price."

A contracting officer has more discretion to pick a higher technically scored proposal if those factors are significantly less important than price.

Here are some examples of successful trade-offs based on GAO decisions:

- An agency was justified in paying 16 percent more when a technical proposal of the winner scored 55 percent higher. (Technical factors were significantly more important than price.)[33]

- An agency was justified in paying 4 percent more for a proposal that scored 16 percent higher. Price was equal in importance (50 percent) to the combined eight technical factors (50 percent).[34]

- An agency properly awarded a lease to an offeror whose technical score was 119 and price was $18.40 sq/ft as opposed to another offeror's price of $12.95 sq/ft with a technical score of 99 points, technical factors being significantly more important than price.[35]

But the contracting officer can still award to the lower-priced, lower-scored proposal if the agency paperwork justifies it. Doing so, however, is tricky. Contractors often believe that "technical being more important than price" prevents the government from awarding a contract to a lower priced, lower technically rated proposal. That's not true. The so-called "quality-price" trade-off in this situation is often done, but it must be done carefully and documented carefully to be done successfully.

GAO gives the following guidance for selecting the lower priced, lower rated proposal:

"Where cost is secondary to technical considerations under a solicitation's evaluation scheme, as here, the selection of a lower-priced proposal over a proposal with a higher technical rating requires an adequate justification, i.e., one showing the agency reasonably concluded that notwithstanding the point or adjectival differential between the two proposals, they were essentially equal in technical merit, or that the differential in the evaluation ratings between the proposals was not worth the cost premium associated with selection of the higher technically rated proposal. Where there is inadequate supporting rationale in the record for a decision to select a lower-priced proposal with a lower technical ranking notwithstanding a solicitation's emphasis on technical factors, we cannot conclude that the agency had a reasonable basis for its decision."[36]

Here's a good example of doing this trade-off correctly:

In a HUD procurement involving CitiWest and Tidewater, Tidewater received a score of 100 points and CitiWest got a score of 90. CitiWest's cost, however, was 15 percent lower. HUD concluded that the 10-point spread in technical proposals did not merit paying 15 percent more and awarded the contract to the lower-rated, lower-priced proposal of CitiWest. GAO said that HUD's documentation justified the decision. An agency may select a lower-priced, lower technically rated proposal if it decides that the cost premium involved in selecting a higher-rated, higher-priced proposal is not justified, given the acceptable level of technical competence available at the lower price.[37]

Here's an example of a trade-off done incorrectly—paying more for slower delivery. Providing a faster delivery only in the short run is unreasonable.

The government wanted 16,000 military steel rings to be delivered at the rate of 3,000 a month, with the first delivery of 3,000 delivered as soon as possible, but no later than within 165 days. Badger Truck Center won, offering the first 3,000 in 150 days but only 1,800 a month after that. A competitor, Novex Enterprises, could deliver the first 3,000 in 165 days, only 15 days after Badger's initial delivery, and could then deliver the government-required 3,000 rings per month after that. Novex's price was lower than Badger's. GAO concluded that Badger's offer failed the "reasonableness" test: "except for the initial quantity, Novex's proposed delivery schedule, which would be completed in 315 days (initial delivery in 165 days and five deliveries at 3,000-unit rate every 30 days), was significantly better than Badger's, which would not be completed until 390 days (initial delivery in 150 days and eight deliveries at 1,800-unit rate every 30 days)."[38]

Being Fair and Reasonable in Administering a Contract

Where does it say that a contracting officer has to be fair and reasonable in administering a contract?

To be exact, there are two places: the common-law-implied duty of good faith and fair dealing and the requirements of FAR 1.602.

Both still demand that the three basic rules of "fair and reasonable" apply: that the contracting officer will think through a decision, write it down, and explain why she has reached the decision she is making.

The Implied Duty of Good Faith and Fair Dealing

When you think about it, do contracting parties really need a contract provision promising to carry out the contract fairly? Not really, although that answer probably seems naive in our litigious society. But for years, judges have built into contracts an implied duty of good faith and fair dealing.

But being *implied*, this duty presents problems. Implied duties under a contract are hard to identify and pin down because they are not written, so any implied duty raises hard questions. Is it fair to make people follow unwritten rules? If someone breaches an unwritten rule, does he have to pay damages? Can unwritten rules even be breached? As we will see, the answer to all three questions is "yes."

In any event, written contracts have unwritten rules. These unwritten rules, called implied duties, are just as binding as the written rules. And they can be breached just like any written rule. The problem with these implied duties is that it's hard to anticipate how they can be broken because they are unwritten.

Although difficult to identify, some violations of this implied duty are obvious. One example, a rare one, shows bad faith on the part of the government.

The Libertatia Associates (TLA) had a grounds maintenance contract at Fort Rucker, Alabama. The COR on the contract told TLA employees that, in the words of the COR, they should think of him as Jesus Christ and the contracting officer as God. Other people heard the COR say that he would run TLA off the contract. Others heard him say to the president of TLA that he would break TLA. The court found that the COR had a "specific intent to injure" the contractor. The COR's "Jesus Christ" comparison "showed the COR to be a contracting official without a proper understanding of his role." His personal animosity was clear from his "break them" statements.[39]

Another example:

When a contractor was trying to negotiate an extension of the contract, a government official adopted a take-it-or-leave-it position on an issue. Worse yet, that position was wrong as a matter of law.[40]

Although it might not seem logical to non-lawyers, bad faith and good faith are not flip sides of the same coin. Proving bad faith was not part of proving that the government didn't act in good faith. They are two different concepts. Good faith is violated by self-interest, whereas bad faith is driven by malice. A person who is selfish is not necessarily out to hurt the other person.

Two men bought from the U.S. government a car confiscated by U.S. Customs in a drug raid. They drove it into Mexico, got arrested for drugs found "unexpectedly" in the car, and spent a year in a Mexican jail for possession of those drugs. They sued the U.S. government, arguing that it had violated the implied duty of good faith because the government had not carefully inspected the confiscated car and found the hidden drugs before putting the car up for auction. Because the car had been confiscated in a drug arrest, "a reasonable purchaser would believe that the vehicles had been adequately searched prior to the sale or at least that the search was not intentionally limited to increase the government's profits." Less government work (inspection of the car), less damage to the car's interior, more government profit was the argument the two men made. Although the government argued that there was no government bad faith, the CFC held there could still be government violation of good faith.[41]

To see what the violation of good faith involves, the CFC in this case gave several examples:

"It may be that plaintiffs can prove that the government failed to conduct an adequate search for the purpose of obtaining higher resale value for the vehicle at auction. This could be a case of the government's appropriating profits to itself at the expense of its contracting partner in direct contravention of the covenant of good faith and fair dealing. Or, if plaintiffs prove they could not have discovered the hidden contraband in the circumstance of the auction sale, and that the government had a policy to search thoroughly any vehicle seized because they contain narcotics, but that the government acted in direct contravention of its stated policy, plaintiffs may be able to show that the government had a duty to notify plaintiffs of the government's failure to search the vehicle thoroughly or a responsibility to put plaintiffs on notice that it would be their responsibility to inspect the vehicle for contraband and to allow them the opportunity to conduct meaningful inspection."[42]

There's an important limit on this implied duty: It's not a catchall duty to be fair in everything the parties do. It's simply a duty to be fair **regarding a clause already in the contract**. The implied duty "does not confer on a party any rights or grounds for recovery other than those that are contractually based. In other words, good faith should not be construed to give rise to new obligations not otherwise contained in the contract's express terms."[43]

A landlord leased offices to the Internal Revenue Service. After the offices were destroyed by arson, the building's owner sued the government, arguing that the government should have told him of the security risk the IRS presented. He lost. His lease with the government had no requirement that the government share with him any information as to the possible threat of harm to the leased premises.[44]

This implied duty typically can be violated in many ways, such as by failing to cooperate in contract performance and interfering with contract performance. One respected government contract authority believes that "By far, the most important implied duty in government contracting is the duty to cooperate."[45]

One of the problems with defining the duty to cooperate is that what one party thinks is "cooperation," the other party often thinks is work well beyond what the contract calls for. Closely related is the duty not to hinder.

Here's the distinction between the two, but notice that the test is the same—reasonableness:

"The implied duty to cooperate imposes an affirmative obligation to do what is reasonably necessary to enable the contractor to perform. Determination of a breach of the duty requires a reasonableness inquiry. The nature and scope of that responsibility is to be gathered from the particular contract, its context, and its surrounding circumstances. In contrast, the implied duty of noninterference is a negative obligation that neither party to the contract will do anything to prevent performance thereof by the other party or that will hinder or delay him in its performance. The Government's actions or inaction must be shown to be unreasonable . . . ."[46]

FAR 1.602-2

Rarely used by courts and boards but still available to a contracting officer in contract administration is FAR 1.602-2. That clause gives the contracting officer a basis to do what is fair and reasonable in the contract administration process.

A contracting officer may terminate, based on FAR 1.602-2, a just-awarded contract for convenience upon discovering that the specification did not adequately describe the government's work.

> "If . . . a contracting officer discovers that the bid specifications inadequately describe the contract work, regulations promulgated under CICA may compel a new bid. Thus, to accommodate CICA's fairness requirements, the contracting officer may need to terminate a contract for the Government's convenience to further full and open competition."[47]

In another case, a court found that a contracting officer had violated this section because the contracting officer had looked at only the government's side of a claim and not the contractor's:

> "The contracting officer had not examined the contractor's daily reports, submitted in support of this claim, but rather reviewed only the inspector's daily logs before making his decision to deny the delay claim. The CO's admitted failure to give any consideration at all to Sergent's arguments and exhibits. By reviewing only the records produced by the government, Mr. Eversole failed to fulfill his duty to be unbiased and impartial."[48]

But overall, FAR 1.602-2 has not been helpful in describing what is fair and reasonable in the contracting officer's administration of a contract.

An "Independent" Judge

A judge is supposed to "call 'em as he sees 'em." In legalese, this means that a judge must make an "independent" decision. That's a decision which, although the judge has thoughtfully considered the opinions of others, is one that he believes to be truly his own, one he is willing to stand by and be responsible for. It is not the decision of the judge's spouse, boss (assuming a distinction between the two), or colleague. It is the judge's **own** decision.

At both major points in the procurement process—when awarding a contract and when issuing a contracting officer's final decision—the contracting officer's decisions must be independent.

In the contract formation process, the contracting officer's decision must be independent. FAR 15.308 requires that the contract award decision be the "source selection authority's independent judgment."

> "The source selection authority's (SSA) decision shall be based on a comparative assessment of proposals against all source selection criteria in the solicitation. While the SSA may use reports and analyses prepared by others, the source selection decision shall represent the SSA's independent judgment."

In the contract administration process, when the contracting officer is acting as a judge in the claims process, case law and the Contract Disputes Act require that the contracting officer's decision be independent.

> "The contracting officer must act impartially in settling disputes. He must not act as a representative of one of the contracting parties, but as an impartial, unbiased judge. If the evidence shows he has failed so to act, there can be no doubt that we have jurisdiction to set aside his decision."[49]

In deciding whether a contracting officer acted independently, some general rules apply.

Rule 1: A contracting officer *must* consider the opinions of colleagues.

A contracting officer "is not required to act in a vacuum."[50] When a contracting officer makes an independent decision, he must consider the input of colleagues—agency lawyers, auditors/accountants, supervisors, and experts, etc. FAR 1.602-2(c) says that the contracting officer shall "request and consider the advice of specialists in audit, law, engineering, information security, transportation, and other fields, as appropriate."

Rule 2: To *not* consider the views of colleagues is wrong.

This goes beyond Rule 1. A contracting officer *must* consider the views of colleagues.

> "A contracting officer may, for the purpose of forming his or her independent judgment, obtain information and advice from advisors and staff offices, particularly in the fields of accounting, engineering and law, areas in which he or she may have little or no expertise. Indeed, it would reflect poor judgment on the part of a CO if he or she did not do so."[51]

Rule 3: A contracting officer may adopt the views of these experts/ colleagues so long as the decision made is the contracting officer's.

In numerous cases, particularly those involving highly technical issues, a contracting officer has an expert prepare a report. When the report is finished, the contracting officer often issues a contracting officer's final decision adopting the expert's report in its entirely. Relying on an expert's report does not necessarily make the contracting officer's decision wrong.

> A construction contractor argued that the contracting officer's final decision was invalid because it was a "wholesale adoption of a litigation expert's report" and not the "personal and independent decision" of the contracting officer as required by FAR and applicable case law principles. The board refused to draw such an automatic conclusion as it set out the requirements of a valid contracting officer's final decision. "It is well established that the contractor is entitled to a decision that has been independently rendered by the contracting officer. A decision issued by a contracting officer acting solely pursuant to the dictates of other, higher-level, personnel in the Government is not valid. At the same time, the regulations and case law anticipate that the contracting officer, particularly in complex matters, will seek and consider advice of counsel and experts as an integral part of the process of formulating a final decision. The contracting officer is not required to be isolated from the advice and guidance of others."[52]

When awarding a contract, a contracting officer may rely on experts and still make an independent decision:

> "[GAO] will not view an SSO's concurrence with the findings of those whose expertise he relies on as evidence that the SSO has abdicated his responsibility to make independent judgments . . . that the mere fact that the SSO adopted language and findings made by his evaluators did not indicate that he failed to exercise his independent judgment . . . [or] where selection authority indicated his concurrence with the findings and recommendations of a contract award panel by marking an X,' . . . ."[53]

The independent decision requirement applies to decisions of the contracting officer. It does not apply to decisions of unwarranted support staff like contract specialists. It is perfectly legal for unwarranted support staff to write up background papers, draft final decisions, etc. the way they are told to by their "boss," the contracting officer. Naturally, a contracting officer may ask for the input of contract specialists, but when the final decision is to be drafted, the fact that support staff does not agree with the decision is legally irrelevant.

Rule 4: When a contracting officer disagrees with the experts, he has to explain why.

A contracting officer is free to disregard the recommendation of an evaluation panel, but if that happens, the basis for the contracting officer's independent judgment must be spelled out. Generalizations won't work.

> "Although source selection officials may reasonably disagree with the evaluation ratings and results of lower-level evaluators, they are nonetheless bound by the fundamental requirement that their independent judgments be reasonable, consistent with the stated evaluation factors, and adequately documented."[54]

Rule 5: A contracting officer can sit on an evaluation panel and still be independent.

The contracting officer may participate in all or various phases of the source selection process and still make an independent decision as required by FAR 15.308.

"[FAR 15.308] does not expressly preclude the SSA from participating in the evaluation process, and we see nothing in an SSA's doing so that is inherently inconsistent with the exercise of independent judgment. We are aware of no other applicable prohibition in this regard."[55]

In fact, it's OK for a contracting officer to play multiple roles in the solicitation process:

"It is neither unusual nor improper for a CO to have multiple responsibilities throughout an acquisition. For example, FAR 15.303(a) specifically designates the CO as the SSA, unless the agency head appoints another individual, and requires that the SSA perform certain enumerated functions such as establishing an evaluation team; approving the source selection strategy or acquisition plan; ensuring consistency among the solicitation requirements, notices to offerors, and proposal preparation instructions; ensuring that proposals are evaluated solely on the factors contained in the solicitation; considering the recommendations of advisory boards or panels; and selecting the source or sources whose proposal is the best value to the government. . . ."[56]

Endnotes

1.   31 U.S.C. § 3553 (2000).

2.   28 U.S.C. §1491(b) (2000).

3.   *First Enterprise v. The United States*, 61 Fed.Cl. 109, 113 (2004).

4.   *M. Steinthal & Co. v. Seamans*, 455 F.2d 1289, 1301-03 (D.C.Cir.1971), *quoted in Kinnett Dairies*, 580 F.2d at 1271.

5.   *KMS Fusion, Inc.*, B-242529, May 8, 1991, 91-1 CPD ¶ 447.

6.   *Universal Building Maintenance, Inc.*, B-282456, July 15, 1999, 99-2 CPD ¶ 32.

7.   *Schlesinger v. United States*, 390 F.2d 702, 708 (Ct. Cl. 1968).

8.   *Granite Const. Co. v. United States*, 962 F.2d 998 (Fed.Cir.1992).

9.   *Opti-Lite Optical*, B-281693, Mar. 22, 1999, 99-1 CPD ¶ 61.

11.   *National Aerospace Group, Inc.*, B-282843, Aug. 30, 1999, 99-2 CPD ¶ 43.

12.   *Id.*

13. *Lockheed Martin Corp.*, B-293679 et al., May 27, 2004, 2004 CPD ¶ 115.

14. *Northrop Grumman Info. Tech., Inc.*, B-290,080 et al., June 10, 2002, 2002 CPD ¶ 136.

15. *Culver Health Corp.*, B-242902, June 10, 1991, 91-1 CPD ¶ 556.

16. *Metro Machine Corp.*, B-281872 et al., April 22, 1999, 99-1 CPD ¶ 101.

17. *The Jonathan Corp.; Metro Mach. Corp.* , B-251698.3, B-251698.4, May 17, 1993, 93-2 CPD ¶ 174.

18. *Lockheed Martin Corp.*, B-293679 et al., May 27, 2004, 2004 CPD ¶ 115.

19. *R&D Maintenance Services, Inc.*, B- 292,342, Aug 22, 2003, 2003 CPD ¶ 162 discussing *Biospherics, Inc.*, B-278278, Jan. 14, 1998, 98-1 CPD ¶ 161.

20. *Northrop Grumman Info. Tech., Inc.*, B-290080 et al., June 10, 2002, 2002 CPD ¶ 136.

21. *Base Technologies, Inc.*, B-293061.2, B- 293061.3, Jan. 28, 2004, 2004 CPD ¶ 31.

22. *Mechanical Equipment Company, Inc.; Highland Engineering, Inc.; Etnyre International, Ltd.; Kara Aerospace, Inc.*, B-292789.2; B-292789.3; B-292789.4; B-292789.5; B-292789.6; B-292789.7, December 15, 2003 released September 14, 2004, CPD ¶ 192.

23. *Creative Information Technology, Inc.*, B-293073.10, March 16, 2005, 2005 CPD ¶ 110.

24. *Id.*

25. *Burns and Roe Services Corp.*, B-296355, July 27, 2005, 2005 CPD ¶ 150.

26. *United Paradyne Corporation*, B-297758, March 10, 2006, 2006 CPD ¶ 47.

27. *S.J. Thomas Co., Inc.*, B-283192, Oct. 20, 1999, B-283192, 99-2 CPD ¶ 73.

28. *Adelaide Blomfield Management Co.*, B-253128, B-253128.2, Sept. 27, 1993, CPD ¶ 197.

29. *Mnemonics, Inc.*, B- 290,961, Oct. 28, 2002, 2003 CPD ¶ 39.

30. *Id.*

31. *Opti-Lite Optical*, B-281693, Mar. 22, 1999, 99-1 CPD ¶ 61.

32. *Shumaker Trucking and Excavating Contractors, Inc.*, B-290732, Sept. 25, 2002, 2002 CPD ¶ 169.

33. *LSS Leasing, B-259551*, Apr. 3, 1995, 95-1 CPD ¶ 179.

34. *William L. Menefee* , B-279272 , May 28, 1998, 98-1 CPD ¶ 144.

35. *1ˢᵗ St. Investments LP*, B-270894, Aug. 15, 1996, 96-2 CPD ¶ 69.

36. *MCR Fed., Inc.*, B-280969, Dec.14, 1998, 99-1 CPD 8.

37. *Tidewater Homes Realty, Inc.*, B-274689.5, Aug. 11, 1998, 98-2 CPD ¶ 40.

38. *Novex Enterprises*, B-297660, Mar. 6, 2006, 2006 CPD ¶ 51.

39. *The Libertatia Associates*, 46 Fed.Cl. 702 (2000).

40. *Isadore and Miriam Klein*, GSBCA 6614, et al., 84-2 BCA ¶ 17,273 (1984).

41. *Francisco Javier Rivera Agredano and Alfonso Calderon Leon v. The United States*, 70 Fed. Cl. 564 (2006).

42. *Id.*

43. *Henry H. Norman v. General Services Administration* , GSBCA 15070, et al., 02-2 BCA ¶ 32,042.

44. *Id.*

45. *Nash & Cibinic Report*, 3 No. 11, p. 78.

46. *Contel Advanced Systems, Inc.*, ASBCA No. 49074, 03-1 BCA ¶ 32155.

47. *Krygoski Const. Co., Inc. v. United States*, 94 F.3d 1537, 1543 (Fed.Cir.1996).

48. *Sergent Mechanical Systems, Inc. v. United States*, 34 Fed.Cl. 505, 523 (1995).

49. *Penner Installation Corp. v. The United States*, 89 F.Supp. 545, 548, 116 Ct.Cl. 550, (1950).

50. *Mike Gibson and Mike Bearden Co-trustees in Dissolution of Delta Products Company*, AGBCA No. 88-139-1, 93-2 BCA ¶ 25,615.

51. *BAE Systems Information & Electronic Systems Integration. Inc.*, ASBCA 44832, 01-2 BCA ¶ 31,495.

52. *Washington Development Group-JWB, LLC v. General Services Administration*, GSBCA 15,137, GSBCA 16,004, July 9, 2003, 03-2 BCA ¶ 32319.

53. *U.S. Facilities, Inc.*, B-293029, B-293029.2, Jan. 16, 2004, 2004 CPD ¶ 17.

54. *Johnson Controls World Services, Inc.*, B-289,942, B-289942.2, May 24, 2002, 2002 CPD ¶ 88.

55. *J.W. Holding Group & Associates, Inc.*, B-285882.3, B-285882.6, July 2, 2001, 2003 CPD ¶ 126.

56. *Digital Systems Group, Inc.*, B-286,931, B-286931.2, Mar.7, 2001, 2001 CPD ¶ 50.

Chapter 2

The Contracting Officer as Sheriff

CONTENTS

FAR 1.602-2 makes the contracting officer the sheriff, guarding the interests of the United States in its contractual relationships:

> "Contracting officers are responsible for ensuring performance of all necessary actions for effective contracting, ensuring compliance with the terms of the contract, and safeguarding the interests of the United States in its contractual relationships."

In many ways, this role overlaps that of the contracting officer as judge, described in Chapter 1, because when the contracting officer is acting as sheriff, protecting the government's interests, she must be fair—on neither the government's side nor the contractor's side. But some of the contracting officer's jobs put her strictly on the side of the government as an advocate of the government's interests.

In this chapter we look at this role in both major parts of the contract process, the solicitation process and the administration process.

In the solicitation process, the contracting officer must protect the integrity of the solicitation process and identify (and mitigate if possible) any conflicts of interest. The contracting officer also must decide whether the apparent winner is responsible—a decision that ensures that the best offer **and** the best offeror win the contract.

Moving then to the contract administration process, we look at how the contracting officer has to watch for fraud, withhold payments to contractors, recover erroneous payments made to a contractor, and monitor who gets the contract check (assignments of claims) and who gets the government contract assigned to it (novation agreements).

THE SOLICITATION PROCESS

In awarding a contract, a contracting officer has so many steps to safeguard that this obligation seems overwhelming. Fortunately for the contracting officer, a couple of issues recur: integrity of the process and responsibility of the vendor.

Protecting the Integrity of the Solicitation Process

One of the contracting officer's main jobs is to protect the integrity of the solicitation process. *Integrity* can be tough to define. It's vague. It's ambiguous. But it's lurking at all points in the solicitation process.

Fortunately, FAR and case law give the contracting officer a lot of help.

Unfair Competitive Advantage

FAR 1.602-2 makes contracting officers

> "responsible for ensuring performance of all necessary actions for effective contracting, ensuring compliance with the terms of the contract, and safeguarding the interests of the United States in its contractual relationships . . . ."

Although this section has been used rarely as precedent, one place it has been used is to allow a contracting officer to throw an offeror out of the solicitation process for various types of unfair conduct. GAO says this FAR section gives the contracting officer the right to do so:

> "Contracting officers are granted wide latitude to exercise business judgment, FAR § 1.602- 2, and may impose a variety of restrictions, not explicitly provided for in the regulations, where the needs of the agency or the nature of the procurement dictates the use of those restrictions. For example, a contracting officer may protect the integrity of the procurement system by disqualifying an offeror from the competition where the firm may have obtained an unfair competitive advantage, even if no actual impropriety can be shown, so long as the determination is based on facts and not mere innuendo or suspicion."[1]

In one case, several employees read other vendors' proposals. The contracting officer properly disqualified the company because of this.

> "Wherever an offeror has improperly obtained proprietary proposal information during the course of a procurement, the integrity of the procurement is at risk, and an agency's decision to disqualify the firm is generally reasonable, absent unusual circumstances."[2]

It's good to note that when a contracting officer decides to disqualify a vendor, she need not prove that an impropriety **actually** happened, as long as the contracting officer's decision is based on facts:

> "A contracting officer may protect the integrity of the procurement system by disqualifying an offeror from the competition where the firm may have obtained an unfair competitive advantage, even if no actual impropriety can be shown, so long as the determination is based on facts and not mere innuendo or suspicion."[3]

Organizational Conflicts of Interest

One way a contracting officer must safeguard the government's interests involves conflicts of interest. FAR gives the contracting officer the job of identifying and dealing with them.

9.504 Contracting officer responsibilities.

(a) Using the general rules, procedures, and examples in this subpart, contracting officers shall analyze planned acquisitions in order to--

(1) Identify and evaluate potential organizational conflicts of interest as early in the acquisition process as possible; and

(2) Avoid, neutralize, or mitigate significant potential conflicts before contract award.

GAO adds that this job is done case by case:

> "Because conflicts may arise in factual situations not expressly described in the relevant FAR sections, the regulation advises contracting officers to examine each situation individually and to exercise 'common sense, good judgment, and sound discretion'

in assessing whether a significant potential conflict exists and in developing an appropriate way to resolve it."[4]

Conflicts of interest come in two sizes—individual and organizational. Because an individual conflict like awarding a contract to a spouse is pretty obvious, these conflicts don't need much attention. But the other type of conflict of interest, the organizational conflict of interest (OCI), is not so obvious.

GAO describes an OCI this way:

> "A potential OCI exists where, because of a contractor's other activities, the contractor may enjoy an unfair competitive advantage, or where award of the subject contract could put the contractor in the position of performing conflicting roles that might bias the contractor's judgment."[5]

FAR 2.101 also defines an OCI, noting that such a conflict exists when

> "because of other activities or relationships with other persons, a person is unable or potentially unable to render impartial assistance or advice to the government, or the person's objectivity in performing the contract work is or might be otherwise impaired, or a person has an unfair competitive advantage."

A contracting officer must watch for three general categories of OCIs: (1) biased ground rules, (2) unequal access to information, and (3) impaired objectivity.

Biased ground rules

A contracting officer should find this OCI easy to spot. It is the most obvious conflict of interest. It's writing the specification and then being able to bid on that specification. Here,

> "the primary concern is that the firm could skew the competition, whether intentionally or not, in favor of itself. . . . These situations may also involve a concern that the firm, by virtue of its special knowledge of the agency's future requirements, would have an unfair advantage in the competition for those requirements."[6]

In carrying out the A-76 process, a consultant and a Navy employee wrote and edited the performance work statement to be used as part of the RFP for contracting out the work. They also wrote and edited the in-house management plan describing how the government would do the work itself.[7]

The other two OCIs are more difficult to see.

Unequal access to information

In watching out for an unequal access to information OCI, a contracting officer must keep a contractor carrying out one government contract from getting access to non-public information that could give it an advantage in getting a later contract.

A subcontractor of a winning contractor had previously monitored a competitor's performance under an earlier contract. During the earlier contract, the sub "had an opportunity to make detailed observations of virtually every aspect of Ktech's [the protester's] work in connection with the prior program, including seeing how the hardware and instrumentation system were being assembled and how the grounding and shielding system was being fabricated. The record thus clearly shows that [the sub] through its prior work as a government contractor had an opportunity to obtain Ktech's proprietary information during the performance of Ktech's prior contract." GAO found an OCI.[8]

Impaired objectivity

This is a little like the old joke about asking a barber if you need a haircut. What answer do you think the barber will give?

According to GAO, there's impaired objectivity when

"a firm's work under one government contract could entail its evaluating itself, either through an assessment of performance under another contract or an evaluation of a proposal submitted to obtain another contract. The concern in such situations is that the firm's ability to render impartial advice to the government could appear to be undermined by its relationship with the entity whose work product is being evaluated."[9]

There was no impaired objectivity where one company monitored its own contract **but did not evaluate** it.

When DoD tracks its vehicles in South Korea, one part of the tracking system uses global positioning system (GPS) equipment. That part was run by Critel. When DoD wanted to get an information management specialist (IMS) to help with the overall tracking system, it hired someone from Critel. An unsuccessful competitor for the IMS contract argued that Critel had a prohibited OCI because the IMS contracted with Critel and the Critel employee would be monitoring Critel's work as GSP equipment supplier.

GAO didn't think there was an OCI. It distinguished between monitoring the system, which was not an OCI, and evaluating it, which could be an OCI. "We find no prohibited OCI here. Under its equipment contract, Critel is required to provide preventative and corrective maintenance and an inspection system covering the required services, and also must maintain and make available to the government records of all inspection work performed. While the IMS contractor is required to develop a quality assurance program to provide surveillance of—that is, to monitor—the required scheduled maintenance, it is not responsible for making judgments as to what maintenance is required or how well the maintenance is being performed." GAO distinguished this case from one where a subcontractor was to establish requirements for tests that it or its prime contractor would perform. That **would** be an OCI.[10]

Responsibility

Before awarding any contract, a contracting officer must determine that the winner is "responsible." The fact that a vendor has the best offer doesn't mean it is a good contractor. A good offer is not enough to win a contract. The vendor must be a good offeror, which means that it has the ability to actually do the work it said it would—that the vendor is responsible.

The Difference between Responsible and Responsive

Responsible is not the same as *responsive*. *Responsive* refers to the offer. *Responsible* refers to the offeror. If the vendor does not promise to do everything the government is asking for, the vendor's offer is not responsive or acceptable. For example, if a vendor makes a product available by January 1, but the government requires it a month earlier, December 1, the offer is not responsive or acceptable.

Two tricky issues confuse this process: (1) different deadlines for responsibility and responsiveness and (2) the involvement of the Small Business Administration (SBA) in responsibility determinations.

Different deadlines

The deadlines for establishing responsiveness and responsibility are different. So the real question differentiating the two concepts is this: By what date must it (responsive or responsible) be satisfied?

Here's where it gets tricky. **Responsiveness** must be satisfied by the due date of an offer, which usually means by the deadline for final proposal revisions. For example, if an offeror persists in offering a product by January 1 when the government needs it a month earlier, by December 1, the proposal is unacceptable. An offer is responsive/acceptable or not when it is submitted.

Responsibility is different in that it can be satisfied at any time up to the date of award of the contract. For example, if a final proposal revision says the item will be made available to the government by December 1 as required but also includes information suggesting that the offeror is not financially stable at the time the offer is submitted, the offer is still acceptable. The offeror has until the date of contract award, which is whenever the government decides to make the award, to prove to the government that it is financially stable.

Role of the SBA

If a contracting officer refuses to award a contract to a small business on the grounds that the small business is not responsible, the contracting officer doesn't have the final say in the matter. The SBA does. If a contracting officer finds a small business nonresponsible, the contracting officer must refer the issue to the SBA. Whatever decision the SBA makes is binding on the contracting officer. If the SBA finds the small business responsible, it issues a Certificate of Competency that conclusively makes the small business responsible.

A related problem is when a contracting officer tries to convert a "responsibility" issue into a "responsiveness" issue. As mentioned above, one of the big differences between responsibility and responsiveness is the point in the solicitation process at which each is judged. Typically, responsiveness is determined earlier in the process, at the time of bid opening or receipt of final proposals. And typically, responsibility is determined later, at the time of award.

For example, when a contracting officer requires a bidder to have permits, a bidder must have the permits simply prior to getting the contract because permits are a responsibility issue. This is true even if the solicitation demands otherwise; for example, that bidders have permits at the time of bid opening, rather than at award.

A solicitation for navigation improvements required bidders to have permits to dump sludge "on or before the date of the bid opening" or the bid would "be considered nonresponsible and rejected." The winning bidder, Bean Stuyvesant, did not include copies of the permits with its bid. A competitor protested, arguing that the winner's bid should have been rejected for lack of permits.

GAO did not agree, basing its decision on the responsive-responsibility distinction. "A requirement for the submission of the permits necessary for performance at a particular site relates to how the contract requirements will be met, rather than to the performance requirements themselves; such a requirement thus pertains to bidder responsibility. A bidder need not demonstrate compliance with solicitation requirements pertaining to its responsibility in order to have its bid determined responsive. Moreover, the fact that the IFB called for submission of a permit showing that the proposed disposal site was "legal to operate" as of the bid opening date does not convert the permit requirement into a matter of bid responsiveness. The terms of the solicitation cannot convert a matter of responsibility into one of responsiveness."[11]

The FAR defines *responsible* as follows:

FAR 9.104-1 General standards.

To be determined responsible, a prospective contractor must—

(a) Have adequate financial resources to perform the contract, or the ability to obtain them (see 9.104-3(a));

(b) Be able to comply with the required or proposed delivery or performance schedule, taking into consideration all existing commercial and governmental business commitments;

(c) Have a satisfactory performance record (see 9.104-3(b) and Subpart 42.15). A prospective contractor shall not be determined responsible or nonresponsible solely on the basis of a lack of relevant performance history, except as provided in 9.104-2;

(d) Have a satisfactory record of integrity and business ethics.

(e) Have the necessary organization, experience, accounting and operational controls, and technical skills, or the ability to obtain them (including, as appropriate, such elements as production control procedures, property control systems, quality assurance measures, and safety programs applicable to materials to be produced or services to be performed by the prospective contractor and subcontractors). (See 9.104-3(a).)

(f) Have the necessary production, construction, and technical equipment and facilities, or the ability to obtain them (see 9.104-3(a)); and

(g) Be otherwise qualified and eligible to receive an award under applicable laws and regulations.

The Test: Reasonableness

To properly find a vendor nonresponsible, a contracting officer must be reasonable.

A decision that follows the law is reasonable. A court can overturn a contracting officer and find a contractor nonresponsible if:

"there has been a violation of a statute or regulation, or alternatively, if the agency determination lacked a rational basis."[12]

The GAO standard is "reasonable when made"; that is, whether the negative determination was **reasonable** based on the information **available** to the contracting officer at the time the nonresponsibility finding was made.[13]

Reasonable . . . :

"Contracting officers are vested with broad discretion in exercising the business judgment involved in a nonresponsibility determination. [GAO] generally will not disturb a nonresponsibility determination absent a showing either that the agency had no reasonable basis for the determination, or acted in bad faith."[14]

. . . when made:

"In our review of nonresponsibility determinations, we consider only whether the negative determination was reasonably based on the information available to the contracting officer at the time it was made."[15]

The "reasonable when made" test makes an important distinction. Often, a vendor might provide the contracting officer with information showing that it is responsible **after** the contracting officer has made the nonresponsibility determination. The contracting officer then, of course, feels stupid for having made the "wrong" decision. But it was not wrong. Because the contracting officer based the decision on the information she had at the time the decision was made, she did the best job possible. She was reasonable. And therefore she was not wrong.

An unreasonable responsibility determination

A good example of an unreasonable responsibility determination is when a contracting officer does not check to see if the offeror has been indicted. In one case, a contracting officer unreasonably found a company, Adelphia, to be responsible.

> "The record does not establish that the contracting officer obtained sufficient information to decide, or for that matter even considered, Adelphia's record of integrity and business ethics. In the absence of any consideration of the involvement, control or influence of the indicted Rigas family members and Adelphia Communications Corporation in the awardee, the contracting officer's statements of general awareness of alleged misconduct on the part of the Rigas family members and Adelphia Communications Corporation is not sufficient to show that the contracting officer's affirmative determination of responsibility is reasonable."[16]

A reasonable nonresponsibility determination

A contracting officer reasonably found a vendor nonresponsible when she used information from her auditors, who had raised serious questions about the vendor's books.

> "While Acquest submitted a great deal of financial information on itself and its related entities, the agency concluded that the information was insufficient to establish financial capability and, in fact, raised more questions than it answered. For example, Acquest's financial statements were considered unreliable, in part, because the net loss for the relevant period was not shown in the equity section of the balance sheet, and a deposit on a land purchase was shown on the November 2000 balance sheet while other documents showed the deposit had not been made until December 2000. Similarly,

although Acquest certified that there had been no material changes in its assets between November 2000 and January 2001, GSA's reviewer found that Acquest's year-end financial statement showed material changes, including a one-third reduction in assets and liabilities, plus an increase in equity although no income was shown. GSA also found that Acquest's equity 'appear[ed] light and no revenues [were] shown;' that there was no current information on a loan that was to be extended to end of January 2001 or on a purchase option that expired on January 28; and that Acquest's proposed rental rate was not sufficient for it to recover its construction costs. In light of these discrepancies and the inadequate rental rate, we think the contracting officer reasonably concluded that Acquest was not financially responsible."[17]

So, the test is, what did the contracting officer know, and when did he or she know it? Simply because a nonresponsible vendor can, after the contracting officer has found a vendor nonresponsible, produce all sorts of wonderful information showing that the company is in fact responsible, the contracting officer's decision is not wrong.

Although it might sound strange, the same offeror in multiple award solicitation may reasonably be found responsible for one award but not responsible for another, especially when the contracting officer gets new information that would make the company responsible for awards yet to be made.

The U.S. Environmental Protection Agency issued a solicitation stating that it would make multiple awards for testing services. Laucks Testing Laboratory was found nonresponsible for one contract because it could not provide the data needed by EPA on a computer disk. Later, Laucks developed the capability to provide the data on the computer disk and ended up getting another EPA contract. GAO saw nothing wrong with this. "We agree with EPA that a bidder's responsibility is to be determined based on any information received by the agency up to the time award is proposed to be made to that bidder. . . . In this regard, although EPA previously determined that Laucks lacked the technical capability to meet the IFB requirements and thus was not responsible, after reopening the IFB to make additional awards, it found that Laucks now has the technical capability to meet the IFB requirements and thus is responsible. An agency can and should reverse a previous nonresponsibility determination based on additional information brought to its attention prior to award."[18]

Due Diligence Investigation by Contracting Officer

How much of a "due diligence" study must a contracting officer make before finding a vendor responsible—or nonresponsible for that matter? A contracting officer cannot "unreasonably" ignore available relevant information. But a contracting officer need not read every piece of paper in the file.

One GAO decision has good examples of what a contracting officer must do and what he need not do in the name of due diligence.

Tri-Technologies, Inc., (Tri-Tech) won a contract even though it was being investigated for fraud in earlier Army contracts. Tri-Tech had not been indicted or debarred for what it had done, one reason being that it was not clear whether the contractor had defrauded the government or had simply made a mistake. A competitor protested, arguing that the Army contracting officer did not thoroughly do her job of investigating whether Tri-Tech was a responsible vendor.

The competitor lost because GAO concluded that the contracting officer had done a good investigation. Before the contracting officer concluded that Tri-Tech should be allowed to compete, in GAO's words, she "both requested and received the following information as part of her review: (1) a "Contractor Performance/Responsibility Review" from an Industrial Specialist at the Army's Tank and Automotive Command (TACOM) . . . (2) additional information from the TACOM Industrial Specialist about current contracts and delivery obligations, via e-mails . . . ;(3) input from the CO's legal advisor regarding what the CO describes as "the responsibility question." . . . In addition, she called a meeting with representatives from various TACOM offices to help her understand the issues involved in allowing Tri-Tech to compete." And before she found Tri-Tech responsible, she knew about Tri-Tech's recent and current performance, was aware of the open fraud investigation, and knew that Tri-Tech had not been suspended or debarred.[19]

It's interesting to note what GAO said the contracting officer in the above case **did not** have to do. GAO said she did not have to address Tri-Tech's problems under the previous contracts either in her written determination that Tri-Tech was responsible or in her decision to allow Tri-Tech to compete: "Given that there is no requirement to even document an affirmative determination of responsibility, we are aware of no requirement that either of these contemporaneous documents address this matter." Nor did she have to "personally review all of the exchanges on multiple contracts (for none of which she was the contracting officer), from the beginning of contract performance to the end, in order to determine for herself whether Tri-Tech did, or did not, commit fraud while performing those contracts." Finally, she did not have to review a thick book of documents the protester had given the government a year earlier describing what the protester had thought was bad conduct on Tri-Tech's part: "We think the CO's reliance on the judgment of the TACOM team about whether these matters do, or do not, constitute fraud, together with her own involvement in certain of these discussions, gave her a sufficient understanding of the situation to provide a reasonable basis for the determination she made."[20]

CONTRACT ADMINISTRATION

In safeguarding the government's interests in the contract administration process, the contracting officer's problems typically focus on several areas: fraud, withholding of payments or recovery of erroneous payments, and assignments.

Fraud

A contracting officer can go only so far in safeguarding the interests of the government when fraud appears. Because a contracting officer is not well trained in this area, the law leaves much fraud resolution to those who are— the agency's Inspector General, the agency's legal staff, or the U.S. Attorney's Office. The contracting officer's limited role here is seen at two points in the contract administration process—fraudulent claims and fraud in delivering something to the government.

Claims

Surprisingly, a contracting officer is actually prohibited by law from handling any claims involving fraud. The Disputes Clause of a contract (FAR 52.233-1) seems to give the contracting officer broad authority to handle all kinds of claims: "claims arising under or relating to a contract." But one type of claim excluded from a contracting officer's authority is a claim that has fraud associated with it.

FAR tells a contracting officer not "to decide or settle . . . claims arising under or relating to a contract subject to the [CDA] . . . involving fraud." 33.210(b). Even if a contracting officer suspects fraud under a terminated contract, it's out of the contracting officer's hands. (FAR 49.106.)

In fact, a contracting officer is wasting time issuing a decision on a claim involving fraud.

"A contracting officer denied a contractor any money under a termination for convenience settlement due to 'apparently fraudulent invoices' in the words of the contracting officer. According to the U.S. Court of Federal Claims, the Contract Disputes Act, 41 U.S.C. Sec. 605(a) 'specifically removes issues of fraud' from his consideration. His decision was 'unauthorized and invalid.'"[21]

Acceptance Following Inspection

Even though the government has accepted what it was buying under a contract, whether it be services, supplies, or construction, the contracting officer has the right to demand that a contractor fix or replace accepted work if there was fraud involved. To do so, the government must prove (1) that its acceptance was induced by its reliance on (2) a misrepresentation of fact, actual or implied, or the concealment of a material fact, (3) made with knowledge of its falsity or in reckless or wanton disregard of the facts, (4) with intent to mislead the Government into relying on the misrepresentation, (5) as a consequence of which the Government has suffered injury.[22]

Contracting officers rarely use this power, however, because civil and criminal statutes give the government better remedies in the event of fraud. As a result, there are very few reported cases in which a contracting officer has invoked this fraud exception to acceptance.

Withholding of Payments

The government has an easy way to collect money from a contractor: it can simply withhold paying the contractor money owed under a contract and use that retainage to pay off the contractor's debt. Two questions are important: What gives the government the right to withhold? How much may be withheld?

What Gives the Government the Right to Withhold?

A number of FAR clauses give the contracting officer the right to withhold payments. For example, FAR 52.232-5, Payments under Fixed-price Construction Contracts, allows a contracting officer to withhold a maximum of 10 percent of a progress payment "until satisfactory progress is achieved."

Other FAR clauses allow the contracting officer to withhold payments. These clauses deal with administration of the Davis-Bacon Act, the Service Contract Act, and the Contract Work Hours and Safety Standards Act. As we will see, how much a contracting officer may properly withhold varies with the particular law involved.

In addition to these rights under FAR clauses and various federal laws, the common-law right of setoff is also available to the government. The setoff principle says that the government has the same right that belongs to every creditor, "to apply the unappropriated monies of his debtor, in his hands, and extinguishment of the debts due to him."[23] The government's right of the setoff actually increases the amount of money the government is entitled to withhold under a particular contract clause.

A Navy contract let the government withhold a maximum of 10 percent of a progress payment "until satisfactory progress is achieved." The contract also let the government collect liquidated damages if a building was not finished on time. The Navy refused to pay an invoice for approximately $120,000 because the contractor's liquidated damages bill would be approximately $180, 000—more than 10 percent. The court concluded the government had the right to withhold this larger amount. The 10 percent limit was not a restriction on the government's current right to retain money due the government for liquidated damages but rather simply a limit on how much the government could withhold to cover future damages arising from the project's not getting finished.[24]

How Much May Be Withheld?

Although the government has the right to withhold progress payments, the amount withheld must be reasonable. It's up to the contractor to prove that the amount withheld was excessive at the time the withholdings were made.

Whether the withheld amount was excessive depends on what law authorized the withholding. Sometimes the contracting officer has to be accurate; other times, the contracting officer has to be only reasonable. And there is a difference, as this case shows:

After employees complained about Davis-Bacon Act (DBA) wage violations, the Forest Service withheld over $37,000 from a contractor. Later, the Department of Labor concluded that the

Davis-Bacon Act violations amounted to only approximately $3,900, roughly 1/10 of the money the government had withheld.

The CAFC said the inaccurate amount was not excessive. The court distinguished between withholding for progress and withholding for DBA: "ordinarily, if the government withholds amounts from progress payments as a setoff, the withholding is proper only if the amount of setoff is found to be properly computed. Where amounts were withheld because of potential DBA violations, a different standard applies. The withholdings are proper as long as the amount withheld depended on a reasonable judgment of the contracting officer that the withheld amounts were needed to protect the employees' interests." Since the test here was reasonableness and not 100 percent accuracy, the government had more room for error in miscalculating the DBA withholding. Here, the contractor gave the contracting officer "only the sketchiest of data highlighting the fact that the appellant could not verify that he had made the contested payments when the Forest Service asked him to do so." This sparse documentation couldn't invalidate the contracting officer's miscalculation.[25]

Recovery of Erroneous Payments

As if a contracting officer did not have enough to do, courts have added more work. In describing the government's alternatives when it has made an improper or erroneous payment of tax dollars, courts hold that the government "has not only the right but the duty to recover the payment . . . ."[26]

There are very few cases in procurement where this duty has been an issue. In one case, the government tenant erroneously paid the landlord's taxes. When the landlord objected to returning the erroneous payment, the court said that the erroneous payment must be returned, using the "right as well as duty" language quoted above. The reason why the money has to be returned is to avoid unjust enrichment of the contractor. As one board said:

> "Indeed, because of the strong government interest in recovering overpayments of public funds, a contracting officer has an affirmative duty to seek recovery of such disbursements and those receiving erroneous payments have a corresponding obligation to find the money."[27]

Assignments

In contract law, there are two types of assignments, and they are distinctly different.

One type of assignment is an *assignment of claims,* in which the assignor (the contractor) gives the assignee (typically, a bank) the money from the contract (or the right to it). The assignee does not do the work under the contract. The other type of assignment is an *assignment of a contract.* Assigning a contract means that the one to whom it is assigned (the assignee) must do the work and must get the money for doing it.

Before discussing how government contract law treats these assignments, it might be helpful to get a better understanding of the concept of an assignment.

An assignment is simply a transfer of something. But assignments can be confused with other types of transfers, such as sales. There's a big difference between an assignment and a sale. For example, when we sell a house, we usually have no further responsibility for the house. A sale divorces us from the house. But in an assignment, there's no divorce. After the assignment is made, the contracting party making the assignment always remains responsible for carrying out the work under the contract. As a result, this original party to the contract, even **after** the transfer of its interest in the contract, remains on the hook to the government. In effect, after an assignment of a contract, both the new party to the contract (the assignee) and the old party to the contract (the assignor) remain responsible for doing the contract work. So in discussing assignments, it's important to distinguish an assignment from a sale.

Of the two types of assignments, it's much easier in government contracting for contractors to do an assignment of claims. Government contract provisions make it easy to assign claims but, importantly, only to a bank. Assignments of claims are in the government's interest, so it wants to encourage them. Assigning claims, which really means the money from the contract, to a bank makes the bank more willing to finance the contractor during contract performance, because the bank has a right to the money from the contract.

An assignment of a government contract, on the other hand, is much more difficult to do because not only money but also performance obligations are being transferred to someone new. The government, therefore, wants to have the right to approve the assignment of the government contract. After all, the government awarded the contract to the original contractor (the assignor) only after concluding that the contractor was responsible. Once the government selects a contractor, a different contractor should not be forced on the government.

The government's approval of the assignment of a contract may come in any one of several forms—typically by the government's signing a novation agreement under FAR 42.1204 and less typically by the government's waiving its rights to approve the new contractor. Finally, one type of assignment of a contract may occur without government approval by novation or waiver. This is the transfer or assignment of a contract made "by operation of law." Because these transfers, such as property passing to heirs or property involved in bankruptcy proceedings under the control of the bankruptcy court judge, happen "by law," they don't need formal government approval.

Assignment of Claims

FAR 52.232-23 covers the assignment of claims. This provision allows a government contractor to freely assign the contract's income stream without government approval. But the assignment may be made only to "a bank, trust company, or other financing institution." The friendly neighborhood loan shark is not included.

Although Congress has made it easy for contractors to assign the income to banks, the banks must follow the assignment of claims requirements to the letter. Failure to do so jeopardizes the bank's assignment.

A construction contractor did an assignment of claims to Banco Bilbao Vizcaya–Puerto Rico ("BBV"). But the bank didn't notify the surety as required by the law, it did not give the contracting officer notice of the assignment as required, and the assignment listed two parties instead of only one as required. So the bank's attempt to get proceeds from the contract were unsuccessful. The CFC ruled that the law must be strictly followed. And because BBV had failed to follow "many" of the law's requirements, the court dismissed the case.[28]

An assignment of claims gets the assignee the right to the money but not the right to sue the government.

First Commercial Funding was an assignee under the Assignment of Claims provisions of a government contract. When the contractor had trouble finishing the project, the contracting officer terminated the contract for default. First Commercial Funding appealed the termination for default but was thrown out of court. There was

> no privity of contract with an assignee under the Assignment of Claims provisions. All the assignee gets is the income, not the right to sue the government.[29]

Assignment of a Contract

As mentioned above, the assignment of a government contract—that is, the work under the contract, as well as the money under the contract—must be approved by the government. This approval can come through the execution of a novation agreement under FAR 42.1204 or by the government's waiver of its right to approve the assignment of the contract.

One of the more difficult issues here is deciding whether to use a novation agreement or a "change of name agreement" under FAR 42.1205. If ABC Corporation has a contract with the government and ABC has changed its name to the DEF Corp., there's really been no change in the contractor. The same warm bodies the government found to be responsible when it awarded the contract to ABC Corporation are theoretically still working on the contract, but now under a new name, DEF Corp. There has really been no change of contractor; there has simply been a change of the contractor's name. For that reason, change of name agreements carry a much lower risk to the government than the assignment of a contract.

In dealing with the approval of the assignment of contracts, a contracting officer must watch for two issues—the government's waiver of its right to approve the assignment of the contract and assignments not requiring approval because they occur "by operation of law."

No government approval needed: waiver

Like any right given to any party in a contract, the right the government has to approve the assignment of a contract may be waived. The typical way the government waives its approval is by freely cooperating and working with the new contractor even though a novation agreement formally granting government approval has not been signed.

In a sense, these waivers don't really harm the government. The whole point of requiring government approvals of the assignment of contracts is to make sure the government finds the new contractor to be someone it wants to work with. So when the government willingly works with the new contractor, the government's cooperation can be considered a waiver of its right to approve the new contractor.

After a construction company did not finish a government project, the surety took it over with government knowledge and worked with the government to get the project finished. When the surety asked the government to pay for costs incurred by the construction company, the government refused, arguing that the surety had not signed a novation agreement. A board made the government pay. The Anti-Assignment Act's protections can be waived "by the government's overall course of conduct. . . . [I]t is unnecessary to identify any one particular act as constituting recognition of the assignments by the government. It is enough to say that the totality of the circumstances presented to the court establishes the government's recognition of the assignments by its knowledge, assent, and action consistent with the terms of the assignments." To the board, the government's course of conduct here indicated its approval. The government knew the construction company was having trouble paying people. Both the company and the surety told the government that the surety had taken over the contract and that the company had given all its rights to the surety.[30]

No government approval needed: transfer by operation of law

If a federal law transfers a government contract to another party, why should or would the contracting officer be allowed to stand in the way of that transfer? That's the theory behind this exception.

One law typically at play here is the bankruptcy law. Under that law, a bankruptcy judge is charged with collecting the assets of one party and finding a way to make those assets more valuable, often by letting someone else manage them. So when a bankruptcy judge has a government contract as an asset, the judge alone can do with that asset whatever seems prudent. A contracting officer has no role in approving the transfer of a government contract when it is transferred in bankruptcy proceedings.

A government contractor filed a claim and later went through Chapter 11 bankruptcy. The approved bankruptcy plan transferred the claim to another company. The government asked a board to throw the claim out, arguing that it was barred by federal law. The board refused. Although the law generally requires the government to approve transfers of ownership of government claims, that did not apply to assignments by operation of law—here the assignment was pursuant to the bankruptcy law and was therefore considered an assignment by operation of law.[31]

Endnotes

1. *Computer Technology Associates Inc.*, B-288,622, Nov. 7, 2001, 2001 CPD ¶ 187.

2. *Id.*

3. *Id.*

4. *American Management Systems, Inc.*, B-285,645, Sept. 8, 2000, 2000 CPD ¶ 163.

5. *Computers Universal, Inc.*, B-292,794, Nov. 18, 2003, 2003 CPD ¶ 201.

6. *The Leads Corp.*, B-292,465, Sept. 26, 2003, 2003 CPD ¶ 197.

7. *The Jones/Hill Joint Venture*, B-286194.4, B-286194.5, B-286194.6, Dec. 05, 2001, CPD ¶ 194.

8. *Ktech Corporation*, B-285,330, Aug. 7, 2000, 2002 CPD ¶ 77.

9. *Computers Universal, Inc.*, Nov. 18, 2003, 2003 CPD ¶ 201.

10. *Id.*

11. *Great Lakes Dredge and Dock Company*, B-290158, June 17, 2002, CPD ¶ 100.

12. *Impresa Construzioni Geom. Domenico Garufi v. The United States*, 238 F.3d 1324, 1333 (Fed.Cir. 2001).

13. *Computer Technology Associates, Inc.*, B-288622, Nov. 7, 2001, 2001 CPD ¶ 187.

14. *Acquest Development LLC*, B-287439, June 6, 2001, 2001 CPD ¶ 101.

15. *Id.*

16. *Id.*

17. *Id.*

18. *American Technical & Analytical Services, Inc.*, B-282277.5, May 31, 2000, 2000 CPD ¶ 98.

19. *FN Manufacturing, Inc.*, B-297172; B-297172.2, Dec. 1, 2005, 2005 CPD ¶ 212.

20. *Id.*

21. *Medina Construction Ltd. v. The United States*, 43 Fed.Cl. 537, 555 (1999).

22. *Bender Gmbh*, ASBCA No. 52,266, 04-1 BCA ¶ 32,474.

23. *Munsey Trust Co.*, 332 U.S. 234, 239 (1947).

24. *Johnson v. All-State Contractors Inc.*, 329 F.3d 848 (Fed.Cir.2003).

25. *Copeland v. Veneman*, 350 F.3d 1230 (Fed.Cir.2003).

26. *Wright Runstad Properties Ltd. Partnership v. The United States*, 40 Fed. Cl. 820 (1998).

27. *B&B Reproductions*, GPO BCA 9-89, June 30, 1995.

28. *Banco Bilbao Vizcaya-Puerto Rico v. The United States*, 48 Fed.Cl. 29 (2000).

29. *First Commercial Funding, LLC., Assignee of Power Construction Group, Inc.*, ENGBCA No. 6447, February 10, 2000.

30. *Safeco Insurance Company of America*, ASBCA No. 52107, 03-2 BCA ¶32,341.

31. *Certified Abatement Technologies, Inc.*, ASBCA No. 39852, 99-1 BCA ¶ 30,389.

Chapter 3

The Contracting Officer as Defendant

CONTENTS

L ike the rest of us, contracting officers always run the risk of being sued by somebody for something. Because contracting officers work for the government administering contracts with contractors, contracting officers face a double threat: potential lawsuits from the government and potential lawsuits from contractors and their employees. This chapter discusses both.

In the first part of the chapter, we discuss a contracting officer's liability for mistakes made in doing his job. Here, we focus on the contracting officer's liability to the government for making improper payments. In the second part of the chapter, we discuss the contracting officer's liability to third parties like the contractor or the contractor's employees hurt performing a contract administered by the contracting officer. This section also discusses the contracting officer's liability under the Federal Tort Claims Act (FTCA).

Contracting Officer's Financial Liability to the Government

There's good news for contracting officers on this issue. And it's not intuitive. *Even though a contracting officer approves contracts and gets heavily involved in the contract payment process, there's not much personal, pecuniary liability for a contracting officer.*

This conclusion comes from the GAO Red Book, which discusses at length how federal law imposes personal liability on "an accountable officer." The Red Book describes who actually is "an accountable officer" (identifying personnel like "certifying officers, civilian and military disbursing officers, collecting officers, and other employees who by virtue of their employment have custody of government funds"), but the Red Book's list does not include a contracting officer.

This is surprising, because a procurement shop gets heavily involved in contract payments—legal and otherwise.

Better yet, from a contracting officer's perspective, the Red Book describes how rare it would be for a contracting officer to be an accountable officer:

> "With rare exceptions, other officials who may have a role in authorizing expenditures (contracting officers, for example) are not accountable officers for purposes of the laws discussed in this chapter. . . ."[1]

The Red Book cites a 1992 GAO opinion as authority. In this decision, a contracting officer and contract specialist messed up spectacularly. Both approved a progress payment to a contractor even though the contract's payments had been assigned to a bank and even though the contract did not allow progress payments. Trying to turn the law on its head, the Air Force wanted to hold these procurement people liable instead of making the accounting and finance officer and the certifying officer liable, as federal law requires. GAO concluded that the Air Force could not make the contracting officer and contracting specialist liable:

> "There is no authority to assess pecuniary liability against the government employee for losses resulting from an error in judgment or neglect of duty. . . ."[2]

In another case, the Department of Veterans Affairs improperly used VA money for three gift certificates to local restaurants and a silk plant in connection with a contest advancing the VA's celebration of Women's Equality Week. GAO refused to hold any procurement employees financially liable:

> "VA's certifying officers necessarily rely on various participants in the procurement and payment process to ensure that only legal and accurate payments are made. However, these officials, including contracting officers and voucher auditors, do not become certifying officers subject to liability for improper payments merely because certifying officers rely on their review or approval of purchases or payments. Therefore, while officials other than certifying officers may be subject to administrative sanctions, our Office has never looked to them for reimbursement in cases of illegal or improper payments."[3]

The Red Book goes on to add that a contracting officer "may be made accountable in varying degrees by agency regulation." Whether this remains true is in question. Although this quote is from the most recent version of the Red Book, it might no longer be good law, as stated in an important 2000 GAO decision:

> "Over the years our Office has taken the position in a number of different contexts that agencies may not hold employees liable for losses caused the government as a result of errors in judgment or neglect of duty in the absence of administrative regulations. . . . On one occasion, we concluded that an agency solely by regulation may establish pecuniary liability for employees supervising a certifying and disbursing process. This conclusion was repeated in passing or in dicta in some other decisions. . . . Regardless of [these decisions], in light of the Supreme Court decisions . . . we believe that an agency may impose pecuniary liability only with a statutory basis. Accordingly, we will no longer accept our earlier case law in this regard as precedent and any decision inconsistent herewith is overruled."[4]

Other government employees, like certifying officials, are not so lucky:

In September 2001 a forest fire in the Gifford Pinchot National Forest (GPNF) led to the Forest Service's contracting with Evergreen Bus Service for busses to carry firefighters. To get paid, Evergreen sent the Forest Service four invoices on Department of Agriculture forms. These invoices, totaling $5,631.85, were paid after the government's certifying officer signed them on September 25. The next day, the government got four more invoices for the same work, in the same amount, but this time on Evergreen stationary, not on USDA forms. Two of these Evergreen invoices even had copies of the USDA forms signed earlier attached to them. The same certifying officer certified them, one two days later and the others eight days later. When the Forest Service realized a mistake had been made, it tried to get the money back from Evergreen, but Evergreen's bankruptcy proceedings prevented that. The Forest Service asked GAO if the employee could not be held liable for the mistake because she paid the invoices in good faith and with reasonable diligence.

GAO said she had to pay the government back. Federal law makes certifying officers repay the government for any "illegal, improper, or incorrect" payments they make. Because the contractor had already been paid once, paying the contractor again was improper, so the certifying officer had to pay the government back unless the employee could come within one of the two exceptions to personal liability. The first exception to personal liability was that the employee used "reasonable diligence." Not here: "We cannot find that the certifying officer, in certifying the September 27 and October 5 payments, acted with reasonable 'diligence and inquiry.' If she had done so, she would have learned that, just days before, she had certified payments to Evergreen for the same services and in the same amounts. The standard of reasonable diligence and inquiry requires an examination of the 'practical conditions prevailing at the time of certification, the sufficiency of the administrative procedures protecting the interest of the Government, and the apparency of the error.' Here, the error was clearly apparent on the face of the invoices that the certifying officer was asked to certify."

The second exception to personal liability was "good faith." That was not the case either: "Our office may relieve liability if the following three conditions are met: (1) the obligation was incurred in good faith; (2) no law specifically prohibited the payment; and (3) the United States Government received value for the payments." GAO found that here, the certifying official here met only two of the necessary three criteria. She was certainly acting in good faith when she certified payments. And it is legal to pay for bus services during a fire. "However, in order to grant relief, we must find that the government received some value for the payments. Clearly, Evergreen had provided no additional bus services beyond those that GPNF had already paid for on September 25, 2001. Accordingly, we are unable to grant relief. . . ." [5]

CONTRACTING OFFICER'S FINANCIAL LIABILITY TO THE PUBLIC

"Mistakes were made," the classic quote from the Clinton White House, is one reason for the Federal Tort Claims Act (FTCA). The government makes mistakes. More accurately, government employees make mistakes.

If an employee of a company makes a mistake, the company can be sued. So can the employee. Can the government be sued for the mistakes of its employees? That depends on whether there has been a waiver of sovereign immunity. Because the government is generally immune from lawsuits, Congress would have to consent to the government's being sued.

The FTCA gave this consent, but it was a very limited consent. The end result is that a contracting officer *acting professionally* is immune from lawsuit. This law waived the government's sovereign immunity and made the government liable for money damages when government employees commit certain "wrongful acts" or torts.

This complex law can be generally summarized like this: If a government employee has a job that must be done—a mandatory duty—but the employee does that job negligently, the government can be sued. But the government cannot be sued if the negligent act of the government employee was a discretionary act. This summary raises four critical issues that typically get litigated: Was the action (1) of a government employee (and not an independent contractor) (2) negligent or one of the "non-enumerated" intentional torts; (3) "within the scope of employment of the government employee;" (4) in the performance of a "mandatory" or "discretionary" duty?

Government Employee or Independent Contractor

The FTCA is a limited waiver of the government's sovereign immunity. It covers only the employees of a federal agency. If an injury was caused by an independent contractor, the contracting officer cannot be liable under the FTCA.

Courts typically find an agency relationship between the government and a contractor if the government has the power to control the detailed physical performance of the contractor or if the government in fact supervises the day-to-day operations of the contractor. Simply because the government *can* inspect or *can* supervise a contractor's compliance with the contract specifications does not establish the agency relationship necessary to bring the case within the FTCA.

Another indicator of an independent contractor relationship is the contractor's having liability insurance. Courts interpret the requirement to have liability insurance as some evidence that the insured is acting as an independent contractor.

Two people were hurt while walking in front of a U.S. Customs Service building. They sued the government. In wonderful legal hyperbole, they claimed that they had been "violently propelled to the ground." They argued that they were hurt because the government didn't properly inspect or repair the sidewalk and didn't provide a safe environment for both of them. The government had a contract with Eastco Building Services. The company was to maintain and repair the sidewalks in front of the building. No government employee supervised these day-to-day operations of the company. The Federal District Court threw the case out, concluding that Eastco was an independent contractor that was itself responsible for problems with the sidewalks. In this case, the government "did not exercise control over the detailed physical performance or supervise the day-to-day activities of Eastco but reserved the right to inspect performance to ensure compliance with the terms of the contract. These factors established that the government was acting 'generally as an overseer' and that no agency relationship existed with Eastco." The court added, "in addition, Eastco maintained liability insurance to cover its operations under the Eastco contract." In fact, the government contract required Eastco to do so.[6]

Negligence or One of the "Non-Enumerated" Intentional Torts

The Federal Tort Claims Act is not all that accurate a name for the law because the law does not let people sue the government for **all** torts. Technically, the FTCA deals with the "negligent or wrongful act or omission" of a federal employee. So negligence, the most common type of tort, is included.

Some "intentional" torts are purposely put beyond the reach of an alleged victim: libel, slander, misrepresentation, deceit, interference with contract rights, assault, battery, or false arrest or imprisonment, except with respect to investigative or law enforcement officers (28 U.S.C. § 2680(h)). But any other intentional torts not expressly excluded by the FTCA are covered.

The FDA posted a company's trade secrets on the agency's website, without telling the company it was doing so. The company sued the government under the FTCA for misappropriating the company's trade secrets and breaching the FDA's confidential relationship with the company. A Federal District Court threw the case out, holding that the case involved interference with contract rights, a tort the government could not be sued on. The appeals court ordered the lawsuit reinstated. To the appeals court, the lawsuit was not one of the expressly excluded intentional torts, like interference with contract rights. Rather, the lawsuit was over misappropriation of trade secrets or breach of confidentiality.[7]

Discretionary Function

Discretion demands immunity. If, for example, the FAR gives a contracting officer wide latitude or discretion to decide which offer is the "best value" to the government, is it fair to make the contracting officer liable for negligence if he makes a bad decision? Would making a contracting officer and the government financially liable for bad judgment lead to better decisions? Or would doing so make a contracting officer reluctant to make any decision? Aren't discretionary decisions best made if the contracting officer is not afraid of financial liability or even the threat of a financial liability lawsuit?

Congress concluded that the best way to let a contracting officer make a discretionary decision is to make the contracting officer and the government immune from lawsuits over the many discretionary actions government employees like contracting officers make as part of their jobs.

What is a discretionary action? It is one that meets two tests, one easy to see and one very difficult to see.

Mandatory?

First, if the government *has* to take the action (or is forbidden to take the action), the action cannot be discretionary. So mandatory actions are not discretionary. Because letting the government carry out policy is the basis for immunity, no policy is being violated when the government violates a mandatory regulation.

The example of the FDA posting a company's trade secrets on the agency's website, without telling the company it was doing so, is relevant again. The company sued the government under the FTCA for misappropriating the company's trade secrets and breaching the FDA's confidential relationship with the company. An appeals court said the action was not discretionary: "Disclosure of trade secrets is not a discretionary function because federal laws prohibit it."[8]

So if a federal statute, policy, or regulation makes an action mandatory, or forbids it, mistakes in doing the action can lead to government liability. These mistake are not immune from lawsuit as a "discretionary" act.

Policy Analysis?

The second part of the discretionary job test is more difficult: Was the challenged action, in the words of the appeals court, "the type Congress meant to protect; i.e., whether the action involves a decision susceptible to social, economic, or political policy analysis"?[9] The theory here is that courts shouldn't let a tort lawsuit be used to let someone second-guess legislative or agency decisions grounded on policy.

This is not an easy call. This same court put it well, referring to

> "the difficulty of charting a clear path through the weaving lines of precedent regarding what decisions are susceptible to social, economic, or political policy analysis. Government actions can be classified along a spectrum, ranging from those 'totally divorced from the sphere of policy analysis,' such as driving a car, to those 'fully grounded in regulatory policy,' such as the regulation and oversight of a bank. . . . But determining the appropriate place on the spectrum for any given government action can be a challenge."[10]

The court gave some helpful guidelines. One is the distinction between design and implementation. "We have generally held that the *design* of a course of governmental action is shielded by the discretionary function exception, whereas the *implementation* of that course of action is not."[11] Another guideline is that "matters of scientific and professional judgment—particularly judgments concerning safety—are rarely considered to be susceptible to social, economic, or political policy."[12]

The court then gave two clear examples:

> "In a suit alleging government negligence in the design and maintenance of a national park road, we held that designing the road without guardrails was a choice grounded in policy considerations and was therefore shielded under the discretionary function exception, but maintaining the road was a safety responsibility not susceptible to policy analysis. . . . Similarly, in a suit alleging government negligence

in the design and construction of an irrigation canal, we held that the decision not to line the canal with concrete was susceptible to policy analysis, but the failure to remove unsuitable materials during construction was not. In three cases concerning injuries resulting from the government's failure to post warnings concerning hazards present in national parks, we held that the government's decision not to post signs warning of obvious dangers such as venturing off marked trails to walk next to the face of a waterfall, and the government's decision to use brochures rather than posted signs to warn hikers of the dangers of unmaintained trails, involved the exercise of policy judgment of the type Congress meant to shield from liability, but that such policy judgment was absent when the government simply failed to warn of the danger to barefoot visitors of hot coals on a park beach, . . . and in an action for the death of a prospective logger 'trying out' for a job with a government contractor at a logging site under the management of a government agency, we held that while the government's authorization of the contract was protected under the discretionary function exception, the government's failure to monitor and ensure safety at the work site was not."[13]

Going back to an example from earlier in the chapter, two people were hurt while walking in front of a U.S. Customs Service building. They sued the government, claiming in their lawsuit that they were "violently propelled to the ground." They argued that they were hurt because the government, among other things, didn't wisely pick or properly monitor the company the government used to maintain and repair the sidewalks in front of the building. No government employee supervised these day-to-day operations of the company. The court threw out the case because the government involvement, if any, was discretionary. "GSA was not required to hire a particular contractor or to engage in a particular degree of oversight over the independent contractor it chose. . . . [T]he selection and supervision of contractors is a discretionary function and cannot form the basis for liability under the FTCA."[14]

Within the Scope of the Employee's Duties

Because a government employee is immune from lawsuit only when acting as a federal employee, one element of proof is that the employee was actually working for the government when the tort occurred.

This issue is one decided by state law. Under some state laws (Ohio's, for example), an employee acting within the scope of his employment has to at least meet the *employer direction and control test:* "[T]he employee was subject to the direction and control of the employer as to the operation of the employee's automobile while using it in doing the work he was employed to do (so that the relation between the employer and the employee and the driving of the automobile will be the relationship of principal and agent or master and servant as distinguished from the relationship of employer and independent contractor)."[15]

A government employee spent four hours at his office on Sunday working to get ready for government business on Monday. On his way home from the base, he was involved in an auto accident with a motorcycle. When the motorcyclist sued him, he claimed that the lawsuit really should be against the federal government because he was acting within the scope of his employment on his ride home. Under Ohio law, however, he was not acting within the scope of his employment because he was not subject to the direction and control of the employer while operating his car on his way home. He had chosen the day and time to make the trip, as well as his route to the office. At the time of the accident, the federal government was exercising no "constraints on Mr. Shimp's time or activities with respect to his employment. No one called Mr. Shimp at home and directed him to go to his office . . . to collect the items which he would need to take Los Angeles the next day. In addition Mr. Shimp was accommodating his own schedule when he went to his office . . . [He] was not required to gather the materials when he did."

The appeals court concluded that his "Sunday drive was on a day of the week when he was not required to go to the Air Force base at all. He had the option of picking up the documents at any time he chose, including the Friday before his trip or the Monday morning just before he left for Los Angeles." The appeals court also considered that he never asked to be reimbursed for the distance he drove between his home and the base. "Although he called his work supervisor shortly after the accident, he did so only because the accident prevented him from traveling to Los Angeles the following day. Shimp simply was not 'subject to the direction and control' of his employer at the time of the accident."[16]

Some victims can't sue either the government or the government's employee. In *United States v. Smith*, 499 U.S. 160, 111 S.Ct. 1180, 113 L.Ed.2d 134 (1991), a government doctor was sued for medical malpractice. The Supreme Court held that the government employee was protected from liability, even where the government had no liability. "The Court expressly recognized that the effect of its ruling was to leave certain tort victims without any remedy—either against the Government or against the employee-tortfeasor. The Court found that this was the intention of Congress." *B & A Marine Co., Inc. v. American Foreign Shipping Co., Inc.* 23 F.3d 709, 715 (2d. Cir.1994).

Endnotes

1.   PRINCIPLES OF FEDERAL APPROPRIATIONS LAW, Vol. II, p. 9-8, (3rd Ed. January 2004).

2.   65 Comp. Gen. 177 (1986) B-241856.2 , Sept. 23, 1992.

3.   *Expenditures by The Department of Veterans Affairs Medical Center, Oklahoma City, Oklahoma*, B-247,563, B-247563.3, Apr. 5, 1996, 96-1 CPD ¶ 190.

4.   *Department of Defense—Authority to Impose Pecuniary Liability by Regulation*, B-280,764, May 4, 2000.

5.   *Forest Service Request for Relief of Liability*, B-303177, October 20, 2004.

6.   *Fisko v. United States*, 395 F.Supp.2d. 57 (S.D.N.Y.2005).

7.   *Jerome Stevens Pharmaceuticals Inc. v. The Food and Drug Administration*, 402 F.3d 1249 (D.C.Cir.2005).

8.   *Id.*

9.   *Whisnant v. The United States*, 400 F.3d 1177, 1180 (9th Cir.2005).

10. *Id.* at 1181.

11. *Id.*

12. *Id.*

13. *Id.* at 1181-1182.

14. *Fisko, supra,* at 65.

15. *Sullivan et al. v. Tedd Shimp,* 324 F.3d 397 (6th Cir.2003).

16. *Id.*

Chapter 4

The Contracting Officer as Plaintiff

If taxpayers and disgruntled employees can be bounty hunters, can a contracting officer be one, too?

For years, bounty hunters have operated under the Federal False Claims Act. This law tries to encourage taxpayers to uncover fraud in government programs by promising them a cut of the fraud recovery the government gets. These lawsuits are called *qui tam* lawsuits. *Qui tam* comes from the Latin phrase meaning "who brings the action for the king as well as himself."[1]

Now this is one government program that really works! By 2003, more than 100 people had collected more than $1 million as bounty hunters. The government recovered more than $8 billion between 1986 and 2004 in *qui tam* suits.[2]

Would that amount be higher if government employees were allowed to be bounty hunters? No one knows the answer, but the question does raise difficult policy issues. For example, since it's part of a contracting officer's job to "safeguard the interests of the United States in its contractual relationships," contracting officers in a sense are already being paid for uncovering fraud.

The courts are still trying to figure out an answer. One thing is clear: the fact that the bounty hunters are government employees is no reason to automatically disqualify them from filing *qui tam* suits. If government employees as a group are not automatically prevented from being bounty hunters, what specific government jobs would disqualify someone from being a bounty hunter?

One case made a distinction between an internal government auditor, whose job was to expose fraud (and thus should not allow him to be a bounty hunter), and another employee, a lawyer, whose job "was not to expose fraud, but to draft contracts and perform other legal services for the Corps," who could be a *qui tam* relator.[3]

A good discussion of the policy issues involved was found in a case dealing with whether a postmaster could be a *qui tam* relator.[4] Mary Holmes, the postmaster in a small Colorado town, knew that a bulk mailer in her area was not paying the correct postage. As a postmaster, Holmes was required to report fraud as part of her job. She told her boss, and eventually the matter was referred to the U.S. Attorney's Office. Holmes filed a *qui tam* lawsuit.

A majority of 7 out of the 10 judges on the entire court allowed Holmes' lawsuit to continue. The law said that these kinds of suits may be brought by the Attorney General or a "person." Because the law entitled a "person" to sue, and clearly the federal employee Holmes was a "person," she should be able to bring these lawsuits.

The government had argued that a federal employee who discovers fraud in the course of employment and is required to report is not a "person" entitled to bring these lawsuits because the acquisition of such information is within the scope of their job. The court, however, did not agree: "This argument finds no support in the ordinary meaning of the word 'person.' In particular, we fail to see how the word could rationally be construed to exclude some, but not all, government employees, and under some, but not all, conditions."

The court also went on to address issues raised by the government on a "policy" basis, as opposed to a strict interpretation of the law. The government was concerned that because Holmes had a duty to report fraud, letting her and other federal employees share in any fraud recovery "would be contrary to federal regulations prohibiting the use of public office for private gain, the use of government property or time for personal purposes, the use of nonpublic government information to further private interests, and the holding of any financial interests that may conflict with the impartial performance of government duties."

Having identified these policy arguments, the court concluded that these were issues for Congress, not the court, to address. "Although the government arguments have some appeal, the fact is that nothing in the law expressly precludes federal employees" from filing these suits. The court pointed out that so far, no court has prevented someone from participating in these lawsuits simply because he or she was a government employee.

Three of the ten judges disagreed with the majority, believing that Holmes' lawsuit should not have been allowed to continue. Significantly, the dissenting judges agreed that federal employees should not be prevented from bringing these lawsuits simply because they are employed by the government. The problem, to these judges, was that Holmes had a specific duty to report this fraud. The dissent focused on another section of the law that discusses lawsuits brought "for the person and for the United States government." Because this phrase distinguishes a person from the United States government, and the United States government is made up of federal employees who are persons, a federal employee must be part of the "United States government" in this phrase, not a "person." Because a federal employee can be only one and not both, federal employees clearly are part of the "United States government." These judges therefore "read this statute as authorizing these actions only by those individuals who are distinct from the government. When a federal employee acting pursuant to job responsibilities obtains information about possible fraud, that employee obtains that information as the government. A federal employee who is involved in an ongoing government investigation pursuant to employment duties is the government."

The dissent also gave a thoughtful discussion of the difficult conflict of interest issue. It noted that federal employees are prohibited from using public government information to further any private interests. Federal employees are also prohibited from using public office for private gain. "Rather than perform their jobs as required, government employees obligated to disclose suspected fraud may inappropriately hide fraud from their supervisors while preparing" bounty hunting lawsuits.

In a footnote, the majority made an interesting point about the conflict of interest issue: An employee filing a bounty hunting lawsuit based on information obtained in the course of employment "might have to forfeit all or part of the recovery obtained."

Undoubtedly, this is an issue that the U.S. Supreme Court will have to resolve some day. So far, it has not.

Endnotes

1. *Erickson v. American Institute of Bio. Sciences,* 716 F.Supp. 908, 909 n. 1 (E.D.Va.1989) (citing W. Blackstone, *Commentaries on the Law of England,* 160 (1768)).

2. http://www.allaboutquitam.org/DOJstats.fy2004.pdf.

3. *Hagood v. Sonoma County Water Agency,* 81 F.3d 1465, 1476 (9th Cir.1996).

4. *United States ex rel. Holmes v. Consumer Ins. Group,* 318 F.3d 1199 (10th Cir.2003).

Chapter 5

Contractor Responsibilities

CONTENTS

Becoming the "other party" to a government contract gets a government vendor involved in a number of unique issues that the vendor would not get involved in if the contract was between the vendor and a typical consumer. One of the biggest differences is that a government vendor gives up rights a vendor normally would have, such as having the contract governed by state law and being able to sue the other party in a local court.

This chapter focuses on the most-litigated issues a contractor faces. First, the chapter looks at the requirement that the contractor verify the authority of a contracting officer. Failure to do so could mean there is no deal with the government. The chapter then looks at the problems a vendor faces when it proposes to use one group of employees if it gets the contract, but ends up using another set of employees after winning the contract. It's the problem of bait and switch. The chapter closes by looking at two fraud landmines: implied certifications make a false claim out of an honest invoice, and the wipe-out damages a contractor faces for false claims.

CHECK CONTRACTING OFFICER'S AUTHORITY

Ideally, on the first day of government service, a contract specialist learns that the government cannot be bound legally to a vendor unless the vendor deals with a government employee that has the authority to make purchases on behalf of the government. The basic concept is that the government is not bound by the acts of one of its employees unless the employee is authorized to do the act. That's why contracting officers have warrants authorizing them to sign contracts. No warrant, no authority, no deal. That's the general rule.

Decisions seem to say that vendors have not learned that principle. According to many contract specialists and contracting officers, vendors **never** ask about the authority of the government employees they are dealing with. So it's no surprise that vendors sometimes get into deals with the government that the government can disavow because the government employee the vendor dealt with did not have the authority to do the deal.

This rule can cause vendors and suppliers that give the government something to end up giving the government that something for free. Two ways a vendor might get paid are as a "third-party beneficiary" or under an "institutional ratification."

Third-party Beneficiaries

Some vendors, such as suppliers or subcontractors, are not a party to the deal between the government and the vendor, but they provide something to the government. When the prime contractor does not pay them, they sue the government under the "third-party beneficiary" rule.

Often, these third-party beneficiaries lose.

The Defense Supply Center Columbus had a contract with Capital City Pipes, Inc., to provide air-duct hose to the government. The supplier, Flexfab, would not sell hoses to Capital City unless payment for the hoses was sent directly by the government to Flexfab. A government Small Business specialist worked out a deal that would do that. But he did not have contract authority, and he did not tell the contracting officers involved about the arrangement for getting the money to Flexfab. After Flexfab delivered the hoses to the government, it was not paid for them as agreed. So Flexfab sued the government for payment but lost. The relevant contracting officers did not know of the arrangement the Small Business specialist had with Flexfab. Because no one in the government with authority had intended to make Flexfab a beneficiary of the deal, Flexfab could not be considered a third-party beneficiary.[1]

In a similar situation, but one involving a contracting officer, Flexfab was found to be a third-party beneficiary. Here, the contracting officer had clearly been involved. He had modified the contract between the government and the prime, with those two parties agreeing that Flexfab would cosign government checks. When that did not happen, Flexfab successfully sued and got paid.[2]

So the general rule is that a government contract "requires that the Government representative who entered or ratified the agreement had actual authority to bind the United States."[3] If a vendor does not check, the vendor

"takes the risk of having accurately ascertained that he who purports to act for the Government stays within the bounds of his authority. The scope of this authority may be explicitly defined by Congress or be limited by delegated legislation, properly exercised through the rule-making power. And this is so even though, as here, the agent himself may have been unaware of the limitations upon his authority."[4]

Although this rule seems harsh (and it is), the rationale for it makes sense to the taxpayers:

> "Clearly, federal expenditures would be wholly uncontrollable if Government employees could, of their own volition, enter into contracts obliging the United States."[5]

The way vendors protect themselves is by dealing with only a "contracting officer." FAR 1.201 defines a *contracting officer* as "a person with the authority to enter into, administer, and/or terminate contracts and make related determinations and findings. The term includes certain authorized representatives of the contracting officer acting within the limits of their authority as delegated by the contracting officer." So it is not only a contracting officer who can bind the government; a contracting officer's representatives can do so as well.

Institutional Ratification

Another way a contractor might get paid, even though dealing with a government employee who does not have authority, is through ratification. This is the contracting officer's after-the-fact approval under FAR 1.602-3 of a previously unapproved act.

Institutional ratification is a more subtle after-the-fact approval used by courts and boards to make sure the government pays for a benefit it has received. Institutional ratification, although rare, can validate an otherwise unauthorized contract.[6]

In these situations, an unauthorized contract can be ratified by the agency when the government receives a direct benefit and the contracting officer involved possesses some level of authority. This is especially true if the government uses a product, benefits from it, and refuses to pay for it.

The Air Force was sued for payment of products and services provided by Digicon under a task order that had not been signed or ratified by a contracting officer. The court concluded that the Air

Force had gotten into a binding, although unauthorized, contract. "In the case of an unauthorized contract, it is well-established that an agency can institutionally ratify the contract even in the absence of specific ratification by an authorized official. Specifically, institutional ratification occurs when the Government seeks and receives the benefits of an otherwise unauthorized contract." Ratification can occur when the government receives a direct benefit and the contracting officer has some level of authority. Here, the government used Digicon's products and services for 16 months.[7]

A lower court had a good discussion of how the CAFC has handled cases involving institutional ratification.

"[The CAFC] discussed Silverman v. United States, which found institutional ratification, and City of El Centro v. United States, which did not. In Silverman, a senior Federal Trade Commission (FTC) official promised a court reporting service that the FTC would pay for hearing transcripts. Based on this representation, the court reporting service sent the transcripts to the FTC, which retained and utilized them. Id. The senior FTC official did not have contracting authority but did have authority to approve vouchers for goods and services. Id. The court held that '[b]y accepting the benefits flowing from the senior FTC official's promise of payment, the FTC ratified such promise and was bound by it.' In City of El Centro, a hospital alleged that the U.S. Border Patrol breached an implied-in-fact contract to compensate it for treatment of illegal aliens who sustained injuries while fleeing U.S. Border Patrol agents. The Federal Circuit rejected the hospital's institutional ratification argument and distinguished Silverman. The Federal Circuit explained that the FTC senior official in Silverman at least had authority to approve vouchers for goods and services, and the government received a benefit from the transcripts, whereas in City of El Centro no official with any contracting authority had promised payment to the hospital, and third parties, not the U.S. Border Patrol, received the benefits."[8]

BAIT AND SWITCH

When a government solicitation says that the government is looking for well-trained people, vendors have an obligation to make sure that the people they propose to use on the contract if they win would actually work on that contract. They cannot bait the government into giving them the contract based on the proposed use of one group of workers and then switch to a different group after winning the contract. If a vendor doesn't exercise due diligence in determining the availability of personnel, the vendor stands to be disqualified from the procurement.

Lining up potential workers can be a real problem for a contractor that is not the incumbent. The qualified workers are probably employed by the incumbent. So the non-incumbents, as well as the incumbent's employees who still want a job even if it's with a new employer, have problems trying to convince the government that they could staff a new contract if they won. On the other hand, things change. People move on to new employers.

Drawing the line between "things change" and "bait and switch" can be difficult. GAO gave an excellent summary of precisely what a prohibited bait and switch looks like:

> "To demonstrate a 'bait and switch,' a protester must show not only that personnel other than those proposed are performing the services—i.e., the 'switch'—but also that (1) the awardee represented in its proposal that it would rely on certain specified personnel in performing the services; (2) the agency relied on this representation in evaluating the proposal; and (3) it was foreseeable that the individuals named in the proposal would not be available to perform the contract work."[9]

The CFC gave another good example of what a bait and switch looks like:

> ". . . bidders proposing people (1) who expressed no willingness to be employees of bidder submitting the employee's name; or (2) who were unwilling or unable to show the level of commitment that the solicitation required of potential employees; or (3) were unable to be the bidder's employees; or (4) who were not directly asked whether they would accept employment."[10]

One way the government can try to get some commitment out of vendors is to get certifications of the availability of personnel from offerors. A material misrepresentation in the certifications—a lie—can make a winning proposal a loser.

The government issued a request for quotations for a vendor to train government employees in the use of a new computer system. A losing vendor, ACS Government Services, protested the award of the contract, arguing, in GAO's words, that the winner's quotation "materially misrepresented the availability of certain personnel proposed. Specifically, ACS contends that three of the individuals offered and certified as available by Metrica (i.e., Messrs. A, B, and C) had never agreed to work for Metrica, nor given their consent to be proposed by Metrica, but instead had exclusively committed themselves to the incumbent ACS. . . . ACS contends that by inaccurately certifying the availability of the individuals proposed, Metrica committed misrepresentations that materially affected the agency's evaluation of quotations and award decision." GAO agreed: "Metrica misrepresented that three of the key personnel that it proposed had agreed to work for the firm. We also find that Metrica included in its quotation the names and resumes of these three individuals without having gained their permission to do so, and cognizant of the fact that the individuals had given exclusive permission to ACS to submit their resumes. Further, we conclude that these actions resulted in a material misevaluation of the key personnel portion of Metrica's proposal."[11]

But it's no bait and switch if an intended hire goes elsewhere. Sometimes a bidder can win a contract based on promising to provide the government with certain persons who end up not working on the contract after it's awarded.

During an Army solicitation, the incumbent contractor, Orion International Technologies, had its employees sign a "no compete" agreement that prevented them only from helping other bidders win the contract. A competitor, Fiore Industries, talked to a Mr. Zucconi, one of the incumbent's employees, before he had signed the "no compete" agreement. Mr. Zucconi agreed to work for Fiore if Fiore won. Fiore did win but did not offer Mr. Zucconi a job. Orion protested, arguing "bait and switch." The court found no "bait and switch." Fiore's bid was responsive. "The extent to which Mr. Zucconi had to commit to Fiore depends on what the solicitation required. Thus, so long as Mr. Zucconi expressed to Mr. Sanchez the requisite level of interest in the project manager position, the agreement between Mr. Zucconi and Orion preventing Mr. Zucconi's involvement with Fiore's bid is irrelevant to the government's decision to award the contract to Fiore."[12]

IMPLIED CERTIFICATIONS

A contractor can violate the False Claims Act (FCA) even though submitting a valid, nonfraudulent invoice. If the good invoice has a bad certification, the FCA can be violated.

Some courts have found an FCA violation when a valid invoice accompanies a certification, for example, that the contract is being complied with when it is not. The result is that a perfectly valid invoice can become a false claim as a result of the false implied certification.

Some examples follow:

- The Court of Federal Claims found that an 8(a) firm had made a false implied certification when it submitted perfectly valid invoices to the government after signing a prohibited co-management agreement with a subcontractor that made the 8(a) firm no longer an 8(a) firm.[13]

- A court found a violation of an implied certification when a Medicare provider submitted invoices for payments knowing that it was not complying with all Medicare requirements.[14]

- An appeals court found a violation of the FCA when a contractor knowingly omitted from progress reports vital information concerning noncompliance with the program it was to implement.[15]

- AAA Engineering and Drafting, Inc., had a contract to do photography for Tinker Air Force Base used a solution containing silver. EPA regulations require that the silver be properly disposed of. The contract AAA had with the Air Force required AAA to comply with these EPA regulations. AAA did not comply with these regulations. It simply poured the silver down the drain. And the president of the company knew the company was not complying. Knowing that the company was not complying with EPA regulations as required by the contract, the company submitted routine, otherwise accurate invoices. Even though there was no *express* certification on the invoices that the company was complying with the EPA regulations or any other regulations, the company had violated the False Claims Act.[16]

But, the issue is not settled. The 5th Circuit refused to find an FCA violation when a contractor submitted progress payment requests and other documents to the government even though the products provided to the government were not meeting the corrosion standards in the contract. Neither the progress payments nor the government receiving reports had any implied certifications.[17]

And the 4th Circuit termed the implied certification theory questionable in that circuit. In one case, the certification was not a prerequisite to payment. The agreement the company had with the government "does not condition payment of invoices on a certification that" the company will do anything.[18]

FRAUD IN CLAIMS

For years, the government has been trying to fight fraud in the claims process. Contractor fraud can be costly. A contractor's misrepresentation of costs in a claim can result in forfeiture of the claim, civil penalties, and damages equal to the amount of the misrepresentation (loaded with freight costs and overhead), plus the government's cost of reviewing the claim.

UMC had a contract with the Air Force for floodlight sets. It submitted a certified delay claim of almost $4 million. UMC consistently argued that the claim reflected incurred costs. UMC, however, had a unique interpretation of the phrase "incurred costs." It submitted as incurred costs material costs which had never been invoiced and in some cases were for material that had never been received. The CFC came down hard on UMC. Federal remedies for fraud are "cumulative and not in the alternative."

The court found UMC liable under several statutes. First, under the Special Plea in Fraud provision of the U.S. Code, fraudulent claims are forfeited. Second, under the False Claims Act, the contractor can be liable for civil penalties if it violates its duty to examine "its records to determine what amounts the government already has paid or whether payments are actually owed to subcontractors or vendors." Third, the Contract Disputes Act allows the government to recover the false or unsupported portion of a claim that can be tied to misrepresentation or fraud. The court found that UMC's actions forfeited the almost $4 million claim; imposed a $10,000 civil penalty; made UMC pay to the government the unsupported portion of the claim, $223,500; and made UMC pay the government's costs of review.[19]

Endnotes

1. *Flexfab, LLC v. United States*, 424 F.3d 1254 (Fed.Cir. 2005).

2. *Flexfab, LLC v. United States*, 62 Fed.Cl. 139 (1996)

3. *City of El Centro v. United States*, 922 F.2d 816, 820 (Fed.Cir.1990).

4. *Fed. Crop Ins. Corp. v. Merrill*, 332 U.S. 380, 384, 68 S.Ct. 1, 92 L.Ed. 10 (1947).

5. *City of El Centro supra*, at, 922 F.2d at 820.

6. *Home Fed. Bank of Tenn., F.S.B. v. United States*, 57 Fed.Cl. 676, 689 (2003).

7. *Digicon Corp. v. The United States*, 56 Fed.Cl. 569, 574 (2005).

8. *Strickland v. U.S.*, 382 F.Supp.2d 1334, (M.D.Fla. 2005). Ck.

9. *Ann Riley & Assocs., Ltd.—Reconsideration*, B-271741, Mar. 10, 1997, 97-1 CPD ¶ 122, at 2-3.

10. *Orion Intern. Technologies v. U.S.*, 66 Fed.Cl. 569, 574 (2005).

11. *ACS Government Services, Inc.*, B-293014, Jan. 20, 2004, 2004 CPF ¶ 18

12. *Orion International Technologies v. the United States, and Fiore Industries, Inc.*, 66 Fed.Cl. 569 (2005).

13. *Ab-Tech Construction, Inc. v. United States*, 31 Fed. Cl. 429, 430 (1994), aff'd without written opinion, 57 F.3d 1084 (Fed.Cir.1995).

14. *BMY--Combat Sys. Div. of Harsco Corp. v. United States*, 38 Fed. Cl. 109 (1997).

15. *United States v. TDC Management Corp.*, 24 F.3d 292, 296, 298 (D.C.Cir.1994).

16. *Debra A. Shaw v. AAA Engineering & Drafting, Inc et al.*, 213 F.3d 519 (2000).

17. *United States of America ex rel. Werner Stegner v. Stewart and Stevenson Services Inc.*, United States Court of Appeals, Fifth Circuit, No. 04-20209, August 8, 2005, available at ftp://opinions.ca5.uscourts.gov/byDate/Aug2005/Aug08/.

18. *United States ex rel. Jose Herrera v. Danka Office Imaging Co.*, 91 Fed.Appx. 862 (4th Cir. 2004).

19. *UMC Electronics Co.*, 43 Fed. Cl. 776 (1999).

Part II

The Contract

The contract that you and I sign in the business world, no matter how much unreadable fine print it contains, is much different from the contracts—plural—that government contractors and contracting officers deal with. Government contracts come in a lot more varieties than the typical commercial contract, tend to be so long and confusing that they are hard to interpret, and contain clauses rarely found in standard commercial contracts. Chalk it up to the government being the 800-pound gorilla.

In Chapter 6, we take a look at the different types of government contracts, first distinguishing the different kinds of agreements—an umbrella term— the government gets into, including grants and cooperative agreements and concession contracts. Many government agencies, like the National Park Service when it looks for vendors to operate campgrounds in national parks, use concession contracts. Their use has raised a number of legal controversies, such as whether an agency's concession contract can be protested.

The chapter then focuses on how express government contracts are created, looking at how government contracts have all the essential requirements of any contract: offer and acceptance, consideration, but also the wild card of "authority"—which government employees are legally competent to bind the government to a deal, an issue that is not as troublesome to the commercial contracting world. The chapter ends with consideration of a contracting officer's worst fear: doing something that somehow ends up being an implied contract binding the government.

In Chapter 7, we take a look at the rules for interpreting the language in government contracts. Over the centuries, judges have developed rules to try and settle controversies over what the language of the contract really means, or worse, controversies over language that one party thought was in the contract. The chapter looks at the various rules, highlighting ways to draft contracts so that arguments over what the contract means can be reduced.

Chapter 8 deals with the reality that, with the government, a deal is not necessarily a deal. The chapter looks at a number of quirks that are found in administering a government contract. These quirks include the changes clause including constructive changes, deadlines that are merely suggestions and not really deadlines, clauses left out of a contract that are really in the contract anyway under the *Christian* doctrine, and the government's right to terminate a contract for convenience even though the government contractor has done nothing wrong and is not in default.

Chapter 6

Types of Government Contracts

Contents

B ecause the government needs so many different things under so many different situations, it needs a wide range of legal instruments to get those things.

The generic word for the piece of paper showing some sort of deal between an agency and somebody else is *agreement*. As we will see, not all agreements are contracts.

Agreements come in all sorts of shapes and sizes. Two common ones are interagency agreements, which describe how one agency will work with another agency, and blanket purchase agreements, which an agency sets up with a vendor to make it easier for the agency to buy certain items repetitively.

Only some kinds of agreements are contracts. Whether a document the government has signed is a contract is important for several reasons. For example, some agreements are contracts subject to the Contract Disputes Act. If a vendor has an agreement with the government that is not subject to the Contract Disputes Act, the vendor's rights and remedies against the government might be limited.

Because the focus of this book is procurement, the focus of this chapter is the procurement contract. We will first discuss the various types of agreements the government gets involved in so that the distinction between generic agreements and binding contracts becomes clearer. The chapter next discusses the procurement contract—the essential elements required for forming an express government contract. Finally, it discusses implied contracts, the kinds of contracts to which contracting officers worry about inadvertently obligating the government.

DIFFERENT KINDS OF AGREEMENTS

Grants and Cooperative Agreements

The government gets into a number of agreements that are not procurement contracts. The most obvious non-procurement agreement is a grant or cooperative agreement. Obviously, a grant agreement describes a deal between the government and a grantee.

The difference between a grant and a contract is the purpose of the agreement. Typically, in a grant, the government gives money to someone to do something that is of interest primarily to the recipient. In a procurement contract the government gets something of interest primarily to itself—goods and services, for example. A grant, when properly used, is not the way the government procures something for itself.

Federal law describes when an agency should use a grant, a cooperative agreement, or a procurement contract.

An agency uses a grant when

> (1) the principal purpose of the relationship is to transfer a thing of value to the State or local government or other recipient to carry out a public purpose of support or stimulation authorized by a law of the United States instead of acquiring (by purchase, lease, or barter) property or services for the direct benefit or use of the United States Government; and

> (2) substantial involvement is not expected between the executive agency and the State, local government, or other recipient when carrying out the activity contemplated in the agreement.[1]

An agency uses a cooperative agreement when

> (1) the principal purpose of the relationship is to transfer a thing of value to the State, local government, or other recipient to carry out a public purpose of support or stimulation authorized by a law of the United States instead of acquiring (by purchase, lease, or barter) property or services for the direct benefit or use of the United States Government; and

> (2) substantial involvement is expected between the executive agency and the State, local government, or other recipient when carrying out the activity contemplated in the agreement.[2]

An agency uses a procurement contract when

> (1) the principal purpose of the instrument is to acquire (by purchase, lease, or barter) property or services for the direct benefit or use of the United States Government; or

> (2) the agency decides in a specific instance that the use of a procurement contract is appropriate.[3]

Grants and cooperative agreements have their own sets of rules. They are not subject to protests, and they do not allow the nongovernment signatories to file a claim under the Contract Disputes Act.

Concession Contracts

Concession contracts are a contentious issue in government contracting. They are "sort of but not quite" procurement contracts. In these types of contracts, the government, strictly speaking, doesn't buy anything. Rather, the government uses concession contracts to give a company a business opportunity on federal land, such as running a video store on the grounds of a military base or running campgrounds in a national park.

Concession contracts have been controversial lately. The National Park Service believes that these contracts are not procurement contracts subject to, for example, either the protest jurisdiction of GAO or the claims jurisdiction of a board of contract appeals (BCA).

Protests

Whether GAO may handle a protest of a concession contract depends on what kind of concession contract it is and how much of "what else" the government is getting, in addition to services or products for taxpayers.

GAO gets its protest authority from the Competition in Contracting Act of 1984 (CICA). This law gives GAO jurisdiction over "a solicitation or other request by a federal agency for offers for a contract for the procurement of property or services." 31 U.S.C. 3551(1)(A).

The typical or "pure" concession contract lets a concessionaire provide services to taxpayers—and nothing more. These, for example, are contracts that "merely authorize a concessionaire to provide services to park visitors."[4] Because these concession contracts do not involve the concessionaire's giving the government anything, other than money, GAO considers these concession contracts to be "pure" concession contracts. A pure concession contract, to GAO, is not subject to the GAO protest authority.

But there are also concession contracts that require a concessionaire to provide not only services to taxpayers but also goods or services to the government under the same concession contract. An example is a tour boat operator that takes visitors to Fort Sumpter, South Carolina, but also cleans (for the government) the offices the concession contractor uses.

So what is GAO's test?

In deciding whether GAO may hear the protest of a hybrid concession contract, it's irrelevant whether the government is paying anything of value to the concession contractor or whether the government is using appropriated funds. A procurement may be subject to GAO review regardless of whether the government was committing money, receiving money, or incurring liability.[5]

Whether GAO will hear protests of hybrid concession contracts depends on how many goods or services come along. The test is *de minimis*—how little.

> "Where the government invites offerors to compete for a business opportunity such as a concession contract, the performance of which also involves the delivery of goods or services of more than *de minimis* value to the government, the contract is one for the procurement of property or services within the meaning of CICA and, therefore, is encompassed within our Office's bid protest jurisdiction. . . . Where, on the other hand, the government invites offerors to compete for a business opportunity that does not involve the delivery of goods or services or that involves the delivery of goods or services that are de minimis in value, the contract is not one for the procurement of property or services within the meaning of CICA; accordingly, it is not within our Office's bid protest jurisdiction."[6]

Summing up all this law, GAO will review a hybrid concession contract if the concession contract requires the vendor to provide goods or services in more than a minimal amount—*de minimis*, or more than a bare minimum.

De minimis

A concession contract made the concessionaire maintain the snack bar, doing things like repairing it and controlling weeds in the area. "In other words, the only services that the concessionaire is required to furnish are those pertaining to the upkeep of the space in which it operates its business. We think that the provision of such services is properly viewed as de minimis, given that the benefit conferred upon the government—which would have no need for performance of the services but for the concessionaire's operation of its business—is minimal."[7]

Not *de minimis*

Concession contracts that went beyond *de minimis* include

> A concession contracts that made the concessionaire provide over $3 million of reconstruction to government-owned facilities[8]

> A concession contract that required the concessionaire "to provide maintenance, repair and other services for government facility, as well as facility improvement valued at over $800,000"[9]

> A ferryboat service concession contract that made the concessionaire provide "janitorial services for agency's docks and piers, equip ferries with public address systems for use by Park Rangers"[10]

Claims

Whether a concession contract is a claim subject to the Contract Disputes Act (CDA) is also a hot issue. The CDA gives a BCA and the Court of Federal Claims (CFC) jurisdiction over claims involving "contracts for the procurement of property, other than real property in being. . . ."[11]

A concession contract, however, "does not constitute a procurement, but is a grant or a permit to operate a business and the government does not commit to pay out government funds or incur monetary liability."[12]

So concession contracts are not subject to the CDA.

But that is not the end of the issue. Because the CFC has jurisdiction under the Tucker Act to handle issues arising under the Tucker Act, the law gives the CFC jurisdiction over any claim against the United States based on an express or implied contract with the United States.[13]

Bill and Kathy Frazier operated Yacht Basin Marina under a concession lease with the Department of the Interior, Bureau of Reclamation. As operators of the concession, the Fraziers sold gas, groceries, fishing supplies and licenses, tourist information, and boat launching and docking. The concession contract/lease was to last for four years. However, the government was considering whether to close the concession area. In the middle of the four-year lease with the Fraziers, the government issued a draft resource management plan that included closing the Fraziers' concession area. The Fraziers sued the government in the CFC, arguing that the plan was in effect an anticipatory repudiation of the contract that still had several years to go and that its issuance resulted in lost profits. The court went on to consider whether the government had breached the lease, concluding that it had not. The court dismissed the Fraziers' case.[14]

EXPRESS CONTRACTS

FAR 2.101 defines a contract quite broadly, to include even an unwritten contract:

> "'Contract' means a mutually binding legal relationship obligating the seller to furnish the supplies or services (including construction) and the buyer to pay for them. It includes all types of commitments that obligate the Government to an expenditure of appropriated funds and that, except as otherwise authorized, are in writing. In addition to bilateral instruments, contracts include (but are not limited to) awards and notices of awards; job orders or task letters issued under basic ordering agreements; letter contracts; orders, such as purchase orders, under which the contract becomes effective by written acceptance or performance; and bilateral contract modifications."

How a government contract gets formed starts out the same way contracts have been formed for centuries—the common law.

> ". . . [T]the common law of contract governs the creation of a contractual relationship between the United States and a private party."[15]

In addition to the usual three common law contract requirements of (1) mutual intent to contract, (2) consideration, and (3) lack of ambiguity in the offer and acceptance, a fourth has been added: (4) authority to bind the government.[16]

Decisions finding any of the first three requirements for an express contract missing are rare. There's a saying in the military that its systems "are designed by geniuses to be used by us idiots." Whether we are idiots or not, the system we procurement professionals work with establishes, quite efficiently, express contracts. The procurement process is so highly structured that using it properly automatically produces a binding legal procurement contract. For example, vendors submit offers or bids that can be accepted by the government. When they are accepted, it's clear that both parties "mutually intend to contract" and that the offer and its acceptance are clear, lacking any ambiguity. And obviously, the contractor's promise to perform the contract work in exchange for the government check (or EFT) is the consideration required. So the highly structured procurement process results, usually, in there being no doubt that the first three contracting requirements have been met.

What typically is the issue in government contract formation is the fourth requirement: authority.

In the material that follows, the first three elements of an express contract are illustrated. Because there are so few cases involving invalid express contracts—government "contracts" missing one of the three essential elements—some of the examples are from cases discussing implied contracts. This makes no difference. For our purposes at this point, whether a required legal element like consideration is missing from a contract, express or implied, is irrelevant. That is because, as we will see in the next section of this chapter, an implied contract needs the same four elements that an express contract needs. The major difference between the two is that there's no piece of paper in an implied contract.

Mutual Intent to Contract

It's pretty obvious from all the time and effort that vendors and the government devote to the procurement process that both intend to contract. So this contract requirement is rarely an issue that is litigated.

In one case, finding no "mutual intent to contract," the fact that the parties never discussed rates of pay or the actual payment to be made defeated a contractor's claim for court reporter services for a cancelled government Equal Employment Opportunity Commission (EEOC) hearing.[17]

On rare occasions, the issue of whether there has been an offer and acceptance is litigated.

Offers versus Quotes

The rules for an offer become important because an offer followed by an acceptance is needed before a binding contract can be formed. In government contracting, offers have various names: a *bid*, as in Invitation for Bids (IFB) in sealed bidding; an *offer*, as in Solicitation for Offers (SFO) or Request for Offers (RFO); or a *proposal*, as in Request for Proposals (RFP). These various offers have different rules for being held open, being irrevocable, and being accepted. But all of these are alike in that they come from the vendor and put the acceptance ball in the government's court. Unless and until the government accepts the offer, there is no contract.

But before there's an offer from a vendor, there might be a *quote* from the vendor. Quotes typically are used in small-dollar items and let the government get an idea of what the marketplace is charging for something in case the government decides it wants to buy it.

GAO gave an excellent description of how a quote and bids/offers are different:

> "We recognize that, in practice, agencies and vendors often treat quotations just as they treat offers. Nonetheless, as a matter of law, quotations are different from bids or offers. The submission of a bid or proposal constitutes, by its very nature, an offer by a contractor that, if accepted, creates a binding legal obligation on both parties. Because of the binding nature of bids and offers, they are held open for acceptance within a specified or reasonable period of time, and our case law has necessarily developed rules regarding the government's acceptance of 'expired' bids or proposals. A quotation, on the other hand, is not a submission for acceptance by the government to form a binding contract; rather, vendor quotations are purely informational. In the RFQ context, it is the government that makes the offer, albeit generally based on the information provided by the vendor in its quotation, and no binding agreement is created until the vendor accepts the offer. A vendor submitting a price quotation therefore could, the next moment, reject an offer from the government at its quoted price."[18]

The difference between a non-binding quote and a binding offer was important when the government accepted a quote that the vendor mistakenly held open until "June 31"—a day on no one's calendar.

The Department of Agriculture asked for quotes from Federal Supply Schedule (FSS) vendors for "change management" software. Agriculture set the quote up properly. Its solicitation said it was looking for information and that any quotations submitted in response were not offers. One vendor gave Agriculture something that respected neither government contract terminology nor the calendar. Its "quote" said, "This offer is valid through June 31, 2003." When Agriculture issued a purchase order to that vendor well after June 31, a competitor protested, arguing that the agency could not accept the quote that had expired. GAO disagreed. "Because vendors in the RFQ context hold the power of acceptance and their submissions are purely informational, there is nothing for vendors to hold open; thus, it simply does not make sense to apply the acceptance period concept or the attendant rules regarding expiration of bids or offers to RFQs."[19]

Acceptance

Because FAR sets clear rules for acceptance of offers or proposals, it's rare to find the issue litigated. In one such rare case, someone tried to buy forfeited property from the U.S. Marshal's Service. Upon submitting the bid, a government employee told that bidder that its bid was the highest so far but that the government would have to wait a short time for more offers. Several days later, the USMS told the bidder that its bid was not the winning bid. When the government did not sell the property to that bidder, it sued, arguing that the government had to sell him the property. The bidder's losing argument was that the government had to accept its offer because it was the highest offer received by a government deadline.

> "Here, there was no unconditional acceptance—the USMS, through its representatives, never stated or otherwise conveyed to plaintiff the message that it had accepted plaintiff's offer. Indeed, the record plainly indicates—and plaintiff does not contest—that the USMS first indicated that plaintiff's offer had not been accepted and then, ultimately, stated that another offer had been accepted."[20]

Consideration

The typical government contract is a something specific in exchange for money. Lack of consideration, therefore, is typically not an issue.

Consideration **does** become an issue with indefinite delivery, indefinite quantity (IDIQ) contracts and requirements contracts. Under an IDIQ contract, the government agrees to buy and the vendor agrees to sell at least a guaranteed minimum amount of goods. Under a requirements contract, the government agrees to buy **all** of its requirements from the vendor.

> "Because the buyer is not obligated to purchase all requirements from the seller, unless the buyer contracts to purchase a minimum quantity, an IDIQ contract is 'illusory and the contract unenforceable against the seller.' The enforcement of such a contract [an indefinite quantity contract, or a requirements contract] would fail for lack of consideration in the absence of a clause stating a minimum quantity or a clause requiring the government to purchase all of its requirements from [the contractor].' Therefore, an IDIQ contract requires the government to order only a stated minimum quantity of supplies or services[,] . . . [and] once the government has purchased the minimum quantity stated in an IDIQ contract from the contractor, it is free to purchase additional supplies or services from any other source it chooses. An IDIQ contract does not provide any exclusivity to the contractor."[21]

So in a requirements contract, consideration is in the form of the government's promise of exclusivity: it will buy whatever it needs from only the requirements contractor. And in an IDIQ contract, the consideration is in the form of the minimum stated quantity.

In rare cases, other kinds of government agreements with vendors have been found to not be a binding contract.

> A forest fire–fighting company, Ridge Runner, signed a government document called an "Interagency Engine Tender Agreement," which described the kind of firefighting equipment the vendor was willing to provide the government. After not getting any calls, the vendor sued the government, arguing that the Department of Agriculture was violating the implied duty of good faith and fair dealing in denying it jobs. The Court of Appeals for the Federal Circuit (CAFC) concluded that the agreement was not a contract because it lacked consideration. "To constitute consideration, a performance or a return promise must be bargained for. And the promise or apparent promise is not consideration if by its terms the promisor or purported promisor reserves a choice of alternative performances . . . [or] if the promises are illusory. Under the agreement, the government had the option of attempting to obtain firefighting services from the vendor or any other source, regardless of whether that source had signed a tender agreement. The Agreement contained no clause limiting

the government's options for firefighting services; the government merely "promised" to consider using Ridge Runner for firefighting services. Also, the Tender Agreement placed no obligation upon the vendor. If the government came calling, Ridge Runner "promised" to provide the requested equipment only if it was "willing and able." It is axiomatic that a valid contract cannot be based upon the illusory promise of one party, much less illusory promises of both parties.[22]

Lack of Ambiguity in Offer and Acceptance

Having an ambiguity in a government contract is not unusual, as Chapter 7 will clearly show. But rarely is there any ambiguity about the basic deal between the government and the contractor.

In one rare case, the parties had strikingly different ideas about the deal.

A property owner sued the government for back rent he thought the Army owed him, but what deal, if any, the parties had was in doubt. The Army thought that the property it was using belonged to a foreign government that was letting the Army use it rent-free, but the property owner believed it was his property and that the Army was renting it for a specific sum, not rent-free. A board concluded there had been no contract.[23]

Authority to Bind the Government: Legally Competent

Asking contracting officers if they are legally competent sounds insulting. It sounds as if their mental competency is being challenged, but it's not. Legal competency goes to the heart of the deal between the government and the vendor. Only if a legally competent person has signed a contract is there a binding contract. A contract's being entered into by someone who is legally competent is one of the requirements of a binding contract with the government.

Usually, in government contracting, the legally competent person for the government is the contracting officer. His agency has given him the authority to bind the government, as shown in his warrant. A warranted contracting officer acting within the limits of his authority is legally competent to bind the government. That's why contracting officers have warrants authorizing them to sign contracts. No warrant, no authority, no deal. That's the general rule.

In view of the importance of warranted authority, it's surprising how seldom vendors ask contracting officers about the contracting officer's authority. If you are a contracting officer, how many times has a vendor asked you what the limits of your authority are—or asked to see your warrant? Rarely is typical. But actual authority is the general rule for government contracts.

Actual authority is just one of several types of authority in the business world. Another type is apparent authority. In the private market, when two vendors make a contract, someone with apparent authority can bind the vendor. That is when a principal lets someone look like its agent but the agent really is not. It's like a Wendy's taking over a McDonald's without the McDonald's removing the golden arches. The facility looks like a McDonald's, but it really isn't a McDonald's. It's now a Wendy's.

In government contracts, when a vendor contracts with the government, the government agent must have actual authority. Apparent authority cannot bind the government. Even if an agency let an unwarranted employee sit in an office with someone else's unlimited warrant on the wall, the government would not be bound if a vendor made a contract with the unwarranted employee.

Exceptions to Delegated (Express) Authority

The basic concept of authority in government contracts—that the government is not bound by the acts of one of its employees unless the employee is authorized to do the act—continues to be eroded. There are exceptions to this most basic of government contracting principles. These exceptions are implied actual authority and institutional ratification.

Implied Actual Authority

Like many things, authority can be express or implied. A warrant shows express authority. Implied authority "comes with the job;" there's no warrant, but the authority to contract is a key or integral part of the employee's work. One court defined *integral* like this:

> "Contracting authority is integral to a government employee's duties when the government employee could not perform his or her assigned tasks without such authority and the relevant agency regulation does not grant such authority to other agency employees."[24]

In other words, the test is whether contract authority is essential or necessary for the person to do his job. So, to see if there is implied actual authority, you have to look at the government employee's duties and the agency's regulations.

Government informers try, usually unsuccessfully, to argue that they are entitled to payment for the help they gave the government. They try to argue that there is a binding contract between them and the government based on the word of, for example, an FBI agent or a DEA official. It's a difficult argument to win because often agency regulations expressly prevent the agency from making a binding commitment.

In one decision, a professional artist was successful in proving that the government employee had implied actual authority, but she lost her case because she couldn't prove that the employee knew about the deal the artist claimed to have with the government.

In 1990, artwork was stored on government premises but was later destroyed. The artist sued the government, claiming that the government's action was a breach of contract. Clearly, there was no express contract between the federal government and her. In trying to prove there was an implied contract, she tried to establish the implied actual authority of the two government employees she dealt with. But the assistant to the Cultural Affairs Officer (CAO) did not have implied actual authority: "Nothing in his position description implies that he led any [government] programs or that contracting authority was necessary for him to discharge his duties successfully." His being responsible for planning these programs wasn't enough to prove that he had contracting authority.

But the court found that his supervisor, the Cultural Affairs Officer, did have implied actual authority. Her job description included "planning, coordinating, and carrying out cultural programs in support of diplomacy objectives." She oversaw all programs and activities at the ACC and reported directly to the country public affairs officer. The only way she could carry out her duties would be to enter into contracts with artists. There was "no reasonably efficient alternative" to the government's giving her authority to contract. If she didn't have the authority to contract, she couldn't do her job well. The CAO had implied actual authority. [25]

Institutional Ratification

Another exception to delegated authority is institutional ratification. This exception is also based on fairness. If the government gets an unauthorized item, uses it, benefits from it, and pays for part of it, should the government later be allowed to argue that there was no authorized authority, so no deal? Although denying there was a deal would be consistent with the general rule, it wouldn't be fair. Because the government benefited from the unauthorized act, it should pay for it, according to the law of institutional ratification.

To understand institutional ratification, we have to talk first about ratification.

Ratification is an after-the-fact approval. It's sort of like the saying, "It's better to ask forgiveness than permission." When someone without authority to commit the government to something has in fact committed the government to it and now wants to make things right, the unauthorized person gets someone who does have authority to now retroactively authorize it. Presumably, this request for permission comes along with a request for forgiveness.

> "Ratification is the affirmance by a person of a prior act which did not bind him but which was done or professedly done on his account, whereby the act, as to some or all persons, is given effect as if originally authorized by him. For ratification to be effective, a superior must not only (1) have possessed authority to contract, but also (2) have fully known the material facts surrounding the unauthorized action of her subordinate, and (3) have knowingly confirmed, adopted, or acquiesced to the unauthorized action of her subordinate."[26]

Institutional ratification is when the institution does all of these.

> ". . .[A]n agency can institutionally ratify the contract even in the absence of specific ratification by an authorized official. Specifically, institutional ratification occurs when the Government seeks and receives the benefits of an otherwise unauthorized contract."[27]

One example of this is the Air Force's institutional ratification of an unauthorized deal after using the product for 16 months.

> The Air Force was sued for payment of products and services provided by Digicon under a task order. The government argued that

it did not have to pay because the contracting officer did not have the authority to sign the contract, nor was the unauthorized contract ever authorized by someone with appropriate ratification authority. The court found an institutional ratification. The Air Force had accepted the task order involved and had benefited from Digicon's products and services for 16 months. It had already paid Digicon over $16 million and tried to get out of the agreement with Digicon under the terms of the contract. In addition, a contracting officer with unlimited authority "was directly involved in the implementation and oversight of the contract. These indicia of intent sufficiently demonstrate the government's institutional ratification of the contract."[28]

IMPLIED CONTRACTS

An oral contract is not worth the paper it's written on, according to Sam Goldwyn. Perhaps that's typical Hollywood delusional thinking because it's not a fair statement of contract law. It's possible for the government to stumble into a binding contract even though there is no written document.

But it is rare.

Nonetheless, contracting officers worry, in the backs of their minds, that they could make a mistake and end up with an implied-in-fact contract. Their worst fear—that a contractor could claim an implied contract in the absence of any writing (essentially a contract out of the blue)—is really unlikely.

Common law sees two kinds of implied contracts: implied-in-fact contracts and implied-in-law contracts.

Implied-in-Fact Contracts

An implied-in-fact contract is just like an express contract, but there is nothing in writing. It is "founded upon a meeting of minds, which, although not embodied in an express contract, is inferred, as a fact, from conduct of the parties showing, in the light of the surrounding circumstances, their tacit understanding."[29]

To prove an implied contract with the government, a contractor has to prove not only the three usual elements of an express contract—mutuality of intent to contract, offer and acceptance, and consideration—but also an additional element: The contractor must prove that the government agent had actual authority to bind the government.

The CFC handled a case in which the court concluded that there **was** an implied contract based on certain facts but there was **no** implied contract based on other facts.

A government employee training center was run by the center's director, who was not a warranted contracting officer. For years, the director contacted various training companies, assigning them certain classes. The companies in turn reserved certain instructors for their assigned courses. When the course was done, they submitted an invoice to the director, who completed and signed an SF-182 requesting payment. In the middle of academic year 2001, a new director told Advanced Team Concepts (ATC) that ATC would not be needed to teach seven courses it had been scheduled to teach that year. For the next academic year, ATC at least got a heads-up. Prior to the start of academic year 2002, the new director circulated the class schedule for the next year to vendors but warned the vendors that the center might change course content and delivery. After ATC had been assigned no courses for that year, it sued the government, arguing that it had implied-in-fact contracts for both of those academic years. The court concluded that the government had an implied contract for the first year's cancelled courses but no implied contract for the second year's courses.

The court found an implied contract for the classes the center had cancelled in the middle of the year because the conduct of the parties provided all the essential elements of a contract. There was just no writing. There was

1. **Mutual intent to contract:** "To find an implied in fact contract, the claimant must demonstrate that there was an unambiguous offer to contract upon specific terms and mutuality of intent between the parties to enter a contract. Here there is no one document reflecting a contract, but instead various documents. The court may read all the documents together in order to find the intention of the parties. The court finds that for academic year 2001 ATC and the center had intent to contract."

2. **Offer and acceptance:** The director of the center prior to an academic year "circulated the schedule to various vendors. The classes taught by ATC were part of the schedule. ATC accepted the offer by the director to provide these classes and scheduled its instructors to teach the courses, thereby committing its resources as done in previous years."

3. **Consideration:** "In consideration, ATC would be paid for its services."

4. **Actual authority:** Even though the director was not a warranted contracting officer, and therefore had no express actual authority, she had implied actual authority: "[I]f the authority to bind the government is central to the duties of the person holding himself out as the contracting officer, implied authority exists." In this case the director had implied authority because she scheduled and paid teachers, proposed schedules of courses, and was authorized to hire contractors by her supervisor and the contracting officer by using the SF-182.

There was no implied contract for the courses during academic year 2002 because there was neither mutual intent to contract nor an unambiguous offer and acceptance. The new director "clearly indicated that there would be a reduced course schedule and that he would contact the vendors personally with regard to the future schedule. This uncertainty of courses for the 2002 year was certainly an ambiguity in offer and acceptance and therefore the court finds no mutual intent sufficient to create an implied in fact contract for that year."[30]

Another way a court could find an implied-in-fact contract typically involve written contracts gone wrong, such as an option not properly exercised.

If a contractor delivers something to the government on the supposition that the option has been exercised and the government uses what has been provided, it's not fair for the government to get something for nothing. In this case, a court might find an implied-in-fact contract just to get a contractor paid.

Sociometrics had a contract for a one-year base with four option years to help put on regional conferences. Sociometrics put on several conferences during the base and option years. One option, however, inadvertently was not exercised and Sociometrics worked on the conference nevertheless. When Sociometrics tried to get paid for the services it had provided under the unexercised option year, the government refused to pay the invoice. The Armed Services Board of Contract Appeals (ASBCA) made the government pay the implied-in-fact contract. Even though the option was not formally exercised, the parties conducted themselves as if it had been. "The government actively encouraged and participated in Sociometrics' efforts."[31]

The case had an added wrinkle: Sociometrics had not been dealing with the contracting officer on this contract. Rather, Sociometrics had dealt exclusively with the contracting officer's representative (COR). But that did not change the board's mind that the government should pay for the work because it was "fair in the circumstances to impute knowledge of the contracting officer's representative to the contracting officer where we can draw no conclusion but that the contracting officer's representative was the eyes and ears of the contracting officer."[32]

It's good to know that, in three situations, creating an implied contract is impossible.

The first situation is when a party argues that there is **both** an express contract and an implied contract. In fact, one of the best safeguards against an implied contract is an express contract. You can't have both at the same time dealing with the same subject matter.

> "The existence of an express contract precludes the existence of an implied-in-fact contract dealing with the same subject matter, unless the implied contract is unrelated to the express contract."[33]

In one case, a newly hired employee of the Indian Health Service had a contract with the agency for repayment of the employee's student loans. But the employee believed he was entitled to more, so he argued that there was an implied contract giving more benefits. The CFC disagreed, finding no implied contract possible because of the existence of a written contract.

> "Plaintiff's express written contracts with the IHS [Loan Repayment Program] covering the loan repayment necessarily defeat his claim that an oral contract providing greater benefits arose as a result of [government employee statements] and the government's erroneous payment. The subject matter of Plaintiff's alleged oral implied-in-fact contract and express written contract with IHSLRP dealt with identical subject matter—the student loan repayments Plaintiff was to receive in exchange for working at the Maniilaq Association."[34]

The second situation is an agency regulation requiring a written document. Routinely, agency regulations require that a contract be written. Any contractor trying to argue that it had an implied contract with the government has to jump this hurdle.

A contractor claimed that the contracting officer told the contractor—orally—that the contractor would get a contract for the next phase of a project. The applicable law required an agency to contract for later phases of the project through solicitations and only after review of proposals. FAR 2.101 says that all contracts "except as otherwise authorized" must be "in writing." The contractor had not submitted a proposal, and there was no written contract. The CFC said there was no implied contract. Quoting precedents, the court said that "agency procedures must be followed before a binding contract can be formed. . . . Oral assurances do not produce a contract implied-in-fact until all the steps have been taken that the agency procedure requires; until then, there is no intent to be bound. Thus, it is irrelevant if the oral assurances emanate from the very official who will have authority at the proper time, to sign the contract or grant."[35]

The third situation is when plaintiffs claim that the implied contract does not have specific terms. For example, one judge refused to find an implied contract where the plaintiffs did not "rely on specific documents or the conduct of any government employee but ask that we look at the overall conduct of the regulators. . . . It is not clear what plaintiffs' alleged implied-in-fact contract provides . . . we cannot know if anyone acting for the United States did so with authority because plaintiffs have not alleged who such persons were or what they did. They have not pinpointed documents or conduct by which the court can establish the elements of an implied-in-fact contract."[36]

Implied-in-Law Contracts

An implied-in-law contract is not a contract at all. It's simply a device, a "legal fiction" that a judge uses to do something fair in a particular case. Such a device implies that the parties had a contract. And by doing so, judges get the result they want.

The classic use of an implied-in-law contract is to fix unjust enrichment. For example, if someone lets a plumber put in a swimming pool knowing that the pool really was supposed to be put in next door, the plumber would get paid by the unscrupulous homeowner because a judge would imply that a contract existed between the homeowner and the plumber. Of course, there never was a contract. There was no meeting of the minds, etc. But it would be unfair for a judge to let the homeowner be unjustly enriched with a free pool and to deprive the plumber of getting paid.

Neither the CFC nor the BCAs have jurisdiction over an implied-in-law contract. But there has to be some leeway in government contracts, and GAO provides it. The GAO Red Book has a nice discussion of how an implied-in-law contract works for ratifications:

> "If an agency determines that it cannot ratify the transaction in question, it should then proceed with the only remaining possibility, a *quantum meruit* analysis. The underlying premise is that the government should not be unjustly enriched by retaining a benefit conferred in good faith, even where there is no enforceable contractual obligation, as long as the 'benefit' is not prohibited by law . . . . This is the pure 'contract implied-in-law' situation. The Court of Federal Claims and the boards of contract appeals decline jurisdiction over contract implied-in-law claims because there is no 'contract' for purposes of their jurisdictional statutes (Contract Disputes Act, Tucker Act). . . . However, GAO regards claims of this type as coming within its general claims settlement jurisdiction. . . . Thus, contract implied-in-law claims can be settled administratively even though judicial review may be unavailable in many, if not most, cases."[37]

Sometimes the phrase *quantum meruit* is used. It means "how much is merited," or fair, and therefore should be granted by a judge. *Quantum valebant* refers to fairness in a services contract context. Often these Latin phrases are used to refer to implied-in-law contracts, but they are also used to refer to implied-in-fact contracts. [38]

Endnotes

1. 31 USC 6304.

2. 31 USC 6305.

3. 31 USC 6303.

4. *Great South Bay Marina, Inc.*, B-296,335, Jul. 13, 2005, 2005 CPD ¶ 135.

5. *Starfleet Marine Transp., Inc.*, B-290181, July 5, 2002, 2002 CPD ¶ 113.

6. *White Sands Concession, Inc.*, B- 295,932, March 18, 2005, 2005 CPD ¶ 62.

7. *Id.*

8. *Great South Bay Marina, Inc.*, B-293649, May 3, 2004, 2004 CPD ¶ 108.

9. *Shields & Dean Concessions, Inc.*, B-292901.2, B-292901.3, Feb. 23, 2004, 2004 CPD ¶ 42, *recon. denied*, B-292901.4, Mar. 19, 2004, 2004 CPD ¶ 71.

10. *Starfleet Marine Transp., Inc.*, B-290181, July 5, 2002, 2002 CPD ¶ 113.

11. 41 USC §602(a)(1).

12. *Frazier d/b/a/ Yacht Basin Marina v. The United States*, 67 Fed.Cl. 57,59 (2005).

13. 28 USC §1491(a)(1).

14. *Frazier v. The United States*, 67 Fed.Cl. 56 (2005).

15. *The United States v. Winstar*, 518 U.S. 839, 116 S.Ct. 2432, 135 L.Ed.2d 964 (1996).

16. *Trauma Service Group v. The United States*, 104 F.3d 1321, 1325, (Fed.Cir.1997).

17. *MTD Trascribing Services*, ASBCA No. 53104, 01-1 BCA ¶ 31,304.

18. *Computer Associates International, Inc.—Reconsideration*, B-292077.6, May 5, 2004, 2004 CPD ¶ 110.

19. *Id.*

20. *L. Dale Jones v. The United States*, 49 Fed.Cl. 516, 517 (2001).

21. *J. Cooper & Associates, Inc. v. The United States,* 53 Fed.Cl. 8 (2002).

22. *Ridge Runner Forestry Inc. v. Ann M. Veneman,* 287 F.3d 1058 (Fed.Cir.2002).

23. *Thai Hai*, ASBCA No. 53,375, 02-2 BCA ¶ 31,971.

24. *Flexfab, LLC v. United States*, 62 Fed.Cl. 139, 148 (2004).

25. *Elaine Leonardo v. The United States*, 63 Fed.Cl. 552 (2005).

26. *Elaine Leonardo* at 63 Fed.Cl. 560-61.

27. *Digicon Corp. v. The United States*, 56 Fed.Cl. 425, 426 (2003).

28. *Id.*

29. *Baltimore & Ohio R.R. Co. v. United States*, 261 U.S. 592, 597, 43 S.Ct. 425, 426-27, 67 L.Ed. 816 (1923).

30. *Advanced Team Concepts, Inc. v. The United States*, 68 Fed.Cl. 147 (2005).

31. *Sociometrics Inc.*, ASBCA No. 51620, 00-1 BCA ¶ 30,620.

32. *Id.*

33. *Schism v. The United States*, 316 F.3d 1259, 1278 (Fed.Cir.2002).

34. *Ruttenburg v. The United States*, 65 Fed.Cl. 43, 49 (2005).

35. *Night Vision Corp. v. The United States*, 68 Fed.Cl. 368, 387 (2005).

36. *Ryan v. The United States*, 57 Fed.Cl. 731, 733-734 (2003).

37. GAO, *Principles of Federal Appropriations Law*, 2d ed., vol. III, ch. 12, pp. 12-82 – 12-83, GAO/OGC-94-33.

38. 13 N&CR ¶ 47.

Chapter 7

Contract Interpretation

CONTENTS

Nobody can write a perfectly clear contract. With complex projects, numerous tasks, and pages of FAR boilerplate, it's hard to write a clearly understood, not-open-to-any-doubt contract. So, among the most common problems in contracting are ironing out what the contract language means, dealing with ambiguities, and trying to get inconsistencies in the contract to somehow hang together.

Rules for interpreting contracts have been developed over centuries. So what are we dealing with in this chapter on contract interpretation? For this chapter, the phrase *contract interpretation* covers a number of different situations.

1. What does a word mean? One situation is when a single word or phrase at the heart of the contract is at issue. For example, a contract requires the funds to be spent by the end of September 05. Is that calendar year (meaning September 2005) or fiscal year (meaning September 2004)?

2. Mixed signals. Another situation is when one part of a contract requires a contractor to do one thing but another part of the contract seems to require something else. For example, one part of the specification calls for a concrete floor while another part of the specification calls for a composition floor. How can the two be reconciled?

3. What gets interpreted? A third situation is when a contract leaves out a critical part of the contract. For example, a contractor is supposed to do work described by a contract at all locations "identified in Attachment A." But the parties forgot to attach Attachment A to the contract, and now the contracting officer has one version of Attachment A and the contractor has another. Which one should be applied?

With all these different meanings, you could say that the phrase *contract interpretation* is itself an ambiguous phrase in need of interpretation.

In the first part of this chapter, we look at the goal of contract interpretation—interpreting a contract to carry out the intent of the parties. The focus of the intent issue is on the "objective intent of the parties." The focus, surprisingly, is not on "subjective intent"—what one of the parties had buried away in its mind and did not share with the other party before entering into the contract. You will see that the cliché "meeting of minds" is not the test.

In the second part of the chapter, we look at the rules judges have developed over the centuries to help solve the most common contract interpretation problems and look at how these rules can be applied to procurement contracts. According to these rules, contract language is either clear or ambiguous. If the words are clear and unambiguous, they should be interpreted according to their **plain** meaning. If, on the other hand, the words are ambiguous, interpreting them is more work. Here we look at the *contra proferentem* rule.

And, finally, in interpreting an ambiguous contract, what help can a court get from other documents or from what the parties actually did? If the contract is ambiguous and therefore no help in interpreting it, what kind of extrinsic evidence can be used to help interpret the ambiguous contract? Lurking in the background of many contract interpretation issues is the extrinsic evidence issue: What evidence outside the contract itself, extrinsic to the contract itself, should be used in interpreting an ambiguous contract?

Before getting into the details of contract interpretation, there is one way the parties can cut to the chase. No contractor can win a contract interpretation argument without proving "reliance"—that the contractor actually based its price, set during the bidding stage, on its interpretation argued during the contract administration stage.[1] As we will see, courts make reliance the last step in contract interpretation. But sometimes the parties can save themselves a lot of trouble by going to the last step first, because if the contractor cannot prove it based its price on this interpretation, its interpretation cannot prevail.

An example of a contractor relying on its current interpretation when it prepared its bid follows.

The U.S. Postal Service issued a solicitation calling for trucks to carry mail long distances. But the solicitation seemed to conflict with federal regulations by saying that drivers could work 12 straight hours even though federal regulations said that drivers could work only 10 straight hours. One company, L.P. Fleming, Jr., Inc., bid the contract assuming *the use of only one driver*. During the contract, federal regulations changed. As applied to Fleming's work, they clearly made him use two drivers. When the USPS refused to increase Fleming's contract to pay for two drivers, Fleming went to the Postal Service Board of Contract Appeals. The Board got Fleming paid for the extra driver. It found that Fleming's interpretation of the contract—that one driver was okay—was reasonable. And Fleming's interpretation was also the one Fleming had relied on in bidding the contract.[2]

An example of a contractor that had not relied on its current interpretation when preparing its bid months earlier follows.

A contractor bid a project intending to put in composition (not concrete) floors. But during contract performance, it argued for an interpretation that the contract demanded only the cheaper concrete floor. According to the board, "Here it is obvious that in the preparation of its bid, which was accepted by the Government, Marden [the contractor] did not rely on an interpretation that composition or latex flooring was unnecessary in the mechanical rooms. Therefore, adherence to well established principles of contract law precludes the contractor's right to recover."[3]

THE GOAL OF CONTRACT INTERPRETATION: FINDING THE INTENT OF THE PARTIES

Contract interpretation—"What do those words mean?"—starts with the obvious question, "What did the parties want them to mean?" The intent of the parties is always the goal of contract interpretation.

But intent can be too easily, and improperly, confused with the famous contract concept of the "meeting of the minds." Because a contract is supposed to be a meeting of the minds, people think that the search for the intent of the parties is a search for what the parties had in their minds when they entered into the contract.

That is not the case. Trying to find out what was inside the heads of the parties, the subjective intent of the parties, is not the goal of contract interpretation. Instead, the goal of contract interpretation is finding the "objective intent" of the parties. If there has been no meeting of the minds, there may be no valid contract. However, the interpretation of a valid contract does not generally consider whether there was a meeting of the minds or whether the minds were ships passing in the night.

What Is "Objective Intent"?

Objective intent tries to outsmart an unscrupulous mind. One party to a contract could play some real games in negotiating a contract. For example, it could use a word that has one meaning to that party but another to the other contracting party. Hidden meanings, the famous phrase "mental reservations," can trick the other party. So, to avoid game-playing, judges look not for subjective intent—what was actually in the mind of one of the contracting parties—but objective intent—what the words of the contract show they meant. So the inquiry is to what's on the outside of the document, the objective intent, and not to what is on the inside of the mind of one of the parties, the subjective intent.

A couple of legal heavy-hitters described how objective intent differs from subjective intent. Justice Oliver Wendell Holmes described how "the words" trump "the minds" of the parties:

> "The making of a contract depends not on the agreement of two minds, in one intention, but on the agreement of two sets of external signs—not on the parties' having meant the same thing, but on their having *said* the same thing. . . ."[4]

Judge Learned Hand described the importance of "the words" and not "the minds" of the parties more colorfully:

> "A contract has, strictly speaking, nothing to do with the personal, or individual, intent of the parties. A contract is an obligation attached by the mere force of law to certain acts of the parties, usually words, which ordinarily accompany and represent a known intent. If, however, it were proved by twenty bishops that either party, when he used the words, intended something else than the usual meaning which the law imposes upon them, he would still be held, unless there were some mutual mistake, or something else of the sort. Of course, if it appear by other words, or acts, of the parties, that they attribute a peculiar meaning to such words as they use in the contract, that meaning will prevail, but only by virtue of the other words, and not because of their unexpressed intent."[5]

What does this improper subjective intent look like? A contractor told the government it would provide a building with a cafeteria but later thought the cafeteria had been taken out of the deal. He was mistaken. Only in his head had the cafeteria been taken out of the deal.

When a developer described its pending offer to GSA, he bragged about the building's cafeteria. The following negotiations did not mention the cafeteria. The lease that was eventually signed also did not mention the cafeteria but was at a lower price than the original offer. When the government demanded that the developer build a cafeteria, the developer claimed that he had lowered his price by eliminating the cafeteria. To him, the lower price and the elimination of the cafeteria were tied together. A court disagreed. "If such a 'tie-in' is what plaintiff really had in mind . . . then the answer is simply that plaintiff failed completely to communicate that purpose to the government. Since contractual obligations are to be ascertained from objective manifestations of intent, plaintiff's mental reservations are legally irrelevant. What matters only is that the plaintiff's offer promised a cafeteria and nothing said or done during the course of the negotiations diminished that manifested intent one iota."[6]

So, in identifying the intent of the parties, the focus is not the hidden, unspoken subjective intent. The focus is the objective intent—the intent expressed by the parties in their contract. In a sense, it's not what's in Carnac the Magnificent's mind. It's what's written in the envelope.

Where Is Objective Intent Found?

Objective intent is found in the words and from the circumstances in which the words were said.

Although the words "this is what we really meant" are perhaps the most famous words in contract interpretation, the way the rules are set up, judges don't want you to **tell** them what you really meant. That's what you supposedly used a contract to do.

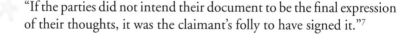

> "If the parties did not intend their document to be the final expression of their thoughts, it was the claimant's folly to have signed it."[7]

So listening to what the parties now claim they meant days, weeks, months, and years after they wrote the contract is the last thing judges what to hear. What judges start with are the words the parties used to show their intent. So trying to find the objective intent of the parties starts with the words of the contract.

But, surprisingly, the words of the contract are only the starting point. The circumstances of the contract must also be considered. Looking at the words of the contract without considering the circumstances they were written in would be seeing only half the picture. "Water, water everywhere but nary a drop to drink" out of context, without considering the circumstances, does not make sense. But if you are talking about the ocean and its saltwater, it does make sense. The same is true when someone tells you what you did was "bad." If a young person living in the late 20th century told you that, it would probably make you feel good. If your boss told you that in the 21st century, you'd probably feel bad. The circumstances words were written in have to be considered when interpreting them.

Trade Practices

One common example of considering the circumstances is trade practice. A word might mean one thing to us lay people but something different to people working in the industry or trade that uses that word. The circumstances the word is used in become important.

In one of the landmark cases, the phrase "new lamps" was in dispute. A NASA contract required the contractor to put in "new lamps" when the project was over. To us lay people, "new lamps" means that any existing lamp previously installed during construction had to be replaced so that all lamps in the building would be new. But to the industry, replacing all lamps is "relamping"; the phrase "new lamps" means replacing only defective, burned out, or broken lamps.

The Federal Circuit concluded it was proper to consider the circumstances in which the words were used.

> "Before an interpreting court can conclusively declare a contract ambiguous or unambiguous, it must consult the context in which the parties exchanged promises. If the context disclosed an ambiguity, trade practice could be used to resolve it. Here, the contractor showed that the electrical industry uses the term 'relamping' to mean a complete change out of lights. Moreover, relamping is rarely performed in new construction. So the circumstances under which a contract was signed can be considered in deciding whether a word is ambiguous. Here 'new lamps' in the lighting industry was not an ambiguous phrase."[8]

Prior Course of Dealing

The circumstances the parties find themselves in also include what they have done in the past under prior contracts—their "prior course of dealing."

Even though each contract stands on its own, what's happened in the past can be relevant. If the government has allowed a contractor to do something in the past, this prior course of dealing can help interpret the current contract. A *course of dealing* is "a sequence of previous conduct between the parties to the agreement which can afford a common basis of understanding for interpreting their expressions and other conduct." (Restatement (Second) of Contracts Sec. 223 (1981)).

The rationale for this rule makes sense:

> "Where there were numerous actions by the Government involving many contracts, there can be no doubt that a contract requirement for the benefit of a party becomes dead if that party knowingly fails to exact its performance, over such an extended period, that the other side reasonably believes the requirement to be dead."[9]

> A GSA contract said the government would reimburse a contractor for taxes the contractor paid if the contractor submitted receipts within 60 days after paying the taxes. The clause warned contractors that receipts submitted after 60 days would not be paid. For seven years, GSA reimbursed a contractor for tax payments even though, each year, the contractor submitted the receipts after the 60-day deadline. When GSA refused to do so in year 8, the contractor took GSA to court and won. To be able to rely on a prior course of conduct, a contractor must prove that the conduct involved the same contracting agency, the same contractor, and essentially the same contract provisions. All these elements are present . . . ."[10]

So a "prior course of dealing" between the contracting officer and the contractor can be used in contract interpretation.

But there's a limit. One time does not make something a "prior course of dealing." In a similar tax reimbursement situation, GSA let a contractor miss the 60-day deadline once. The GSBCA concluded that a one-time government slip does not make a course of dealing.[11]

So "We've done it that way before" doesn't usually work. A contractor would have better luck arguing "But we've **always** done it that way."

So in trying to find the intent of the parties, a judge looks not only at the words of the contract but also at the circumstances surrounding the negotiating of the contract.

THE TWO STEPS OF CONTRACT INTERPRETATION

Over the centuries, judges have made up rules of contract interpretation. We will look at these rules in this section. We will see that the rules can get confusing.

But there is an easy way to deal with **any** contract interpretation issue. That's because there really are only two steps in interpreting a contract.

- STEP 1: If the words are clear and unambiguous, find the **plain meaning** of the words. If the words being interpreted have a plain meaning, forget about STEP 2.

- STEP 2: If the words are not "clear and unambiguous" but instead are ambiguous, **resolve the ambiguity** by applying a different set of rules.

STEP 1: If Words Are Clear and Unambiguous, Find Their Plain Meaning

The first rule of contract interpretation is to discover the "plain meaning" of clear and unambiguous words used in the contract.

> "When construing a contract, a court first examines the plain meaning of its express terms."[12]

Sometimes how this rule is applied is obvious, and sometimes it is not. In the next two examples, a judge finds a plain meaning in the words. In the first case, most of us would agree with the interpretation. In the second case, the plain meaning is not all that plain.

In the first case, a court concluded that the plain meaning of "Replacing dead trees" for free meant replacing dead trees regardless of when they died—before or after the contractor signed the contract.

One paragraph of a landscaping contract required the contractor to "replace dead, dying or unsightly plants, trees and shrubs or plant material as deemed necessary by the COTR at no additional expense to the Government. . . ." Unlike other clauses that had dollar limits, there were no dollar limits on "additional expense" for this task. Two months after the contract was signed, the government made the contractor replace a tree that had not bloomed. The contractor filed a claim arguing that it was not responsible for trees that died before it signed the contract.

A board agreed with the government. "We find that the plain language of the contract supports the government's interpretation. As detailed above, paragraph C.9.2.9 states that '[t]he Contractor shall replace dead, dying or unsightly plants, trees and shrubs or plant material as deemed necessary by the COTR at no additional expense to the Government. There shall be no dollar limitation on the Contractors costs associated with any plant replacement.' This unconditional language makes no distinction between plants that were dead at the beginning of the contract and plants that died during the course of the contract . . . . Nothing in the contract can be read to mean anything other than what is plainly stated."[13]

But another judge using a plain meaning rule came to a conclusion that was not so obvious.

A contract promised a vendor that the government would pay damages including "out-of-pocket" expenses caused by a government delay. A judge held that the plain meaning of "out-of-pocket" would not include attorneys' fees incurred by the contractor in preparing a claim and litigating it after the contracting officer denied it, even though very definitely those attorneys' fees literally came out of the contractor's pocket. To the court, the attorneys' fees were not "things of the same general kind of class as those specifically mentioned, i.e., losses due to plaintiff's inability to harvest timber under the contract. Attorneys' fees are simply not within that general kind of class. The plain meaning of [the clause] does not permit plaintiff to recover attorneys' fees incurred in connection with claim preparation or litigation in this court."[14]

It's important to briefly add here a point to be discussed in detail in Section C of this chapter—extrinsic evidence. The parties often want a judge to ignore the words of the contract and consider "other things" not in the contract, like something said by the contracting officer at a prebid conference or testimony by the parties long after the contract was signed describing what they **really** meant. Courts call this "extrinsic evidence." When the words of a contract are clear and unambiguous, there is no need to use extrinsic evidence. So what the parties might have said, etc., is irrelevant.

> "If the terms of a contract are clear and unambiguous, they must be given their plain meaning, and extrinsic evidence, such as evidence of the parties' intent, is inadmissible to interpret them."[15]

> A landowner had a contract with the U.S. Army Corps of Engineers to let the Corps "deposit fill, spoil and waste material" on the designated land and to "perform any other work necessary and incident to the construction" of a dam. At the end of the project, the landowner sued, claiming that the Corps had left fill on his land in excess of what it had orally promised. The CFC agreed with the landowner, honoring the oral agreement he had with the Corps. The CAFC reversed, holding that the agreement with the Corps was clear and unambiguous so the court could not consider any evidence of oral agreements between the parties.[16]

So the plain meaning approach gets this plain meaning **only** from the contract itself.

STEP 2: If the Words Are Ambiguous, Get Interpretive Help from Wherever You Can Find It

By definition, ambiguous words cannot have a plain meaning. So when the contract is ambiguous, it becomes necessary to look for help interpreting the contract from outside the contract.

Dealing with an ambiguous contract brings up three issues:

1. What makes a contract ambiguous?
2. What are the rules for interpreting an ambiguous contract?
3. What gets interpreted? Can evidence **other than the contract** can be used to clear up the ambiguous language?

What Makes a Contract Ambiguous?

Drafting a contract that is not ambiguous is difficult.

When the new owners of the World Trade Center bought the property months before the events of 9/11, they insured the property for $3.6 billion "per incident." When the property damage totaled well in excess of that amount, the lawyers had to argue over whether the two planes attacking one location constituted one incident or two incidents.

If the government orders simply a sandbag, is it supposed to come loaded with sand?

If a contract tells a building maintenance company simply to "stock the restroom," is the toilet tissue to be one-ply or two-ply?

Two people disagreeing about what a contract means doesn't make a contract ambiguous. To judges, a contract is ambiguous if it is susceptible to more than one reasonable interpretation, each of which is consistent with the contract itself.[17]

> Conditions at a construction site, as well as the words in a contract, can create an ambiguity. Although it's usually words that are ambiguous, a situation—like the conditions found at a prebid site investigation for a construction contract—can be ambiguous. A contractor, Conner, was going to bid for a contract with the government to put in ductwork at an Army hospital. When company employees went to a prebid inspection of the work site, the employees couldn't get a good look at the area above the ceiling because pipes and ductwork filled that area. And they did ask the government to give them more information or a better view. After winning the contract, the company filed a differing site condition claim but lost. The fact that Conner and other bidders could not perform a site inspection through no fault of their own "creates a glaring inconsistency. Conner was therefore obligated to have made further inquiry with the Corps to bring the contradictory and ambiguous situation to the attention of government officials who would then have been put on notice that plaintiff lacked information necessary to formulate its bid . . . ."
>
> *Conner Brothers Construction Co. Inc. v. The United States*, 65 Fed. Cl. 667 (2005).

Requirement 1: For words to be ambiguous, there must be two reasonable interpretations of the words

Here's an example of a contract with two reasonable interpretations:

A NASA contract used language that had two reasonable interpretations. The contract required the contractor at the end of the project to install new lamps in the building. To NASA, this meant that all lamps, even brand-new ones, had to be replaced. To us lay people, that is a reasonable interpretation. But the contractor had a different interpretation of "new lamps." The contractor used the lighting industry's interpretation of "new lamps," which meant simply replacing only burned-out bulbs.[18]

Notice that the "two reasonable interpretations" rule talks about "a" reasonable interpretation. It doesn't mean that the interpretation being argued is the only right interpretation. The interpretation being advanced must simply be one that is within the zone of reasonableness. So a party claiming an ambiguity does not have to prove that its interpretation is the only justifiable one. It must be "a" reasonable interpretation, not "the" reasonable one.

Here's an example of a contract with only one reasonable interpretation:

A contract between the government and a contractor had an item called "telecommunications and data cabling." Two contract documents said the telephone company would provide the cabling. But another part of the contract, the specification called "telephone and data systems equipment," stated that the contractor shall "provide a complete system of cabling from the main terminal to the workstations; . . . ." A judge found the contract ambiguous because one part of the documents required the contractor to provide the cabling while another said the telephone company would.[19]

Requirement 2: The ambiguity must be hidden (latent)

The second requirement is that the ambiguity must be latent or hidden, not patent or obvious. The logic of the requirement is, to pardon the expression, patent: it makes the contractor who does not clearly understand the meaning of language in a government document ask the government for clarification **before** bidding. The bottom line is that the patent ambiguity doctrine gets the government off the hook. If the ambiguous words are a patent ambiguity—are obvious—and the contractor never asked for government clarification—the government cannot be responsible for the ambiguity.

One student of mine had a memorable description of the difference between *latent* and *patent*: "The love in her eyes was patent but the malice in her heart was latent."

Cases finding patent or obvious ambiguities are rare. A patent ambiguity was found in one decision where one part of a solicitation said that award would be based on a lowest-priced technically acceptable basis but another part of the same solicitation said that award would be based on the trade-off method, with price being significantly less important than technical factors. That's impossible: price is either **the** factor or only **one** factor. Any bidder should have seen that ambiguity.

A construction contract had a base line item and several option items for an addition to a fitness center and the renovation of the existing fitness center. The very first Base Schedule line item, item number 0001, covered "all design activities to include new additions . . . , renovation areas . . . , all site work . . . , and comprehensive interior design." Construction of the addition would be done under one base line item, and renovations would be done under an option line item.

The government interpreted the contract to require all design work, of base items as well as option items, covered by line item 0001. But the contractor wanted more design money for option items; to the contractor, it did not made sense for companies to bid design money for option work the government wasn't even sure would be done. The ASBCA said there was no ambiguity but if there was, it was patent. "Although the contractor thought the contract requirements were very clear, he could only reach that conclusion either by ignoring the reference to 'renovation areas' in item number 0001 or by assuming that related only to option items. When we do the same, the reference to 'renovation areas' creates an ambiguity so glaring as to impose a duty upon ECI to inquire about the government's intentions prior to submitting its bid. Because ECI made no such inquiry, the ambiguity must be resolved against it."[20]

So if the ambiguity is obvious or patent, shame on the contractor for not asking for clarification of the language during the bidding stage. Reasonable interpretation or not, an ambiguity that is patent requires a contractor to inquire about its meaning at the bidding stage. If no inquiry is made, a contractor cannot take advantage of the ambiguity in carrying out the contract.

Requirement 3: The contractor did not know that the government had a different interpretation

Another requirement has been added by a recent Federal Circuit decision. Prior to this decision, *contra proferentem* made the government responsible for an ambiguity only if it was latent or hidden; but if an ambiguity was patent or obvious, the bidder had to tell the government and resolve the ambiguity.

But the Federal Circuit has added to the patent ambiguity exception another one: if a bidder knows its interpretation is in conflict with the government's at the solicitation stage, the bidder must resolve it. The bidder cannot take advantage of its interpretation knowing that the government has a different interpretation.

When the government wants after-hours air-conditioning, it often pays for it on a zone basis. This is similar to a daytime zone and nighttime zone in some homes. The word "zone" was ambiguous. It was possible that the prospective landlord had a meaning of the word "zone" in mind different from what the contracting officer had in mind, and it was also possible that the offeror was holding his cards close to his vest and didn't explain to the government how it intended to charge the government for overtime. So interpretation of the word "zone" came down to the third, and controlling, issue: whether the bidder had actually and reasonably relied on its current interpretation months earlier when it had prepared its bid. The appeals court was concerned that the contractor could knowingly take advantage of the government's drafting of a particular contract provision, even though the ambiguity was not patent. This problem was one the appeals court wanted to deal with.

> "Where an ambiguity is not so glaring as to rise to the level of patency, if the contractor knows or has reason to know that the drafting party, unaware of the contractor's interpretation, holds an interpretation different than its own, the result should be no different than if the ambiguity were patent."[21]

In other words, bidders should not be able to take advantage of obvious contract drafting errors or drafting errors—obvious or not—they know about.

What Are the Rules for Interpreting an Ambiguous Contract?

Over the years, judges have used a number of ways to deal with an ambiguous contract. The Federal Circuit sees "several legal rules for choosing between competing interpretations of an ambiguous contract provision. The general rule is *contra proferentem* . . . ."[22]

Contra proferentem

This **is not** the rule: "Ambiguities in a document are to be resolved against the drafter."

This **is** the rule: "A reasonable interpretation of a latent ambiguity will be construed against the drafter."

Because the government is usually the drafter of government contracts, this rule is often construed against the government. According to the CAFC, there are four requirements for *contra proferentem* to apply:

> "The essential ingredients of the rule are: (1) that the contract specifications were drawn by the Government; (2) that language was used therein which is susceptible of more than one interpretation; (3) that the intention of the parties does not otherwise appear; and (4) that the contractor actually and reasonably construed the specifications in accordance with one of the meanings of which the language was susceptible."[23]

NASA made a contractor replace all the bulbs in a building the contractor had just finished, relying on the contract that said the contractor would install "new lamps." Because the electrical industry uses the term "relamping" to mean a complete change-out of lights, Metric argued the government interpretation was wrong. The CAFC agreed with the contractor and construed the language against the drafter, NASA.[24]

Order of Precedence Clause

A clause familiar to procurement is FAR 52.215-8, Order of Precedence—Uniform Contract Format. It makes some parts of a contract more important than others when interpreting a contract:

> Order of Precedence—Uniform Contract Format (October 1997)
>
> Any inconsistency in this solicitation or contract shall be resolved by giving precedence in the following order:
>
> (a) The Schedule (excluding the specifications).
>
> (b) Representations and other instructions.
>
> (c) Contract clauses.
>
> (d) Other documents, exhibits, and attachments.
>
> (e) The specifications.

On occasion, this clause is **some** help.

But its use is limited for several reasons. First, according to case law, this clause is a clause of last resort. A contract should be read to avoid a conflict, so as to make unnecessary invocation of the Order of Precedence clause.[25] Second, this clause resolves only conflicts between these parts of the contract. It does not help resolve the typical problem—a conflict **within** the specification itself or **within** the Schedule. And, finally, it does not deal with all the types of contract interpretation issues the parties could be faced with.

What Gets Interpreted?

The parties often want a judge to ignore the contract and consider "other things"—things not in the contract, such as something said by the contracting officer at a prebid conference, or testimony by the parties long after the contract was signed describing what they **really** meant. Courts call this "extrinsic evidence" or "external evidence." *Intrinsic* refers to something inside or inherent in something; *extrinsic* means something that is not inside but rather outside something, here outside the actual contract.

Judges don't like extrinsic evidence. The contract itself is supposed to spell out the deal. When the parties, long after the contract is signed, urge a judge to ignore the words in the contract and to consider what was said, supposedly, in the course of drafting the contract, or what the parties had done on other occasions way back when . . . the parties make the contract meaningless. Allowing extrinsic evidence to help resolve contract interpretation claims would cast "a long shadow of uncertainty over all transactions."[26]

A solicitation for government work in Italy said that offers were due by 2 PM local (Italian) time. But the Navy website said that the due date of the solicitation was "1400 hrs (U.S. Time Zones)." A vendor who was late wanted the Navy to use U.S. time. A court refused. "Incorporating the 'U.S. Time Zones' language from the website into the solicitation would be to impermissibly rely on extrinsic evidence to interpret an otherwise plain and unambiguous term within the solicitation."[27]

When courts talk about extrinsic evidence, two other phrases come up: parol evidence and integrated agreements.

The **parol evidence** rule is not really a rule of interpretation. More accurately, the parol evidence rule "defines the subject matter of interpretation" by limiting the use of extrinsic evidence.[28]

"The parol evidence rule provides that when a document is integrated, '. . . a party to a written contract cannot supplement or interpret that agreement with oral or parol statements that conflict with, supplant, or controvert the language of the written agreement itself.'"[29]

An **integrated contract** is one that takes all previous negotiations, all promises, and all contract drafts and makes one "whole" document. (*Integrate* means "make whole.") If the parties want a promise or negotiation point to be included in the final document, it better be in there in writing.

Technically, the parol evidence rule prohibits two things. First, it prohibits the use of extrinsic evidence to **contradict** language in a partially or **fully integrated** agreement. Second, it prohibits the use of extrinsic evidence to **add to or modify** the terms of a **fully integrated** agreement.[30]

What's the difference? And what difference does it make? The Court of Claims gave a good answer to both questions:

> "Where the parties intend that their written agreement shall not only be final, but be also the exclusive statement of all their agreement, even a consistent prior oral agreement is superseded and overridden by the written agreement, termed a completely integrated agreement. Where there is no such intention, the agreement is only partly integrated and a consistent, oral collateral agreement is effective to supplement a written agreement."[31]

So an integrated agreement cannot be contradicted by outside sources of interpretation, extrinsic evidence, or parol evidence. That's a good start.

The typical government contract is a **partially integrated agreement** because it follows the Uniform Contract Format.[32] A highly respected treatise in government contract law believes that many government contracts would be considered partially integrated agreements.

> "The scope and complexity of problems encountered throughout the performance of the government contract ordinarily involve contingencies not expressly provided for under the terms of the agreement. Resolution of such problems often requires information outside the contract documents. The written contracts in many instances cannot be characterized as the 'complete and exclusive' agreement of the parties and therefore should be considered to be partially integrated."[33]

So when interpreting the typical government contract, the parol evidence rule prohibits the use of extrinsic evidence to contradict language in the contract.

Even better is a completely integrated agreement because the parol evidence rule prohibits the use of extrinsic evidence to add to or modify the terms of a fully integrated agreement.[34]

A company, Freedom NY, had a contract with the Defense Logistics Agency to prepare combat rations for the government. During negotiations over a proposed time extension, the contractor sent the government letters, later referred to as a "side agreement," claiming that the government would give the contractor another contract for more rations if the contractor were "otherwise qualified."

Eventually, both parties signed the modification, called Modification 25, which gave the contractor an extension of the delivery schedule and a price adjustment. In return, the government was released from any potential claims that had arisen to date. The modification included an integration clause that stated that "both parties expressly state that the aforesaid recitals are the complete and total terms and conditions of their agreement." The government, however, never gave Freedom NY any additional contracts, so the contractor sued for breach of contract of the "side deal." The CAFC concluded that the parol evidence rule excluded any evidence of the side agreement because the modification was a fully integrated agreement. "One attempting to add terms to a contract with the integration clause carries an extremely heavy burden of overcoming this attestation to the document's finality and completeness."[35]

How does a contract become an integrated agreement? Just by saying so. When the parties declare the agreement to be an integrated agreement, they generally are making it a fully integrated agreement so that extrinsic evidence cannot be used to contradict the language of the contract or to add or modify terms of the contract.[36]

There is no required form for an integrated agreement or merger clause. One example of an integration clause found in a Federal Circuit decision said "Both parties expressly state that the aforesaid recitals are the complete and total terms and conditions of their agreement."[37]

Endnotes

1. *Lear Siegler Management Servs. Corp. v. United States*, 867 F.2d 600, 603 (Fed. Cir.1989).

2. *J.P. Fleming, Inc.*, PSBCA No. 5197, February 3, 2006.

3. *Edward R. Marden Corp. v The United States*, 807 F.2d 701, 705 (Fed.Cir.1986).

4. Holmes, *The Path of the Law*, 10 Harv. L.Rev. 457, 463 (1897).

5. *Hotchkiss v. National City Bank of New York*. 200 F. 287,293 (S.D.N.Y 1911), *aff'd*. 201 F. 664 (2d Cir 1912), *aff'd*, 231 U.S. 50,34 S.Ct. 20,58 L.Ed. 115 (1913)) quoted in *L.S.S. Leasing Corp. v. United States*, 695 F.2d 1359, 1364 (Fed.Cir 1982).

6. *David Nassif Associates v. The United States*, 214 Ct.Cl. 407, 557 F.2d 249 (1977).

7. *California Sand & Gravel, Inc.,* 22 Cl.Ct 19, 26 (1990).

8. Metric Constructors, Inc., 169 F.3d 747 (Fed.Cir. 1999).

9. *Gresham and Co. Inc. v. The United States*, 470 F.2d 542, 554 (Ct. Cl. 1972).

10. *4J2RIC Limited Partnership v. GSA*, GSBCA 15584, 02-1 BCA ¶ 31742.

11. *Roger Parris dba Manchester Realty v. GSA*, GSBCA 15512 01-2 BCA ¶ 31 ,629.

12. *Textron Def Sys. v. Widnall*, 143 F.3d 1465, 1468 (Fed.Cir.1998).

13. *Brooks Range Contract Services, Inc.,* DOTCAB No. 4456, DOTCAB No. 4457–4458, November 29, 2004.

14. *Precision Pine and Timber. Inc. v. The United States*, 63 Fed.Cl. 122 (2004).

15. *Barron Bancshares, Inc. v. United States*, 366 F.3d 1360, 1376 (Fed.Cir.2004).

16. *McAbee Construction, Inc. v. United States*, 97 F.3d 1431 (Fed. Cir. 1996).

17. *Community Heating and Plumbing Co. v. Kelso*, 987 F.2d 1575, 1579 (Fed.Cir. 1993).

18. *Metric Constructors, Inc. v. National Aeronautics and Space Administration*, 169 F.3d 747 (Fed.Cir.1999).

19. *Nielsen-Dillingham Builders, J.V v. United States*, 43 Fed.Cl. 5 (1999).

20. *ECI Construction. Inc.,* ASBCA No. 54344, 05-1 BCA ¶ 32, 857.

21. *HPI/GSA 3C. LLC v. Perry*, 364 F.3d 1327, 1334 (Fed.Cir.2004).

22. *HPI/GSA 3C. LLC, supra* at 1334.

23. *Id.*

24. *Metric Constructors, Inc. v. National Aeronautics and Space Administration*, 169 F.3d 747 (Fed.Cir.1999).

25. *Sun Microsystems Federal. Inc. v. Department of the Army*, GSBCA 13615-P, 96-2 BCA ¶ 28,507.

26. *Trident Ctr. v. Connecticut Gen. Life Ins. Co.*, 847 F.2d 564, 569 (9th Cir.1988).

27. *Conscoop-Consorzia Fra Coop. Di Prod. E. Lavoro v. U.S.*, 159 Fed.Appx. 184, 185-186, (Fed.Cir.2005).

28. RESTATEMENT OF CONTRACTS, SECOND, § 213

29. *Schism v. United States*, 316 F.3d 1259, 1278 (Fed.Cir.2002) (en banc).

30. J. Cibinic and R.C. Nash, Jr., ADMINISTRATION OF GOVERNMENT CONTRACTS 188 (George Washington University 3d ed. 1998).

31. *Sylvania Electric Products, Inc. v. United States*, 458 F.2d 994, 1006 (1972).

32. Cibinic and Nash, *supra* at 189.

33. Cibinic and Nash, *supra* at 191.

34. Cibinic and Nash, *supra* at 188.

35. *Freedom NY v The United States,* 329 F.3d. 1320 (Fed.Cir.2003).

36. *Freedom NY, supra* at 1328.

37. *Freedom NY, supra* at 1323.

Chapter 8

Contract Administration Quirks

CONTENTS

B ecause a government contract is a contract, many of the rules that apply to contracts in general—contracts that business people get into all the time—apply to government contracts. But because a government contract is with the government (obviously), carrying out a government contract is not always identical to carrying out the typical commercial contract. This chapter looks at several of the unique aspects of administering government contracts.

In this chapter, we will see that, with the government, a deal is a deal as described in the contract

1. Unless the government intentionally and unilaterally changes it using the Changes clause

2. Unless the government inadvertently changes it through a constructive change

3. Although the deadlines in the contract are not really deadlines, just suggestions

4. Although clauses left out are in there anyway

5. Although the deal can be ended by the government prematurely without paying breach of contract damages

THE GOVERNMENT INTENTIONALLY AND UNILATERALLY CHANGES IT USING THE CHANGES CLAUSE

The Changes clause in government contracts is unique in the business world. Sears or Home Depot will not give you and me a Changes clause in any contract we have with those companies. Normally, in the business world, a deal is a deal. If you want to change the deal, you can but only if the other party agrees. But in government contracting, a deal is a deal unless it is changed under the Changes clause, with or without the contractor's consent.

134

The heart of the Changes clause is section (a):

Changes-Fixed Price (Aug 1987)

(a) The Contracting Officer may, at any time, without notice to the sureties, if any, make changes within the general scope of this contract in any one or more of the following:

(1) Drawings, designs, or specifications . . .;

(2) Method of shipment or packing;

(3) Place of delivery.

The Changes clause is a very important clause. It allows the government to respond quickly to changing needs, such as changes in congressional or agency priorities. And if the contractor doesn't want to make the change, the government can force the contractor to make it.

But everything has its limits, and that includes the Changes clause. A contracting officer may not use it to change everything in the contract. The clause itself has two self-imposed limits: the change must be "within the scope of the contract," and only those parts of the contract listed in the clause (like the drawings, designs, or specifications) may be changed.

Within the Scope of the Contract

With such a handy clause, there's sure to be mischief. One example of this is what is called a cardinal change. The dictionary defines *cardinal* as "principal," "fundamental," and "chief." Courts and the Government Accountability Office (GAO), however, don't look on cardinal changes very kindly. They see the Changes clause as a device that could be used to make an end run around full and open competition. So the test of "beyond scope" really focuses on competition and the change's effect on it. The government may not modify a contract to where it is "materially different" from the original contract. In other words, does the original contract as modified require "essentially the same performance"? If so, it need not be competed. But if it's not, it should be.

One court used this definition:

> "A cardinal change . . . occurs when the government effects an alteration in the work so drastic that it effectively requires the contractor to perform duties materially different from those originally bargained for."[1]

Here's how GAO describes its test:

> "In assessing whether the modified work is essentially the same as the effort for which the competition was held and for which the parties contracted, we consider factors such as the magnitude of the change in relation to the overall effort, including the extent of any changes in the type of work, performance period, and costs between the modification and the underlying contract."[2]

A broader scope of work to start with, in the original contract, allows a broader change in that scope. If an agency uses the changes clause to get "more" under a procurement, vendors might see its use of the clause as an end run around full and open competition. The vendors might believe that the "more" should have been competed among all vendors instead of obtained from only the incumbent vendor. But if an agency has given vendors the chance to bid on a contract that has a broad scope, the losing vendors can't fairly complain when the broad scope is used to get—through a modification to the contract—something the losing offerors think should be a separate procurement.

For years, H.G. Properties (HGP) housed the National Park Service's Western Archeological and Conservation Center (WACC). WACC has about 5 million museum objects and gives advice on archeology to parks in the western United States. As the contract with HGP was about to end, the Park Service issued a solicitation for, in its terms, a "Cadillac" or state-of-the-art facility for WACC. When the awarded contract was modified, a competitor protested the change as beyond scope. The CAFC disagreed. The broad scope of the original solicitation let the Park Service make a broad modification. The original solicitation "encouraged bidders to submit suggested modifications to the solicitation so as to create a state of the art facility. Accordingly, the 'scope' of the contract would be understood to embrace changes or modifications to these requirements."[3]

Indicators of Beyond-Scope Work

Type of Work

As mentioned above, one indicator of a beyond-scope change is a change in the type of work. But, as one GAO decision shows, garbage collection is still garbage collection, even if it is changed to be done with contractor, not government, equipment.

Mark Dunning Industries (Dunning) had a contract to collect and dispose of garbage at Fort Rucker, Alabama. The contract was comprehensive, covering the waterfront of garbage collection. Dunning was to pick up residential, commercial, industrial, and community area garbage. One of the contract tasks let Dunning use front-loading government vehicles to collect the garbage. But the front-loading government vehicles weren't very reliable, so the Army changed the contract to have Dunning provide these trucks as part of the contract. The price of the contract was increased about 20 percent. GAO found the change to be within scope.

GAO emphasized that "[t]he Army's modification did not make any changes to the original nature and purpose of the contract. First, the front-loading refuse collection service is but one of the multiple refuse collection services [that were] to be performed under the contract, the bulk of which were to be performed using the contractor's trucks. Moreover, the contract specifically included as one of the multiple line items the requirement that the contractor would perform the very front loading refuse collection services that were the subject of this modification, albeit with government-furnished vehicles." In addition, GAO noted that the change was made because the government's equipment was broken. Therefore, "[s]ince the essence of the requirement was for the contractor to provide front loading refuse collection, the Army's modification, merely shifting the responsibility for the vehicles and the containers needed to carry out the services to the contractor, did not substantially change the contract, nor make it essentially different."[4]

Large Changes—Up or Down—in Contract Cost

Large cost increases are one factor to be considered, but costs, curiously, are not a surefire indicator of a beyond-scope change.

In one case, increasing the contract amount by 80 percent was a beyond-scope change.

The government wanted to have a "flexible" contract for custodial services. The winning offeror would give the government an "Add/ delete of Service Cost Sheet" right after winning the contract. The sheet would list the winning contractor's prices to be used in negotiating with the Air Force for adding services or deleting them after award. The government expected the additions or deletions to be minimal. Once the contract was awarded, however, the winning contractor's cost sheet itself was deleted, making service changes negotiable one-by-one and at much higher costs.

The court acknowledged that whether the contract is "materially different" could be measured by the difference in costs between the contract as awarded and as modified. But the amount of increase alone isn't the only factor. The change in costs must be put in context: the context of what the original bidders thought they were getting into if they won the contract. A 100 percent increase in funding, under the circumstances, was not considered a cardinal change in one precedent. In that case, the government had estimated the number of hours the eventual winner of a security services contract would have to provide. Because the hours in the contract that all the bidders had fought for were simply an estimate, there had been no "beyond scope" change when the actual number of hours under that contract was increased to double the original amount due to an emergency. But here, there had been no such change in circumstances and the contract price had increased by 80%. The change therefore was beyond scope.[5]

Modifications of a contract that **reduce** the scope of the contract might be beyond scope and have to be competed.

A contract called for providing and recycling but **not** disposing of something. The government modified the contract to require providing and recycling **or** disposing of something. The "disposing" was not only a much cheaper task; "disposing" also had more competitors waiting in the wings to do the work if the agency would compete the work as modified. GAO held that the reduction was beyond the scope of the original contract, so the modification should have been competed. "Here, the RFP did not anticipate that the contractor could be relieved of the recycling requirement or that a disposal effort could be ordered in lieu of recycling. Furthermore, .

. . the costs of leasing plastic media with no recycling requirements is as much as 50 percent less . . . ." Also, there were at least four competitors who could do the work.[6]

THE GOVERNMENT INADVERTENTLY CHANGES THE DEAL: CONSTRUCTIVE CHANGES

The money a contractor gets under a government contract normally may be increased only if the government voluntarily issues a modification of the contract, usually under the contract's Changes clause.

One classic exception to this rule is a constructive change. When there is a constructive change, judges in effect become contracting officers. As contracting officers, the judges find that although the government did not expressly change the contract, something the government made the contractor do changed the contract, and therefore the contractor should get paid for the "change." Judges, of course, do not have warrants, so a judge cannot order a formal change. But judges can construe things anyway they want to. So in these instances, what the government did is **construed** by the judge as a change to the contract, hence the phrase *constructive change.*

Because constructive changes are so important and so common, we need a good definition:

> "A constructive change occurs where a contractor performs work beyond the contract requirements, without a formal order under the Changes clause, either due to an informal order from, or through the fault of, the government. Before the contractor can recover, it must show that the government ordered it to perform the additional work. The contractor cannot merely show that the government disapproved a mode of performance. Rather, the contractor must show that the government actually compelled the additional work. The government order need not be formal or in writing. The additional work must be beyond the requirements of the pertinent specifications or drawings. At the same time, the additional work performed by the contractor cannot be beyond the general scope of the contract. Drastic modifications or fundamental alterations ordered by the government beyond the scope of the contract will constitute a breach of contract. The additional work must therefore be beyond the requirements of the contract, albeit still within the general scope of the contract."[7]

When a constructive change happens, the contracting officer typically does not think he is changing the contract. For example, when asked by a contractor to interpret words in a contract, the contracting officer tries to correctly interpret the contract; the contracting officer thinks he is simply interpreting the contract. But if a contractor disagrees, files a claim, and convinces the judge his interpretation is the correct one, the contracting officer will learn—years after making the interpretation—that his interpretation was wrong and had changed the contract. So in a sense, no contracting officer knowingly issues a constructive change; only a judge "issues" a constructive change. There should be no stigma attached to a contracting officer who learns he has made a constructive change to a contract. The contracting officer was administering the contract as he believed to be fair, but a judge disagreed and the judge had the last word.

A constructive change can sneak up on a contracting officer and can appear in all sorts of disguises. The most common types are extras and defective specifications.

Extras

Generally, extras are candidates for a constructive change. Judges don't like the government getting something for nothing. So when a contracting officer makes the contractor do more expensive work but refuses to pay for it, a judge can bring out the constructive change theory to make the government pay for the extras.

Note: Although the focus in a constructive change is on the contracting officer's making the contractor do more work, it's important to realize also that not only a contracting officer can make a constructive change. So can other government employees, as we will see later.

The U.S. Postal Service issued a solicitation calling for trucks to carry mail long distances. But the solicitation seemed to conflict with federal regulations by saying that drivers could work 12 straight hours even though federal regulations said that drivers could work only 10 straight hours. One company, L.P. Fleming, Jr., Inc., noticed the difference but thought nothing of it since all USPS solicitations it had seen had that same language in them. Moreover, when the head of the company described how he intended to do the work— using only one driver—to a USPS contract specialist, the contract specialist never voiced any opposition to Fleming's plan and in fact recommended that Fleming get the contract.

During the contract, federal regulations changed. As applied to Fleming's work, they clearly made him use two drivers. After ignoring the earlier federal regulations, the USPS now enforced the changed regulations on Fleming, making him spend money for two drivers. When the USPS refused to increase Fleming's contract to pay for two drivers, Fleming went to the Postal Service Board of Contract Appeals. The Board got Fleming paid for the extra driver. The Board found that Fleming's interpretation of the contract—that one driver was okay—was reasonable and in fact "was shared by the government at the time of award and thereafter. Under these circumstances, that interpretation of the contract language governs. Therefore, when the contracting officer directed Fleming to perform the contract in accordance with the revised federal regulations, that direction had the effect of changing the contract provisions governing the allowable driving time. . . ." It concluded by making the USPS pay for the extra work.[8]

The board came to this conclusion after addressing two important points in contract interpretation—reasonableness and reliance. Fleming's contract interpretation was reasonable ("Its drivers were regularly able to complete the trips" under the solicitation's time limits). And Fleming's interpretation was also the one he had relied on in bidding the contract.

Defective Specifications

Sometimes the extra work comes not from a wrong interpretation of a contract but from a defective specification in the contract.

Lamb Engineering and Construction won a contract to modify ammunition storage buildings at Camp Navajo in Arizona. The specification in the contract let Lamb use dirt from one part of the camp (a borrow area) to fill holes in the ground caused by the project. During the bidding stage the government had told bidders, including Lamb, that the winning contractor could use this dirt "as is." The dirt was in such good condition that none of it had to be broken up, none of it was rock, and none of it was hard material. But in fact Lamb had to pay for "screening" some of the material and for breaking up other parts of the material. When Lamb did not get the additional cost of this extra work, it went to the Armed Services Board of Contract Appeals. The Board found a constructive change. "To the extent that the contract indicated that the existing arch cover and the borrow stockpile would be suitable, Lamb attempted to perform in reliance on the government's detailed design specifications . . . and incurred increased costs in screening clay clods or clumps and other deleterious items. . . . The specifications were defective and extra work resulted from the ensuing constructive change."[9]

A Constructive Change by Other Government Employees

No discussion of a constructive change is complete without stressing that government employees **other than** the contracting officer can end up making a constructive change to a contract. And this is true regardless of what the contract's clauses say.

A government inspector looked at a newly installed roof that would let ponding water evaporate in 48 hours, the industry standard. But that was not good enough for him. He made the contractor change the roof to make water evaporate in 24 hours. A SBCA made the government pay for the contractor's extra work. "Inspectors with authority to accept or reject work have been held to bind the government when they improperly reject the work. An extremely rigid, unreasonable, and arbitrary course of conduct by a government quality assurance representative constitutes an improper disruption of a contractor's performance that can work a constructive change entitling the contractor to an equitable adjustment under the changes clause." The contract contemplated that there would be some ponding. "Where there are no contract provisions establishing acceptance criteria, the standard used to pass on contract work is a standard customary within the industry. The rejection of the contractor's work . . . was unjustified."[10]

In this case, the inspector cost the government money even though the contract clauses seemed to prohibit it. The contract said that "no understanding or agreement between the contractor and any Government employee other than the contracting officer would be effective or binding upon the Government." The board fit its decision into the terms of the standard clause. The inspector "was acting with the authority of the contracting officer in performing his inspection duties to obtain compliance with his interpretation of contract requirements."[11]

Deadlines That Are Not Really Deadlines, Just Suggestions: Notice Requirements

Rule 1: Read the contract. Rule 2: Don't believe everything you read in the contract. These rules pretty well sum up the way courts and boards see deadlines in FAR clauses. They see deadlines as merely suggestions.

For example, several clauses, including the heavily used Changes clause, say that a contractor "must" do something in 30 days. For example, the Changes clause for fixed-price contracts, FAR 52.243-1, has a 30-day "deadline:"

> "The Contractor must assert its right to an adjustment under this clause within 30 days from the date of receipt of the written order. However, if the Contracting Officer decides that the facts justify it, the Contracting Officer may receive and act upon a proposal submitted before final payment of the contract."

The Changes clause at FAR 52.243-4 has two deadlines: a 20-day and a 30-day deadline:

> (d) . . . no [equitable] adjustment . . . shall be made for any costs incurred more than 20 days before the Contractor gives written notice as required.

> (e) The Contractor must assert its right to an adjustment under this clause within 30 days . . . .

But the deadlines in these clauses are not faithfully and literally applied by courts and boards.

One reason is that these deadlines are not like a statute of limitations designed to end a contractor's right to do something. They are more like a warning, forcing the contractor to tell the government something; for example, that the contractor thinks the government has made a constructive change to its contract. If a contractor intends to get an equitable adjustment for the constructive change, the government has to know why the contractor thinks the government made a constructive change. So a deadline in a FAR clause helps force the contractor to give the government notice.

But if the government already knows about it, why demand that the deadline in the clause be slavishly observed? If the clause is designed to make sure the government knows something, and the government in fact already knows it (even without the contractor's giving the government notice), why allow lack of formal notice to defeat any right the contractor might have to an equitable adjustment?

In the classic decision that used this relaxed approach, the court gave this "wholesome" explanation:

> "To adopt [a] severe and narrow application of the notice requirements . . . would be out of tune with the language and purpose of the notice provisions, as well as with this court's wholesome concern that notice provisions in contract-adjustment clauses not be applied too technically and illiberally where the government is quite aware of the operative facts."[12]

What, then, are the rules on deadlines?

First, the rules shift the focus from "strictly following the deadlines" to "what harm has the government suffered because the contractor did not follow the deadlines"? In legalese, the issue is "prejudice." It's a "so what?" It's a contractor saying, in effect, "I was late, but so what? What was the harm to the government because I was late?"

Second, if the government wants to make a deadline a requirement and not a suggestion, it must tell the contractor what happens if the deadline is **not** met. Warning a contractor of the consequences of not following a deadline makes the time limit a real deadline.

Here are examples from two recent cases that have considered deadlines and have ignored them.

Notice under the Changes Clause

In one recent case, the government attorney argued that the claim was too late. This led to the board's making the seemingly irrational criticism of the government that the government had cited "no case law in support of enforcement of the time frames set out in the Changes clause, but rather relies on its understanding of the language." The board went on to note that the government had not addressed "the fact that established case law and precedent have established that the time frames are not to be applied to time bar a claim in most instances. Decisions of various boards and courts have made it clear that the 30 and 20 day time frames in the Changes clause, such as those in issue here, are not generally enforced . . . ."[13]

In this case, the contractor had to build a stone wall. When it took more stone to build the wall than the contractor had anticipated, the contractor filed a claim under the Changes clause asking for an equitable adjustment for the extra stone. The government fought the claim by arguing that the contractor had not observed the time limits in the Changes clause.

The board refused to throw the claim out.

> "The law is settled that generally courts and boards do not bar a claim for failure to comply with contractually required notice provisions absent a showing that the government has been prejudiced by a lack of notice. Even then, overwhelming precedent favors the imposition of a higher burden of persuasion upon the contractor rather than outright denial of the claim. There had been some limited situations where a claim was first introduced well after final payment or when some clear and significant prejudice has been shown. None of those situations have been identified in the current record before us."[14]

No Prejudice

It's "comparatively rare" that the government can prove prejudice.[15]

An old case is one of the few but often-cited examples of prejudice to the government involved a time lag of 5½ years and what the contracting officer would have done if he had had a chance to deal with the issue back then.

> A contractor waited for 5½ years to file an acceleration claim. When it did file the claim, the contracting officer testified "that if he had been apprised in the early stages of the contract that an acceleration claim would be filed, he might have taken a different course on extension of the contract completion time." He also testified "that the government could not evaluate plaintiff's claim in 1965, as adequately as in the latter part of 1959 or 1960," and gave as his reason that defendant "could do nothing about the claim in 1965, whereas in 1959 it would have been possible to take other action . . . ."[16]

But in another more recent case involving a "late-notice" contractor, the government could not prove any prejudice. Although the board identified one potential type of harm—the cost of fixing something had gone up while the contractor was delaying its notice to the government—that type of prejudice had not happened in this case. The decision also shows how it's not necessary that the contracting officer get the notice; notice the government gets from reports or site visits of inspectors or contracting officer's technical representatives counts as notice to the contracting officer.

Parker Excavating had a contract to bury electrical cables at Fort Carson, Colorado. The contractor used a horizontal drill to prepare the dirt for the cables but unexpectedly ran into buried and abandoned foundations of demolished buildings on 19 different occasions. Trying to drill under these conditions increased the equipment costs to repair and replace parts of the drilling equipment. When Parker filed a claim for differing site condition, the government denied it for various reasons, including that the equipment operator was at fault and that the contracting officer had not received notice required by the differing site condition clause on all 19 occasions. The Armed Services Board of Contract Appeals concluded that Parker had encountered a differing site condition and should be compensated for it.

The Board did not let lack of formal notice get in the way. "The written notice requirements are not construed technically to deny legitimate contractor claims when the government was otherwise aware of the operative facts. Some of the daily contractor Quality Control Reports put the government on notice of the conditions encountered. . . . in addition, we have found that the government was aware of the conditions from meetings and site visits. The burden is on the government to establish that it was prejudiced by absence of the required notice. Here the government has made no showing of prejudice from the passage of time or an inability to minimize extra costs resulting from any delay in receiving prompt written notice."[17]

Making Deadlines Firm

If the government wants to make a deadline firm, it must say what the deadline is and what happens if the deadline is not met. In one case, the court required strict compliance with the termination for convenience settlement proposal deadline because the clause said that if the proposal was not submitted within one year from the effective date of termination, the contracting officer could unilaterally determine the amount due and the contractor would lose the right to appeal the determination.[18]

In addition, a GSA clause requires a government lessor to apply for reimbursement of a tax increase within 60 days after paying the tax. The clause warns lessors that if the 60-day limit is not met, the lessor loses its right to reimbursement. The General Services Board of Contract Appeals has ruled that the 60-day deadline must be strictly observed.[19]

CLAUSES LEFT OUT THAT ARE IN A GOVERNMENT CONTRACT ANYWAY: THE *CHRISTIAN* DOCTRINE

The *Christian* Doctrine, named after a 1963 decision of the Court of Claims, holds that a mandatory clause inadvertently omitted from a government contract is in the contract nonetheless. It's not a doctrine used by all courts. The U.S. Court of Appeals for the District of Columbia Circuit has said, "Our court has never adopted the Federal Circuit's Christian doctrine."[20]

The issue usually becomes whether the omitted clause was so fundamental to government procurement that leaving it out was wrong.

The U.S. government had a contract for transporting Portuguese nationals from home to work in the Azores. It told the contractor that the contract was being terminated for convenience pursuant to the short-form termination for convenience clause. Unfortunately for the government, there was no termination for convenience clause in the contract, long- or short-form; also among the missing was a termination for default clause. The contractor argued that the government could not terminate the contract because there was no clause in the contract letting the government do so. The board concluded that there was no short-form termination for convenience clause in the contract because such a clause was discretionary with the contracting officer. A discretionary clause cannot be considered a mandatory clause. The board cited precedent holding that "the *Christian* case does not require the incorporation of a clause whose applicability is based on the exercise of judgment or discretion."[21]

The CAFC gave a nice summary of what the *Christian* Doctrine covers and what it does not.

"... the Christian Doctrine applies to mandatory contract clauses which express a significant or deeply ingrained strand of public procurement policy: a clause requiring plaintiff to exhaust administrative remedies before bringing suit for breach of lease; a clause promoting uniform treatment of "major issues" such as cost and pricing data when more than one military department is purchasing an item; a clause outlining proper pre-award negotiation procedures; and a clause implementing requirements of Buy American Act. . . . However, the Christian Doctrine has also been employed to incorporate less fundamental or significant mandatory procurement contract clauses if not written to benefit or protect the party seeking incorporation . . . [like] a missing "Mistake in Bids" clause required under [the regulations to] be incorporated into the contract as requested by the government because the clause was written for the protection of contract bidders." [Internal citations and punctuation omitted.][22]

Examples of clauses incorporated into a contract under the *Christian* Doctrine are

The "Disputes Concerning Labor Standards" clause[23]

The "Disputes" clause[24]

The "Assignment of Claims" clause[25]

The "Default" clause[26]

The "Fair Labor Standards Act and Service Contract Act-- Price Adjustment" clause[27]

The "Changes" clause[28]

A small business set-aside clause making the small business contractor do at least 50 percent of the work[29]

The Service Contract Act provisions[30]

The "Payments" clause[31]

A "Government Furnished Property" clause[31]

The "Protest After Award" clause[33]

THE GOVERNMENT PREMATURELY ENDS THE AGREEMENT: TERMINATIONS FOR CONVENIENCE

A deal is a deal unless you are the government and have a termination for convenience clause as part of the deal. When you and I sign a contract, we don't have the luxury of deciding, unilaterally and on the cheap, that we don't want to carry out the contract any longer. If we want to unilaterally get out of the deal, we become liable for breach of contract damages. These damages would include all the profit the other party would have made if we had stuck to our deal, so-called anticipatory profits.

The government is different. It has the clout to set new rules for the deal— rules more favorable to itself.

This is not unfair. If somebody wants to contract with the federal government, the contractor knows going into the deal that the government might end the contract before the contractor has had the chance to make all the profit the contractor expected. And it's not as if the government's termination for convenience will do any real harm to the contractor. The government will pay the contractor all costs to date and the profit on that work. In addition, the government will pay for the lawyers and accountants of the contractor as they determine what those costs are. But, unlike you and me, the government will not have to pay anticipatory profits as damages.

The heart of the clause is section (a):

> **Termination for Convenience of the Government (Fixed-Price)** (May 2004)
>
> *(a) The Government may terminate performance of work under this contract in whole or, from time to time, in part if the Contracting Officer determines that a termination is in the Government's interest. The Contracting Officer shall terminate by delivering to the Contractor a Notice of Termination specifying the extent of termination and the effective date.*

The critical issue here is what is "the convenience of the government"? How far can the government push convenience? The answer is that the government can push convenience really far. An improper termination for convenience is rare.

That seems surprising. What is the convenience of the government? A word that vague invites overuse, but only on rare occasions does the government accept that invitation. Although the courts and boards have been vigilant to guard against gross abuses,

> "[i]t is not the province of the courts to decide *de novo* whether termination was the best course. In the absence of bad faith or clear abuse of discretion the contracting officer's election to terminate is conclusive."[34]

Let's look at these grounds, bad faith and abuse of discretion, that the government must have to terminate a contract for convenience improperly.

Bad Faith

Contractors trying to prove a bad faith termination for convenience have a really hard time doing so.

> "The contractor's burden to prove the Government acted in bad faith, however, is very weighty. . . . Any analysis of a question of Governmental bad faith must begin with the presumption that public officials act conscientiously in the discharge of their duties. . . . Due to this heavy burden of proof, contractors have rarely succeeded in demonstrating the Government's bad faith."[35]

So it's in only a rare case that the government terminates a contract for convenience in bad faith.

Here's one:

> "Although wartime situations no longer limit use of the practice, the Government's authority to invoke a termination for convenience has, nonetheless, retained limits. A contracting officer may not terminate for convenience in bad faith, for example, simply to acquire a better bargain from another source . . . ."[36]

Abuse of Discretion

Not only is a bad faith termination for convenience hard to prove, it's also hard to prove the government abused its discretion in terminating for convenience.

Decisions show two common situations that are **not** an abuse of discretion: a termination for convenience after discovery of a cardinal change and a termination for convenience to further full and open competition.

Cardinal Change

A cardinal change is a significant change to the work under a contract. It's so significant that if the changed work were to be competitively bid, more or different bidders would try to get the contract. If the government discovers after the contract has been awarded that the work is significantly different from what it expected, a cardinal change, the government can terminate the contract for convenience and resolicit the work with a solicitation that accurately reflects the government's new understanding of the work.

A government contract anticipated that approximately 10 percent of the work would be asbestos removal. It turned out, however, that the asbestos removal work would be about 50 percent of the contract. Believing that this large increase in work constituted a cardinal change, the contracting officer terminated the contract for convenience and resolicited the work. The terminated contractor argued that the termination for convenience was an abuse of discretion, but the court disagreed: under the circumstances, the contracting officer had ample justification for conducting a reprocurement competitively under CICA. "With this change in the scope of contract work, different bidders, like asbestos removal firms, may have entered the competition on the contract."[37]

Further Full and Open Competition

Clearly, a cardinal change defeats full and open competition. But a cardinal change isn't the only justification for a termination for convenience. Trying to further full and open competition, even without a cardinal change, is a proper exercise of the contracting officer's discretion to terminate a contract for convenience.

In estimating the work expected under a Navy contract for automotive and related vehicle parts and accessories for the United States Public Works Center on the island of Guam, the government greatly underestimated how many parts the government would need. After awarding the contract to T&M Distributors, Inc., the government learned that its estimate was wrong by 450 percent. Instead of having a value of about $1 million, the contract's value was over $5 million. The government terminated the contract for convenience, which the contractor opposed. The court held that the government was correct. The government did not have to prove a cardinal change to justify the termination for convenience. All the contracting officer had to demonstrate was that the statutory requirements for full and open competition had been affected. The court found this to have occurred: "It is not unreasonable for the contracting officer to find that a 450 percent error in the original solicitation could have affected the pool of bidders. That having been the case, we are not prepared to say he acted unreasonably or abused his discretion in concluding that the circumstances called for a new procurement with corrected requirements to satisfy CICA's requirements of full and open competition." [38]

Endnotes

1. *AT&T Comunications Inc. v. Wiltel*, 1 F.3d 1201, 1205 (Fed.Cir.1993) (quoting *Allied Materials & Equip. Co. v. United States*, 215 Ct. Cl. 406, 409, 569 F.2d 562, 563-64 (1978)

2. *Poly-Pacific Technologies, Inc.*, B-296029, June 1, 2005, 2005 CPD ¶ 105.

3. *HG Properties A, L.P. v. The United States & Quality Leasing & Development*, 68 Fed. Appx. 192 (Fed.Cir.2003).

4. *Atlantic Coast Contracting Inc.*, B-288969.4, June 21, 2002, 2002 CPD ¶ 104.

5. *Cardinal Maintenance Services, Inc., v. The United States*. 63 Fed.Cl. 98 (2004).

6. *Poly-Pacific Technologies, Inc., supra.*

7. *NavCom Defense Electronics, Inc. v. England*, 53 Fed.Appx. 897 (Fed.Cir. 2002).

8. *J.P. Fleming, Inc.*, PSBCA No. 5197, February 3, 2006.

9. *Lamb Engineering and Construction Co.*, ASBCA No. 53304, 06-1 BCA ¶ 33178.

10. *A & D Fire Protection, Inc.*, ASBCA No. 53,103, 02-2 BCA ¶ 32053.

11. *Id.*

12. *Hoel-Steffen Construction Co., v. United States*, 456 F. 2d 760 (Ct. Cl. 1972).

13. *Flathead Contractors, LLC*, AGBCA No. 2005-130-1, January 18, 2006, 06-1 BCA ¶ 33174.

14. *Id.*

15. *Central Mechanical Construction*, ASBCA Nos. 29431-33, 85-2 BCA ¶ 18061 (1985).

16. *Eggers & Higgins & Edwin A. Keeble Associates, Inc. v. United States*, 185 Ct.Cl. 765, 776-777, 403 F.2d 225, 231 (1968).

17. *Parker Excavating Inc.*, ASBCA No. 54637, 06-1 BCA ¶ 30796.

18. *Do-Well Machine Shop, Inc. v. United States*, 870 F.2d 637 (Fed.Cir.1989).

19. *4J2R1C LP v. General Services Administration*, GSBCA No. 15584, 02-1 BCA ¶ 31742.

20. *Amfac Resorts, L.L.C. v. U.S. Dept. of the Interior*, 282 F.3d 818, 824, 350 U.S.App.D.C. 191, 197 (D.C. Cir. 2002) *reversed on other grounds, National Park Hospitality Ass'n v. Department of Interior*, 538 U.S. 803, 123 S.Ct. 2026, (2003).

21. *Empressa de Viacao Terceirense*, ASBCA No. 49827, 01-1 BCA ¶ 30796.

22. *General Engineering & Mach. Works v. O'Keefe*, 991 F.2d 775, 779-780 (Fed.Cir. 1993).

23. *M.E. McGeary Co.*, ASBCA No. 36788, 90-1 BCA ¶ 22512.

24. *Fireman's Fund Insurance Co.*, ASBCA No. 38284, 91-1 BCA ¶ 23439.

25. *Rodgers Construction, Inc.*, IBCA No. 2777, 92-1 BCA ¶ 24503.

26. *OFEGRO*, HUDBCA No. 88-3410-C7, 91-3 BCA ¶ 24206; and *H&R Machinists Co.*, ASBCA No. 38440, 91-1 BCA ¶ 23373.

27. *Telesec Library Services*, ASBCA No. 42968, 92-1 BCA ¶ 24650; and *Ace Services, Inc. v. General Services Administration*, GSBCA No. 11331, 92-2 BCA ¶ 24943.

28. *GAI Consultants, Inc.*, ENGBCA No. 6030, 95-2 BCA ¶ 27620.

29. *Unit Data Service Corp. v. Department of Veterans Affairs*, GSBCA No. 10775-P-R, 93-3 BCA ¶ 25964.

30. *Miller's Moving Co.*, ASBCA No. 43114, 92-1 BCA ¶ 24707.

31. *General Engineering & Machine Works*, ASBCA No. 38788, 92-3 BCA ¶ 25055.

32. *Rehabilitation Services of Northern California*, ASBCA No. 47085, 96-2 BCA ¶ 28324.

33. *Labat-Anderson, Inc. v. U.S.*, 42 Fed.Cl. 806, 857 (1999).

34. *John Reiner & Co. v. United States*, 163 Ct.Cl. 381, 325 F.2d 438, 442 (1963).

35. *Krygoski Const. Co., Inc. v. United States*, 94 F.3d 1537, 1541 (Fed.Cir.1996).

36. *Id.*

37. *Id.*

38. *T & M Distributors, Inc. v. United States*, 185 F.3d 1279 (Fed.Cir.1999).

Part III

Lawsuits over Government Contracts

The complexity of government contracts is most obvious when there is a controversy with one. For our purposes, a controversy can either be a protest, which is a lawsuit by an unsuccessful vendor trying to get the government contract, or a claim, which is typically by a government contractor tried to get more money out of the government.

These procurement lawsuits are much more complex than the typical lawsuit. Chapter 9 tries to prove that. It starts out talking about what a typical lawsuit looks like and how a typical lawsuit gets resolved. It then looks at a typical federal lawsuit and describes how much more complex they are. Finally, the chapter examines the typical procurement lawsuits: protests and claims.

In Chapter 10, we look more carefully at protests, looking at the "what," "when," and "how" of protests before GAO and the CFC.

In Chapter 11, we look more closely at claims, again from a "what," "when," and "how" perspective of claims before the boards of contract appeals (BCAs) and the CFC.

And finally, in Chapter 12, we look at how the government might end up paying for the costs of protests and claims. Significantly, just because the government loses a lawsuit, that's no reason the government pays attorneys' fees. As long as the government has a good argument in a losing lawsuit, it won't pay the costs of litigation.

156

Chapter 9

Federal Litigation: Suing the Federal Government

CONTENTS

Whoever came up with the expression "Don't make a federal case out of it" knew how hard it is to sue the federal government. Anybody who wants to sue the federal government has to satisfy a number of complex requirements. Suing someone in a state court is much different and not nearly as complex. It's much easier to have your case heard there.

The complexity of the process is apparently what the founding fathers wanted. When they wrote the Constitution, they could have made life really easy for litigants. They could have let anybody sue everybody in any federal court for any reason to get whatever kind of help a court thought would be fair.

But they did not take the easy way. They made federal courts "courts of limited jurisdiction." So federal courts are available to litigants who can "make a federal case out of it."

Government vendors are no different than other litigants. If a vendor wants to sue the government in any procurement forum—Court of Federal Claims, Government Accountability Office (GAO), or a board of contract appeals (BCA)—it must meet these complex requirements. Whether it's a disappointed bidder trying to file a protest or a government contractor trying to file a claim, a number of legal hoops must be jumped through.

This chapter discusses the minimum requirements for any lawsuit against the federal government. It lays the groundwork for understanding the two typical procurement lawsuits, protests and claims, discussed in Chapters 10 and 11. It also lays the foundation for Chapter 12, Costs of Litigation, a discussion of the availability of attorneys' fees and costs available in protests and claims.

To make it easier to understand the complexity of lawsuits against the federal government, this chapter moves in a two-step process from the general to the specific to the really specific. The "general" is a typical lawsuit at any level of government—federal, state, or local. The "specific" is a typical lawsuit against the federal government. The "really specific" is a typical procurement lawsuit against the federal government.

The section titled "Any Lawsuit" discusses what is involved in **any lawsuit** at any level of government—federal, state, or local. It discusses these typical lawsuits: injured pedestrian vs. a negligent driver, irate neighbor vs. irate neighbor. You might be surprised by how little we know about a real lawsuit because much of what we think is legal reality is actually Hollywood fiction. In describing "any lawsuit," we discuss the four elements of any lawsuit—what branch of government gets involved (typically, the judicial branch); the jurisdiction of the court; the level of the court; and the help or relief the court can offer.

The section titled "Any Lawsuit against the Federal Government" discusses what is involved in a **typical lawsuit against the federal government.** As you will see, a lawsuit against the federal government is much more complex than neighbors suing neighbors. Lawsuits against the federal government involve not only the four requirements described above but also two additional elements, sovereign immunity and standing. All of these elements—the four "any lawsuit" elements and the two additional ones—are discussed in that section.

The section "The Two Typical Procurement Lawsuits against the Government: Protests and Claims" focuses on the two **typical procurement lawsuits against the government**, protests and claims.

To simplify this complicated material, we'll take two shortcuts. One shortcut is that the material in this chapter deals with only civil law. Any case that comes before a judge has to be either a criminal case or a civil case. Criminal cases are lawsuits brought by a government (local, state, or federal) to punish those who break the criminal laws. The punishment can be imposed through money (fines) or jail. Civil lawsuits, on the other hand, are generally brought by taxpayers suing each other, although on occasion people sue the government. So to simplify things, we will take a shortcut and focus solely on civil cases.

A second shortcut is that we will focus on trial courts, not appellate courts. Hollywood has shown us plenty of trial judges in shows ranging from "Perry Mason" back in the 20th century to the current "Law & Order" series. These judges sometimes have juries to help them do their work. They make sweating witnesses on the witness stand answer all sorts of insulting questions put to them by nasty lawyers, and they usually rule right from the bench orally, making people go to jail or pay someone some money.

Much less frequently, we see appellate judges on television. One of the most noticeable examples was the litigation over the 2000 election, which involved the Florida Supreme Court. The litigation gave the average taxpayer an inside view of the rarely seen appellate process. Appellate judges don't deal with juries, don't listen to witnesses, and don't act all by themselves. They join other judges on a panel of three to nine or more judges to hear lawyers argue points of law apparently messed up by trial judges, and they usually issue written decisions, not immediate rulings from the bench.

Appellate judges do not necessarily give litigants any type of relief. These judges typically decide whether the trial court judges were right. If an appeals court decides the trial court was wrong, the appeals court can return the case to the trial court to fix it.

What most people don't realize—and it's important that they do—is that appellate courts don't try the case all over again. All they do is see whether the trial court based its decision on facts and not guesswork and whether the trial court applied the law in the right way. And even if the trial court made a mistake, the error could be harmless to the trial court's decision. Harmless error avoids the trial court's having to try the case all over again. So the appellate court has a much narrower job to do: see if the trial court did its job without fatal error.

ANY LAWSUIT

In a typical lawsuit, any taxpayer who can find the courthouse asks a judge in the judicial branch to apply state or local law to give the plaintiff some kind of help, usually money. If one of the parties does not get the result it wanted, it can appeal to an appellate court.

Significantly, a defendant typically can't beat the lawsuit by claiming that it is immune from lawsuits. As we will see later in this chapter, immunity from lawsuit—the government's sovereign immunity—is one big issue that a lawsuit against the federal government must deal with.

A typical lawsuit has four essential elements. And although we will see many differences in lawsuits in this book, we will also see these four constants in all lawsuits: (1) the branch of government the "judge" works for—legislative branch, judicial branch, or executive branch; (2) the jurisdiction of the forum; (3) the law that gets applied—federal, state, or local; and (4) the type of relief or help a plaintiff can get—money or something else, like an injunction (nonmonetary).

Branch of Government: Judicial, Legislative, or Executive?

All countries need a government to make laws, to carry them out, and to enforce them. In a dictatorship, all three jobs can be done by one tyrant.

In our country, and indeed in most countries, the government is based on a theory of the separation of branches of government. Rather than concentrating the job of making the laws (legislative branch), carrying out the laws (executive branch), and interpreting/enforcing the laws (judicial branch) all in one entity, most governments divide up these three responsibilities and entrust them to separate and independent branches of the government.

Most judges are in the judicial branch. But the executive branch can have "judges," too. Some communities have a Department of Motor Vehicles "judge" to whom you can argue that you did not deserve a traffic ticket. And some legislators can be judges: Some communities let their local city or town councils make zoning changes that pit a landowner against the neighbors, leaving the local legislature to decide who wins. So it's possible for all three branches to get involved in lawsuits.

In general, though, the typical lawsuit involves a judge working for the judicial branch of government.

The Jurisdiction of a Forum

Jurisdiction has two aspects: subject matter jurisdiction and jurisdiction over the person being sued. We'll focus on the first one. The subject matter of some state and local courts, for example, is limited by the maximum dollar amount for which a plaintiff can sue. A Small Claims Court might be able to hear only cases under, for example, $5,000.

The Law the Judge Applies

Because our country is made up of local, state, and federal governments, all three levels of government may make laws for a judge to apply. Typically, a local judge applies local laws passed by a local legislature, such as a City Council. A local judge could apply state law but does not apply federal law.

The same is true with a state court judge, who applies state law. A federal judge typically applies federal law.

There are exceptions, however, as we will see in greater detail later. In some cases, Congress has told federal judges that they may be guided by the applicable state law. One example of this is the Federal Tort Claims Act (FTCA), which involves a federal judge deciding whether a federal employee is immune from lawsuit. Another exception is when there is no federal law on an issue before a federal judge. In that case, the federal judge is like a kid in a candy store, picking the law to follow based on the "best in modern decision and discussion."

Relief

Relief means the type of help a judge may give. Most plaintiffs want money from the defendant.

But sometimes they want something different. A plaintiff might want to stop someone from doing something and therefore seeks an injunction.

Or a plaintiff might want a judge to decide conflicting rights of the parties; for example, whose interpretation of a contract is the correct interpretation of the contract. In this case, a plaintiff would ask for a declaratory judgment, a judgment declaring the rights of the parties to the contract.

On rare occasions, one of the contracting parties might want a judge to require the reluctant other party to go through with the contract. For example, a home buyer might have a sales contract with the home seller that obligates the seller to sell the house to the buyer at some point. If, for example, the housing market involved has become hot and prices in the market have increased greatly, a home seller might not want to carry out the contract with the home buyer because the home seller might like to get more money from a different buyer now that the market is hot. The home buyer in that case would go to court asking the judge to order the specific performance of the contract between the buyer and the seller.

So, generally, four kinds of relief are available in a typical lawsuit: money damages, injunctions, declaratory judgments, and the specific performance of a contract.

Any Lawsuit against the Federal Government

As we see from the media daily, the federal government gets sued for all sorts of things. Some of these lawsuits argue that something the government did was unconstitutional; that something an agency did was illegal; or (of importance to us and to be discussed in a later chapter) that something went wrong with a federal contract.

Like the typical lawsuit described above, a typical lawsuit against the federal government involves a judge in the judicial branch being asked for relief such as money damages, an injunction, or a declaratory judgment.

But there are several additional issues found in federal lawsuits that make them different from a typical lawsuit.

The first difference is that the judge takes a harder look at the plaintiff. A federal judge has to ask, "Does the plaintiff have the right to bring this lawsuit? Does the plaintiff have **standing**?"

The second difference looks at the court where the case is being heard. Now the federal judge asks, "Has the government waived **sovereign immunity** to be sued in this court?"

After looking at how the four elements of a typical lawsuit apply to a lawsuit against the government, we'll look at these two unique additional issues that affect those lawsuits.

Branch of Government

Most cases against the federal government are fought out in Federal District Court. So the judicial branch of government is typically the forum for litigation against the federal government.

But as we all know, the other two branches, the legislative and the executive, get involved in resolving controversies against the federal government. Congress gets involved when, for instance, it passes legislation benefiting one or more persons or companies. In addition, as we will see later, an arm of Congress, GAO, is a major player in procurement litigation because it is one of the forums that litigates protests.

And the legislative and the executive branches also get involved in resolving controversies, such as those which arise when an agency issues licenses, such as the Federal Communications Commission issuing television licenses.

Procurement lawsuits, as we will see shortly, can involve all three branches of the federal government. For example, protests can be resolved by GAO in the legislative branch, by the U. S. Court of Federal Claims (CFC) in the judicial branch, by the agency awarding the contract in the executive branch, or by more than one of the branches.

Jurisdiction of a Forum

The subject matter jurisdiction of the federal court is typically a lawsuit between residents of different states (diversity jurisdiction) or questions involving the Constitution, federal laws, and federal regulations (federal question jurisdiction). In discussing the typical lawsuit against the federal government, we will discuss federal question jurisdiction.

The Law a Judge Applies

The federal judge typically applies federal law and not state law. There are, however, several exceptions to this rule allowing a federal judge to apply state law.

Federal Tort Claims Act

On occasion, Congress has told federal judges to apply state law. When Congress passed the FTCA, which is discussed elsewhere in this text, it told federal judges to use state law in deciding, for example, whether a federal employee is protected under the FTCA because the employee is acting within the scope of employment.

No Federal Law

Another exception is when there is no federal law on a topic. In this no-man's land, the federal judge can look to state law or general common law for an answer.

> "Since federal law does not answer the issue, we look to general property and contract law principles as they are embodied in state law pronouncements."[1]

Relief

Generally, federal judges can give litigants any one or more of the four forms of relief typically available in any lawsuit: money, injunctions, declaratory judgments, and specific performance.

But, as we will see, these four remedies are not always available in procurement cases. A contractor filing a claim can get money only for a government breach of contract; and in a protest, the court may issue an injunction and make a declaratory judgment under some circumstances but may not order not specific performance of a contract, like a judge faced with a home buyer–home seller controversy.[2]

Standing of the Plaintiff

The issue of standing begins our departure from the more straightforward state court rules to the more complex federal court rules.

In a typical federal lawsuit, simply because a taxpayer can find a federal courthouse, the taxpayer cannot necessarily sue someone in that courthouse. Only a plaintiff with standing can bring a lawsuit. And there is no assurance that the plaintiff has standing simply because the plaintiff pays taxes.

This is one significant difference between the typical federal lawsuit and lawsuits at the state and local levels, where standing is not an issue. As we will see, standing is an issue in protests and claims.

Standing is frustrating. As one commentator put it,

> "Standing has been labeled one of the most amorphous concepts in the domain of public law, and has been referred to as 'a complicated specialty of federal jurisdiction,' and criticized as being both 'needlessly complex and needlessly artificial.'"[3]

Surprising examples of plaintiffs lacking standing in a federal courthouse are taxpayers objecting to Congress's spending money on a war or members of Congress arguing that one of their laws is not being carried out properly.

Although these examples might seem surprising, their outcomes are realistic. An unelected judge does not want to get too involved in issues better left to the elected officials in the executive branch or legislative branch.

Sovereign Immunity

Historically (and this means going back many centuries), a sovereign like a king could not be sued unless the sovereign had consented to be sued. This is the concept of sovereign immunity.

Because the federal government is a sovereign, it enjoys sovereign immunity. It cannot be sued unless Congress has waived the government's sovereign immunity. This waiver comes in the form of a "consent statute," which is a law passed by Congress and signed by the President waiving the government's sovereign immunity and consenting to the government's being sued.

Sovereign immunity is not an issue in a lawsuit in a federal court between residents of different states. But it certainly is an issue if the lawsuit is against the federal government. Whether a judge has jurisdiction to hear that kind of a case depends on whether the government has waived its sovereign immunity.

Jurisdiction and sovereign immunity are closely related. Jurisdiction describes the kinds of cases a judge can hear, whether it's a lawsuit against a next-door neighbor or a government. Sovereign immunity is related to jurisdiction because a court has jurisdiction over a case in which the federal government is a defendant **only** if Congress has waived the federal government's sovereign immunity. If you want to sue your neighbor, all you have to prove is that the court has jurisdiction; your neighbor doesn't have immunity from suit. But if you are suing the government, you have to prove both that the court has jurisdiction and that the government has waived its sovereign immunity. If so, the court has jurisdiction. So while the jurisdiction of a court describes the types of cases it can hear involving a neighbor or the government, sovereign immunity whittles away the kinds of cases a court has jurisdiction over when the federal government is the defendant.

THE TWO TYPICAL PROCUREMENT LAWSUITS AGAINST THE GOVERNMENT: PROTESTS AND CLAIMS

With this background on lawsuits in general, and lawsuits specifically against the federal government in mind, we now move to the two typical procurement lawsuits the government faces—protests and claims.

One of the problems with distinguishing between these two radically different types of lawsuits is the terminology. In our everyday language, a controversy can be called many things: people protesting what's happening, people claiming they are not being treated fairly, people disputing somebody else's conclusion. So in everyday language, the terms *protests*, *claims*, and *disputes* are used interchangeably.

But in the procurement field, these terms are *terms of art*. This means that they have a special, unique meaning in procurement that is different from what they mean in everyday language.

So the first thing to keep in mind in discussing procurement litigation is the sharp distinction between the two battles, protests and claims.

A *protest* is a lawsuit by a loser trying to get the contract.

A *claim* is a lawsuit by a contractor trying to get more money under the contract. A claim may also be filed by a contractor asking the government to interpret words used in a contract or provide some other type of help.

This section discusses protests and claims in terms of the *who* (standing), *where* (jurisdiction), and *why* (relief). The *when, what,* and *how* of protests and claims are discussed in Chapter 10, Protests, and in Chapter 11, Claims.

Protests

A losing vendor can file a protest in any or all of three forms: the agency awarding a contract, GAO, or the U.S. Court of Federal Claims. Although all three forms have a specific process for dealing with claims, only two, GAO and the court, have reported decisions. For that reason, this section discusses only protests to these two forums.

The Court of Federal Claims (CFC)

Some laws Congress passes are so complex that Congress set up special courts to handle them. For example, the U.S. Bankruptcy Courts handle our country's complex bankruptcy laws, and the U.S. Tax Court deals with the equally complex Internal Revenue Code.

We won't debate where the FAR falls in terms of complexity when compared to bankruptcy laws and tax laws. But by any standard, procurement is legally complex. Congress recognized this when it set up the Court of Federal Claims to deal with procurement litigation, both protests and claims.

Up until 1982, the Court of Claims had a trial part and an appellate part. In 1982 the trial part became the U.S. Claims Court and the appellate part was incorporated into the U.S. Court of Appeals for the Federal Circuit. In 1992 the Claims Court was renamed the Court of Federal Claims.[4]

Federal courts are typically classified as Article I or Article III courts, after the particular section of the U.S. Constitution that set the court up. Article III courts have judges with lifetime appointments. Article I courts are set up by Congress, and their judges do not have lifetime appointments. The CFC is an Article I court. Its judges are appointed by the President, with the consent of the Senate, to 15-year terms.

Branch of government

The court is in the judicial branch of government.

CFC protest jurisdiction

About one-third of the court's caseload involves government contracts—protests and claims. The other matters the court handles include tax refund suits (about 25 percent of the court's caseload), Fifth Amendment takings (10 percent), civilian and military pay questions, and intellectual property issues.[5]

Prior to 1996 the CFC handled only pre-award protests. So when the ink dried on the award document, the court could not handle a protest of that award.

But in 1996 Congress expanded the court's jurisdiction to include post-award protests. The court now has protest jurisdiction over

> "an action by an interested party objecting to a solicitation by a Federal agency for bids or proposals for a proposed contract or to a proposed award or the award of a contract or any alleged violation of statute or regulation in connection with a procurement or a proposed procurement."[6]

Law applied by the CFC in protests

The court, like any other federal court, applies federal law and, as needed, state law.

CFC protest relief

It would be nice if every federal court could give all four forms of relief. But they cannot, and the CFC cannot.

It would also be nice if at least the CFC had consistent forms of relief for the two types of cases it handles, protests and claims. But that is not the case. In fact, it's backward. In a protest, the primary relief is an injunction against performance and a declaratory judgment that the government messed up the solicitation process. If that relief is given, money, in the form of bid preparation and proposal costs, is available.[7]

What the CFC cannot provide a protester is what the protester wants most—the contract. But a court cannot tell an agency to whom to award a contract.

So a homebuyer has greater rights than a government contractor. When people buy a home, they typically sign a sales contract with the seller of the house. The contract requires the seller to go through with the deal sometime in the future. But what happens if the property values increase after the contract has been signed and the seller wants to try to get more money for the house, either by trying to get more money out of the other party to the sales contract or by trying to sell the house to somebody different? If a seller refuses to carry out the sales contract, the home buyer has a good remedy available in a courtroom: a judge could order the home seller to carry out the sales contract. The judge would order "specific performance of the contract." The seller would then be forced to perform the contract and sell to the buyer.

Getting back to a government contractor, can a vendor ask the CFC to order specific performance of a government contract, that is, to order the government to award the protester the contract? The answer is "No."

LABAT-Anderson was a government contractor managing a government supply depot. After the government decided to take distribution services back in-house to be performed by government employees, LABAT protested to the court. It asked the court for an order prohibiting the government from taking the work in-house until the government re-solicited the contract using the A-76 process. To the court, however, the protester was asking for an injunction since any order the court might issue would require the government to award a contract to LABAT. Although the court was authorized to "award any relief that the court considers proper, including injunctive relief," the court's jurisdiction "does not include the authority to award a contract."[8]

CFC protest standing

Having described standing as a confusing concept, now is the time to add that, for protests, standing is made easier to work with because GAO and the CFC apply the same test for determining whether a protester has standing to bring a protest.

In protests, standing depends on two issues: "prejudice" and an "interested party."

Prejudice

Curiously, the test for standing starts out with the question "So what?" If a protester argues that the agency did not evaluate its proposal correctly, broke the law, bribed the contracting officer, or made some other mistake, the first issue the CFC must deal with is standing, which in turn requires that the CFC look at "prejudice"—harm—a "So what?"

"In order to establish standing, ITAC must show that it is an 'actual or prospective bidder or offeror whose direct economic interest would be affected by the award of the contract or by failure to award the contract,' i.e., that ITAC was an interested party, prejudiced by the award to RSIS. The Court of Federal Claims did not decide the question of prejudice because it determined that there was no error in the procurement process, stating that '[i]f the court finds error, the court then examines whether the error was prejudicial to plaintiff.'. . . This approach was erroneous. In fact, because the question of prejudice goes directly to the question of standing, the prejudice issue must be reached before addressing the merits. As we said in Myers, 'prejudice (or injury) is a necessary element of standing.'"[9]

Prejudice here means "harm." It's important to point out that prejudice in protest/standing issues does not mean prejudice in the sense of EEO prejudice. Prejudice simply means the government did something wrong during the solicitation process that hurt a vendor who had a real good chance of winning a contract.

"To establish prejudice, ITAC must show that there was a 'substantial chance' it would have received the contract award but for the alleged error in the procurement process. . . . In other words, the protestor's chance of securing the award must not have been insubstantial."[10]

The CAFC went on to show how ITAC qualified as an interested party, having been prejudiced by the government's actions:

"ITAC argues that the award to RSIS should be set aside on a variety of grounds. If ITAC were successful, the award would be set aside, and ITAC might secure it. ITAC also argues that the Air Force improperly failed to conduct 'discussions' with ITAC and that, if it had, ITAC would have been able to cure deficiencies in its bid. There is no question here that ITAC was a qualified bidder and that its proposal would have been improved and its chances of securing the contract increased if the problem with its cost estimate had been cured. The Air Force's decision letter stated that '[a]ll offerors provided proposals which met minimum contract requirements' and 'all proposals were fundamentally sound.' Under these circumstances, ITAC has established prejudice (and therefore standing), because it had greater than an insubstantial chance of securing the contract if successful on the merits of the bid protest."[11]

It's important to add that prejudice can become an issue at two points in the process:

> "To prevail in a bid protest, the protestor must show that the procuring agency acted without a rational basis or contrary to law and that the error prejudiced the offeror's posture in the procurement process. . . . Prejudice thus frequently is addressed at two separate stages of a bid protest, first in analyzing whether the protestor has standing to pursue its claims and then near the end of the analytical process in determining whether the protestor is entitled to relief. The second analytical step has also been described as follows: 'for [plaintiff] to prevail it must establish not only some significant error in the procurement process, but also that there was a substantial chance it would have received the contract award but for that error.'"[12]

Interested party

In addition to proving prejudice, a protester must also prove it is an "interested party" to have standing to raise the protest. Only an interested party has standing.

One big problem in defining *interested party* is that Congress has not defined it for the federal courts. The law giving the Court of Federal Claims more protest authority did not have a definition of *interested party* in it. This law, the 1996 Administrative Dispute Resolution Act, gave the court the authority to hear the cases of "interested parties," but the act did not define the term.

So judges had to come up with a definition. Their definition uses the one Congress in the Competition in Contracting Act told GAO to use:

> "Standing is limited to actual or prospective bidders or offerors whose direct economic interest would be affected by the award of the contract or by failure to award the contract."[13]

So to be an interested party, the protester must have been an actual or potential bidder.

In protests, if you don't put in a bid, it's hard to win a protest. It's **possible** for a non-bidder to win a protest, but rare. So, protests are like lotteries in more ways than one. One similarity is a variation of the rule that if you don't buy a ticket, you can't win the lottery.

Rex Service Corp. was once the only approved source for "thumbwheel switches," a component in aviation control transponders. When the government issued a solicitation for these switches in 2004, Rex protested, claiming that the government had violated the Procurement Integrity Act. But Rex let the deadline for submitting a bid pass without putting one in. The agency later denied Rex's protest and gave the contract to a new supplier of the switches. Rex then protested the contract award to the Court of Federal Claims. The court threw the protest out, concluding that Rex was not an interested party because Rex had not submitted a bid. Since Rex had not submitted a bid, it was not an "actual" bidder. Nor was Rex a "prospective bidder." Precedent said that "in order to be eligible to protest, one who has not actually submitted an offer must be expecting to submit an offer prior to the closing date of the solicitation." Here, because Rex could have bid but chose not to, it could not be considered a prospective bidder and was not an interested party.[14]

In addition to non-bidders failing the standing test, winning vendors can fail the interested party test. Curiously, the fact that a vendor won a contract does not mean the vendor is an interested party entitled to participate in a protest by another vendor against the contract award. Winners do not have an unconditional right to defend the agency's selection by participating in the protest.[15]

Tanner won a protested contract and wanted to defend its contract, so it asked the CFC to let it intervene. The court's rules allowed intervention either as a matter of right or by permission of the court. Intervention as a matter of right was allowed only if a statute authorized intervention or where necessary to protect someone's interest "unless the applicant's interest is adequately represented by the parties." Neither condition was met here. There was no statute that would let Tanner intervene. Also, the government would adequately represent Tanner's interest. Tanner had one alternative. It could participate as an *amicus curiae*, a friend of the court. That way Tanner could, without the court's prior consent, file briefs responding to the motions of other parties. It could also appear at all public hearings. What Tanner could not do as *amicus* would be to file initial motions, take discovery, or participate in settlement discussions.[16]

Another vendor that lacks standing is a vendor that "withdrew its proposal, or a case in which a disappointed bidder could not receive the award even if successful in its challenge to the winning bidder's proposal."[17]

Sovereign immunity

Congress has consented to the government's being sued in the CFC for protests.

> "Congressional consent to suit in the Court of Federal Claims, which thereby waives sovereign immunity, must be explicit and strictly construed. Consent to suit in this Court is granted by 28 U.S.C. § 1491(b)(1)."[18]

The Government Accountability Office (GAO)

GAO is a favorite forum for protesters. It's easy—a protest can even be filed by e-mail. GAO's accessible—a protest can be filed at GAO 24/7. And it's cheap—you don't need a lawyer.

But a lawyer can be very useful to a protester in a GAO protest. If a protester has a lawyer, that lawyer can get access to much more agency information because of a device known as a protective order. Information will be disclosed to the lawyer but is protected from being disclosed by the lawyer to the client.

Branch of government

GAO is a branch of Congress, the legislative branch. In addition to its protest work, GAO is a think tank for Congress. When members of Congress want a study of a particular issue done, they ask GAO to do it.

Jurisdiction

GAO has authority to deal with protests involving "the procurement of goods and services" by the government.[19] And although those kinds of procurements are the bulk of GAO's work, some types of agency contract awards don't involve the procurement of goods and services.

Concession contracts

A good example is concession contracts. These are contracts through which the government offers vendors business opportunities. One example is a contract for someone to provide a service like running a Park Service campsite.

When the government awards a concession contract, GAO doesn't believe the government is procuring goods and services. To GAO, the government is selling a business opportunity when it awards a concession contract. So generally GAO will not hear protests of concession contracts.

But if the concession contract includes more than a minimal amount of services, GAO will hear a protest of the award of a concession contract.

The Park Service awarded a concession contract to a vendor to operate ferry services carrying visitors to Fort Sumter. But that wasn't all. The vendor was also to clean and repair the office space that the Park Service would provide as part of the concession contract. Because the concession contract included services, GAO concluded it had jurisdiction over the protest.[20]

Outleases

In addition, GAO will not hear protests when the government owns land and is looking for a tenant to use that land. These "outleases" of government property are not considered a procurement and therefore cannot be protested to GAO.

Task orders

Nor will GAO generally hear protests of individual task orders under indefinite delivery/indefinite quantity (IDIQ) contracts.

Several years ago, Congress encouraged agencies to use IDIQ contracts to speed the procurement process. One concern at the time, however, was that the easy use of these contracts would be reduced by protests of the task orders issued under them. One solution was a law that limited the protests of task orders. As a result, GAO cannot handle protests of task orders issued under IDIQ contracts except on the ground that the task order increases the scope, period, or maximum value of the IDIQ contract.

But, as always, there are exceptions to this seemingly blanket prohibition on protests of task orders. For example, someone protesting a task order might really be protesting the underlying IDIQ contract. If so, GAO will hear the protest—not of the task order but of the underlying contract.

A federal law established a preference for contracting with local, small, and small disadvantaged businesses for work associated with base closures. A contracting officer was supposed to determine whether there is a reasonable expectation that offers would be received from local companies. After the Corps of Engineers intended to award to one company both an IDIQ contract and a task order, a company protested, arguing that the contracting officer had made no such determination. When the company protested to GAO, the government asked GAO to throw the protest out because it was a protest of a task order. GAO refused. The protest was really about the underlying contract, and the contracting officer's failure to do his job under federal law and regulations. "Since we are charged by statute with reviewing protests alleging that a solicitation does not comply with applicable procurement statutes and regulations, we conclude that Ocuto's protest is properly within our bid protest jurisdiction."[21]

GAO will also consider protests of a task order when an agency tries to get around the law and regulations by, for example, using a non-appropriated fund instrumentality or a cooperative agreement or grant instead of a contract.[22]

Protests of subcontract awards

Protests of subcontract awards are rare and happen only in two limited cases. GAO refers to these exceptions as subcontracts **"for"** the government and subcontracts **"by"** the government.

A subcontract **"for"** the government

A prime contractor can go out and buy something for the government acting as the government's purchasing agent. This is a contract awarded by a prime but "for" the government. For the contract to qualify as a subcontract "for" the government, the losing vendor would have to prove that (1) the prime contractor was acting as a purchasing agent for the government; (2) the agency relationship between the government and the prime contractor was established by clear contractual consent; and (3) the contract stated that the government would be directly liable to the vendor for the purchase price.[23] GAO "will consider a protest of that buy only if asked by the agency."[24]

A subcontract **"by"** the government

In this subcontract, the prime plays only a minor role in awarding the contract. It's the government that does all the hard work. GAO says a subcontract procurement was "by" the government "where the agency handled substantially all the substantive aspects of the procurement and, in effect, 'took over' the procurement, leaving to the prime contractor only the procedural aspects of the procurement, i.e., issuing the subcontract solicitation and receiving proposals. . . . In such cases, the prime contractor's role in the procurement was essentially ministerial, such that it was merely acting as a conduit for the government. On the other hand, we have found subcontractor procurements were not 'by' the government where the prime contractor handled other meaningful aspects of the procurement, such as preparing the subcontract solicitation and evaluation criteria, evaluating the offers, negotiating with the offerors, and selecting an awardee."[25]

The Agency for International Development (AID) had a contract with SRA International, Inc. AID needed a grants management software program so AID asked SRA to get one. SRA got one from Infoterra, Inc. When a competitor of Infoterra, STR L.L.C., found out about the subcontract, STR protested to GAO, arguing it was a subcontract for or by the government. GAO dismissed the protest. The subcontract was not a subcontract "for" the government because the prime was not a purchasing agency and AID did not ask GAO to review the protest. The subcontract was not a subcontract "by" the government because the government played only a minor role in the award.

Here, the prime, SRA, did all the hard work. "SRA personnel played a major role in the evaluation of proposals and selection of an awardee. In this connection, the evaluation team consisted of both government representatives and SRA employees, with the two subgroups providing differing types of substantive input into the evaluation/selection process. . . . It is also clear from the record that the SRA team members were full participants in the deliberations that led to recommendation of the Infoterra product. While we recognize that it is apparent from the foregoing that government personnel, as well as SRA personnel, played major roles in the evaluation, government involvement in the evaluation/selection process is not enough to make the procurement "by" the government . . . we consider a procurement to be "by" the government only where the agency controls the procurement process to such an extent that the contractor has no real input into substantive decisions, which was clearly not the case here."[26]

___

Protests of contract administration activities

As the above examples show, typically the government procures goods and services through the solicitation process. But sometimes the government also procures goods and services during a contract administration phase, such as when it modifies a contract to procure more (or fewer) goods and services. So although GAO's protest jurisdiction typically involves the solicitation process, GAO on occasion gets involved in the contract administration process.

When GAO does get involved in the contract administration process, it's typically because of change orders the government wants to issue. When the government realizes it has to change contract work, it can modify the existing contract to give the incumbent contractor the work or it can solicit the changed need from vendors using full and open competition. GAO can handle protests of whether changes to a contract should have been competed under full and open competition rather than awarded sole source to the incumbent contractor.

What GAO is looking for is whether the change is within the scope of the contract and within one of the designated areas of the contract covered by the Changes clause; for example, the method of shipment or packing.

On occasion, GAO gets in involved in parts of the contract administration process **other** than changes. For example, GAO can review the use of a termination for convenience as a protest remedy. Normally, whether an agency properly used a termination for convenience is a matter for the claims process. On rare occasions, however, the government uses the Termination for Convenience clause in the protest process to right some wrong done during the solicitation process. In that event, GAO reviews the agency's use of the termination for convenience remedy.

___

Fisher-Cal Industries, Inc., won an Air Force contract that had to be terminated for convenience due to solicitation problems. The termination for convenience brought a protest in turn from Fisher-Cal, which argued that its prices had been exposed to the general public and to its competitors so it could not fairly compete in any re-solicitation. GAO concluded that the Air Force had used the Termination for Convenience clause properly to correct problems with the solicitation process. GAO did not have much sympathy for Fisher-Cal's exposed price and the unfairness it presented to the re-solicitation process. "The possibility that the contract might not have been awarded based on a true determination of the most advantageous proposal has a more harmful effect on the integrity of the competitive procurement system than the disclosure of the price of an improperly awarded contract."[27]

Government employees and A-76

One of the longest running—but losing—battles government employees have endured is the fight to get government employees more actively involved in challenging agency decisions in the A-76 process that take away the jobs of these employees. Over the years Congress has relaxed some of the rules, but generally it has limited how much input these government employees have in the A-76 process.

For years GAO held that the Competition in Contracting Act (CICA) did not allow "representatives of in-house government competitors to pursue a protest" before GAO. Even after the 2003 changes to A-76, this remained GAO's position. But Congress did expand the definition of an *interested party* that could file a bid protest in A-76 issues to provide that "the term 'interested party' includes the official responsible for submitting the Federal agency tender in a public-private competition conducted under Office of Management and Budget Circular A-76. . . ." But that was as far as Congress let GAO go.

Today, not even the head of the employees' union has standing.

The Department of Labor (DOL) decided that some of the accounting functions its employees currently performed should be competed under A-76. Mr. Lawrence C. Drake headed the union most affected by this decision. Mr. Drake wrote GAO, asking GAO to consider him "an interested party" for protests of the DOL A-76 process because he was president of the affected union. GAO refused. If he represented a majority of the employees, he "would have the right to intervene in a protest filed by an interested party, including the [agency tender official]" quoting from the Congressional history. But since he did not, he had no standing.[28]

The law GAO applies

The law GAO uses in deciding protests usually is precedent from its previous cases and federal law. It looks to state law only as a last resort.

"Where controlling federal law exists, state law may only be considered where the result would not conflict with federal laws or policies, or otherwise interfere with the exercise of federal powers."[29]

Whether federal procurement laws may preempt local and state laws is an issue with difficult Constitutional questions. To what extent can the federal government make states do something or not do something? Although this issue rarely affects procurement, in one interesting example involving utilities at a military base, GAO concluded that the federal government could preempt state law because Congress said it could.

Virginia Electric and Power Company (VEPCO) and Baltimore Gas & Electric Company (BG&E) submitted a bid to the U.S. Army Corps of Engineers for the privatization of utilities at five military installations. Federal law let DOD get some of its utility needs from a state or local utility using competitive procedures. A local utility protested, arguing that state law had given it a monopoly over utilities in the state so any other provider would have to get approval from the state legislature and other local bodies. GAO did not agree, pointing to a line of Supreme Court cases showing "congressional preemption that invalidated state regulations that prohibited what federal procurement statutes required. . . . Here, there is a federal statute that mandates a particular procurement approach."[30]

Relief available at GAO

The relief that GAO can give a protester is, curiously, labeled only a "recommendation" to the agency. Routinely, virtually all GAO recommendations are followed by the agencies. These recommendations include a range of alternatives, such as putting a successful protester back in the competitive range, reevaluating proposals, reconsidering award decisions, and awarding protest costs, including attorneys' fees.

Standing

The test for standing to raise a protest before GAO is similar to the test used by the CFC in that the GAO test uses the same phrases, *interested party* and *prejudice*.

An interested party

GAO defines an *interested party* as "an actual or prospective supplier whose direct economic interest would be affected by the award of a contract or the failure to award a contract."[31]

A more workable definition is that a "protester is not an interested party where it would not be in line for contract award if its protest were sustained."[32]

In a sealed bid, the second-low bid would be an interested party to protest a contract awarded to the low bidder. But if the third-low bidder wanted to be an interested party, it would have to protest the agency's treatment of not only the winner but also the second-low bidder so that the protester (the third-low bidder) could be in line for award and therefore an interested party. So to be an interested party in these price-oriented awards, a protester must challenge not only the winner's award but also the evaluation the agency did on any vendors between the protester and the winner. In other words, an interested party must clear the deck of all vendors, including the winner and everybody in between.[33]

An interested party must also have submitted a technically acceptable offer. Otherwise, it would not be in line for award. For example, a vendor quoting a nonconforming product would not be in line for award so it cannot be an interested party.[34]

But as always, GAO has found exceptions:

> "[W]e have found a firm to be an interested party even though its product sample had been properly rejected as failing to comply with various required salient characteristics of the solicited product, where its protest alleges that the product samples of the awardee did not comply with the salient characteristics and where the awardee was the only other offeror eligible for award. . . . In addition, we will consider a protest where an offeror protests that it was denied equal treatment because the agency rejected its nonconforming offer while accepting a competitor's similarly nonconforming offer. . . . In other words, we view a protester as an interested party where the basis for protest is that the protester and the awardee were treated disparately, even where we agree that the protester's offer was unacceptable."[35]

In a best value trade-off solicitation—one based on price and other (non-price) factors—it is easier to be an interested party. All the protester generally has to argue is that if the agency had properly done its evaluation job, the protester would have been the best value, it would have won the contract, and so it is an interested party.

But this argument does not always work.

> "[S]ince as a result of the agency's evaluation, which we find reasonable, McDonald's technical proposal was ranked seventh, and since in addition to Greenhut's, several other higher-rated, reasonably priced proposals remained eligible for award, McDonald is not an interested party to challenge the agency's tradeoff decision because, even if its protest were sustained, those intervening offerors, not McDonald, would be in line for award."[36]

Prejudice

In the NBA it's called "No harm, no foul." In procurement, it's called "prejudice."

Making a mistake in the solicitation process does not mean the government loses a protest. Before the government can lose, a vendor has to prove an extra fact: that the government mistake probably was fatal to the vendor's chances of winning the contract. Unless a vendor can prove that the government's mistake probably cost the vendor the contract, the vendor cannot win a protest at GAO.

GAO says that

> "[p]rejudice is an essential element of any viable protest and even where the record establishes a procurement deficiency, we will sustain a protest on this basis only where it results in competitive prejudice to the protester."[37]

To prove competitive prejudice,

> "a protester must demonstrate that, but for the agency's actions, it would have a substantial chance of receiving award."[38]

The United States Marine Corps issued a Request for Quotations (RFQ) to upgrade hardware and software. Technical factors were significantly more important than price. During price discussions, the Marines told Sytronics that its high price was "high," but told Nexjen that its low price was "excessive." When the Marines awarded the contract to NexJen with its lower-priced, lower-rated quote, Sytronics protested, arguing that the government's discussions helped Nexjen get a lower price. GAO agreed, finding that the agency improperly favored Nexjen when it advised Sytronics that its high price "appeared high," while it advised Nexjen that its low price "appeared excessive." GAO said that "a vendor would reasonably view the term 'excessive' as sending a stronger message than the term 'high.'" GAO also found that these price discussions prejudiced Sytronics: "The conduct of the price discussions may have led to a greater price advantage for Nexjen. Accordingly, we find that Sytronics has been competitively prejudiced by the agency's conduct of this procurement because, but for the flaws in the conduct of the procurement, Sytronics would have had a substantial chance for award."[39]

Sovereign immunity

Sovereign immunity is not an issue for protests before GAO. The government has consented to be sued on protests before GAO. The Competition in Contracting Act gave GAO protest authority.

Claims

The Court of Federal Claims (CFC)

Branch of government

As mentioned above, the court is in the judicial branch of government. (The following text is stated earlier in the chapter, but is repeated here for those readers who are skipping through the book.)

Some laws Congress passes are so complex that Congress has set up special courts to handle them. For example, the United States Bankruptcy Courts handle our country's complex bankruptcy laws, and the United States Tax Court deals with the equally complex Internal Revenue Code.

We won't debate where the FAR falls in terms of complexity when compared to bankruptcy laws and tax laws. But by any standard, procurement is legally complex. Congress recognized this when it set up the Court of Federal Claims to deal with procurement litigation, both protests and claims.

Up until 1982 the Court of Claims had a trial part and an appellate part. In 1982 the trial part became the United States Claims Court and the appellate part was incorporated into the CAFC. In 1992 the Claims Court was renamed the Court of Federal Claims.[40]

Federal courts are typically classified as Article I or Article III courts, after the particular section of the U.S. Constitution that set the court up. Article III courts have judges with lifetime appointments. Article I courts are set up by Congress, and their judges do not have lifetime appointments. The CFC is an Article I court. Its judges are appointed by the President, with the consent of the Senate, for 15-year terms.

Jurisdiction in claims

General rule

The jurisdiction/sovereign immunity of this court is based on the Tucker Act, which gives the court jurisdiction over "any claim against the United States founded upon any express or implied contract with the United States."[41] So generally, the court has jurisdiction over claims involving a government contract.

But the fact that the Tucker Act gave the court jurisdiction does not mean that **all** government contracts can be litigated there. In a distinction that perhaps only lawyers can see, the jurisdiction of the court is separate from a litigant's right to sue in that court. As the CAFC said in a recent decision,

> "The Tucker Act itself does not create a substantive cause of action; in order to come within the jurisdictional reach and the waiver of [sovereign immunity in] the Tucker Act, a plaintiff must identify a separate source of substantive law that creates the right to money damages."[42]

Since the Contract Disputes Act (CDA) gives the parties to a procurement contract the right to appeal a contracting officer's final decision to the CFC or a BCA, the CDA gives this "separate source of substantive law."

Recurring jurisdictional issues

The CFC has several continuing jurisdictional issues: its jurisdiction over claims under contracts with non-appropriated fund instrumentalities (NAFIs) like the U.S. Mint or the Post Exchanges (PX) operated by the military and its jurisdiction over implied-in-law contracts.

NAFIs: A non-appropriated fund instrumentality (NAFI) is, as its name suggests, a government entity that uses money that did not come from Congress.

What difference does that make? Well, years ago the Court of Claims held that its jurisdiction was limited

> "to claims against government instrumentalities whose judgments could be paid from appropriated funds. The Court of Claims reasoned that when the government assumed no liability for a federal entity, the government could not be said to have consented to suit against that entity."[43]

Congress has resolved the "can anybody sue a NAFI" question by identifying in the CDA some NAFIs that could be sued. So now the CFC can hear claims against some NAFIs, such as military Post Exchanges.

But that's it.

Congress did not, however, alter the general rule excluding NAFIs from Tucker Act jurisdiction, nor did Congress waive the protective basis of sovereign immunity to allow suit other than against the few enumerated exceptions.[44]

One NAFI Congress did not make subject to the Tucker Act is the U.S. Mint. So a contractor trying to get the CFC to hear a claim against the Mint will lose.

A contractor filed a claim against the Mint in the CFC. Both the CFC and the CAFC concluded that the government had not waived sovereign immunity and thus had not consented to the Mint's being sued. The Mint operates without one penny from Congress. The only money the Mint uses is money it gets from selling items like commemorative coins to consumers in general, as well as selling coins to the Federal Reserve System. When Congress expressly waived the government's sovereign immunity for some NAFIs, like Post Exchanges, Congress did not waive sovereign immunity for the Mint. So the four-part test the Supreme Court set for NAFIs applied to the Mint. A NAFI that meets all four parts cannot be sued in the CFC. The test is (1) it does not receive its money by congressional appropriation; (2) it gets its money primarily from its own activities, services and product sales; (3) it could not get appropriated funds to operate without Congress passing a law giving it money; and (4) Congress clearly wanted to keep the agency separated from general Federal revenues. The Mint met all four, so Congress had not consented to having the Mint sued.[45]

The CFC and GAO deal with some NAFIs differently. Revolving funds are an example. According to the CAFC, GAO sees a revolving fund (i.e., a single account to which an agency deposits its receipts and from which that agency draws its expenditures) as "permanent or continuing appropriations" and so they do not qualify as NAFIs. . . . The GAO's determinations do not control the [CAFC's] analysis of Tucker Act jurisdiction. For example, the GAO's determination that the Fed was not a NAFI led the government to assert that the Dual Compensation Act . . . applied to Fed employees. We ruled to the contrary; Fed employees do not fall under the Dual Compensation Act because the Fed is a NAFI. The GAO's definition is clearly inconsistent with our precedent. Were we to apply the GAO's definition to either the Fed or the Finance Board, neither one could be ruled a NAFI—directly contradicting our holdings. . . . The GAO's approach remains misplaced in an assessment of Tucker Act jurisdiction. Revolving funds are not necessarily "continuing appropriations," and they will not disqualify an agency from being classified as a NAFI."[46]

So generally, the CFC cannot hear claims involving the Federal Reserve System, the Federal Housing Finance Board, Federal Prison Industries, or the United States Mint "because the United States has not assumed the financial obligations of such entities by appropriating funds to them."[47]

It's interesting to note that a BCA does not have the same problem. It could hear a NAFI case. A board can hear a claim by a non-appropriated fund instrumentality barred from the court.[48]

Implied contracts: The CFC has jurisdiction over contracts "express or implied," according to the Tucker Act. But *implied* does not mean "all implied contracts." An implied contract can be either an implied-in-fact contract or an implied-in-law contract. The CFC has jurisdiction over only an implied-in-fact contract, not an implied-in-law contract.

> "Under the Tucker Act this court's contract-based jurisdiction extends only to contracts either express or implied in fact, and not to claims on contracts implied in law."[49]

An implied-in-fact contract is one that has all the elements of a contract without the paperwork. We discussed implied-in-fact contracts in Chapter 6.

But an implied-in-law contract is not a contract at all. It is what we call a "legal fiction." It's a fiction because a judge makes up an implied-in-law contract so that the end result is a fair one. Because a judge does not have a warrant, he cannot enter into express contracts or implied-in-fact contracts for the federal government. But judges can certainly construe what has taken place to be something that sort of looks like a contract. These situations typically involve cases where the government has received a benefit from a contractor but there is no "legal" way to pay the contractor.

But again, the CFC has no jurisdiction over implied-in-law contracts.

> **Law applied:** The court applies federal law as it has been interpreted by the U.S. Supreme Court and the CAFC. The court may look to precedents set by BCAs, but those decisions are not binding on the court.[50] In addition, one judge on the court is not bound by the decisions of any other judge on that court. The judges certainly consider the conclusions reached by their colleagues on the court, but they are not bound by those decisions.

CFC relief in claims

The first place to look for the kind of relief a contractor can get in the claims process is the contract and its clauses. Many clauses describe what remedy a contractor can get if the government doesn't comply with the clause. For example, many clauses call for an equitable adjustment, which means more money to a contractor. So, contractors filing claims with the CFC can obviously get money as one form of relief. This is one reason it's called the U.S. Court of Federal Claims.

But sometimes money is no help at all. When the government and a contractor are arguing over whether the contract's requirement that the contractor "stock the restroom" means to provide one-ply or two-ply paper hand towels, money isn't the issue. The issue is, what does the contract require? So sometimes the usual type of help a court gives, monetary damages, is inadequate, making nonmonetary relief a requirement.

Outside the government contracting world, a court can typically give three different kinds of nonmonetary help: injunctions, declaratory judgments, and specific performance of a contract. An injunction stops things. A declaratory judgment declares the rights of the parties. And specific performance of the contract requires a reluctant contracting party to perform the contract the parties had previously contracted for.

Life would have been easy if Congress had allowed the government contracting world to have those three nonmonetary remedies as well. But that's not the case. Congress has given the CFC this nonmonetary relief jurisdiction:

> "The Court of Federal Claims shall have jurisdiction to render judgment upon any claim by or against, or dispute with, a contractor arising under section 10(a)(1) of the [CDA], including a dispute concerning termination of a contract, rights in tangible or intangible property, compliance with cost accounting standards, and other nonmonetary disputes on which a decision of the contracting officer has been issued under [section 605 of the CDA]."[51]

So, under the CDA, only one of these three nonmonetary remedies is available. The CDA lets government contractors force the contracting officer to interpret contract terms, in a sense making declaratory judgments available.

But the CDA does not allow the government and a contractor to get injunctions against each other, although the government can stop a contract by terminating it. Nor does it let the parties demand specific performance of the contract, although the government can issue a cure notice demanding that the contract be performed, with the threat of a default hanging over the contractor's head if it is not.

Declaratory judgments

The CFC has jurisdiction over contract interpretation issues:

> "The Tucker Act grants the Court of Federal Claims jurisdiction to grant nonmonetary relief in connection with contractor claims, including claims requesting an interpretation of contract terms."[52]

But when judges get involved in interpreting a contract, they start to get involved in administering a contract. And judges don't want to administer contracts. As part of the judicial branch of government, they want to decide cases and leave contract administration to contracting officers. Since the CDA gives a contractor the right to file a claim—while the contract is still going—over issues involving the interpretation of contract terms, however, judges can't avoid getting involved in the contract administration process.

But how deep into contract admin issues should judges go? One answer, the easy answer, is not at all. If the contractor wants to challenge what the contracting officer wants him to do, the contractor should just do whatever the contracting officer demands and ask for an equitable adjustment to get paid for the contested work when the contract is over.

But in some cases this easy answer doesn't make sense. For example, if a janitorial contract requires the contractor to "stock the restroom" but does not describe the quality (one-ply or two-ply) of hand towels, a judge would decide whether the ambiguous phrase "stock the restroom" means one-ply or two-ply paper. In a janitorial contract, that's a fundamental question to the contract.

The easy answer also doesn't make sense when a case has a special need for early resolution of a legal issue, such as when the government exercises an option that the contractor says is an illegal exercise of the option. Here the issue is not "what does the contractor have to do under the contract" but rather "does the contractor even have to perform the option." That kind of issue should be resolved early and not after the contract is over.

So the CAFC has resolved the issue of its role in the admin process by giving judges the discretion to decide some admin issues but not others.

Here's the test: The CFC should consider

> "the appropriateness of declaratory relief, including whether the claim involve[d] a live dispute between the parties, whether a declaration will resolve that dispute, and whether the legal remedies available to the parties would be adequate to protect the parties' interests."[53]

The appeals court gave a good example of routine matters of contract performance that judges should stay out of:

> "While a contractor may want to know ahead of time how a contract issue will be resolved—such as whether the contractor will be entitled to additional compensation under the changes clause for a particular item of work directed by the contracting officer—such cases do not ordinarily put into question whether the contractor is obligated to perform at all. . . . It would normally be appropriate in such cases for the court . . . to decline to issue a declaratory judgment and to await a later equitable adjustment claim by the contractor."[54]

But they can hear contract admin issues that involve a fundamental question of contract interpretation or contract performance.

This debate over a judge's role in contract administration usually comes up in the context, legally, of whether a judge can issue a "declaratory judgment" resolving the rights of the parties.

CW Government Travel Inc. (Carlson) had an Army contract that made Carlson the "exclusive" provider of certain kinds of travel services for the Army. So when the Army issued a solicitation that seemed to involve the same kinds of services, Carlson asked the contracting officer to confirm that its work under the existing contract would be transferred to the new contract. The contractor did not ask for money damages. After Carlson did not get the answer it wanted from the contracting officer, it went to the CFC. The CFC did not think it was getting involved in day-to-day routine contract administration. The case met at least the first element of the three-part "court-intervention" test: a "live dispute" over whether the government would repudiate its contract. The court refused to dismiss the cae.[55]

Quantum meruit—unjust enrichment

Quantum meruit is Latin for "how much money should be paid, regardless of the laws of contracts." When the CFC sees unjust enrichment, it can make sure justice is done by finding an implied-in-fact contract.

An implied-in-fact contract could be used when the express contract is unenforceable. For example, if an initially valid contract is improperly assigned and becomes invalid, the CFC can find the existence of an implied-in-fact contract to make sure the contractor gets paid.

"Assuming arguendo that the [contract was illegally transferred], the voiding of th[e] contract did not automatically nullify the further dealings between plaintiff and defendant. . . . In this case, plaintiff and defendant, with the approval of the CO, fully carried out the contractual obligations embodied in the contract . . . . In similar circumstances, courts have found that an implied-in-fact contract for a quantum meruit arose."[56]

CFC standing in claims

Standing in claims is easier. Some clear examples: A contractor has standing to bring a claim. On the other hand, a subcontractor cannot bring a claim unless the claim is sponsored by the prime.

Sovereign immunity

Generally, the government has waived sovereign immunity in claims as a result of the CDA. The real issues over sovereign immunity in claims are those addressed above in the jurisdictional section, such as non-appropriated fund instrumentalities.

> ### Constitutional "taking" issues
>
> The CFC can hear a contract case that a BCA cannot hear. A board cannot hear an issue involving the taking of a person's land, but the CFC can.
>
> When the government leases out its land, the lease involves both contract rights and property rights. So breaching the lease could be considered not only a breach of contract rights but also a breach of property rights. Although BCAs can hear cases involving breach of contract, they cannot hear a "breach of property rights" argument like that made by a tenant on government land claiming that the government has so restricted the tenant's use of the land that the government has taken the tenant's property rights under the Fifth Amendment to the U.S. Constitution.
>
> The Army leased out some of the land it owns at Fort Leavenworth, Kansas, to Bruce Zoeller. After the Army ended the lease, which it had the right to do, Mr. Zoeller claimed that the Army had destroyed "native perennial" plants that remained on the land he was leasing and that the government "taking" of them should be compensated under the Fifth Amendment. The court denied this taking claim. "A breach of contract scenario does not necessarily foster a taking's claim. . . . Taking claims rarely arise under government contracts because the government acts in its commercial or proprietary capacity in entering contracts, rather than in its sovereign capacity. Accordingly, remedies arise from the contracts themselves, rather than from the constitutional protection of private property rights."[57]

Boards of Contract Appeals

Branch of government

The BCAs are part of the executive branch.

Jurisdiction

The CDA gave the boards jurisdiction over "any express or implied contract for (i) the procurement of property, other than real property in being; (ii) the procurement of services; (iii) the procurement of construction, alteration, repair or maintenance of real property; or, (iv) the disposal of personal property."[58]

So the boards typically have jurisdiction over claims filed by contractors under the CDA.

In addition, boards have jurisdiction under their own charters. And in rare cases, this lets a board hear a case that the CFC could not hear under the CDA and, in fact, that the board could not hear under the CDA.

Federal Prison Industries operates under the trade name UNICOR. It operates solely on money received from the sale of the products it makes; it does not use any appropriated funds. Logan Machinists Inc. had a contract with UNICOR to provide drawer slides to be used in UNICOR furniture. After the contract was terminated for default, Logan used the disputes clause of the contract to appeal the termination for default to the BCA. Despite this clear contract language, the government asked the Board to throw the appeal out. It argued that, despite what the contract promised, the CDA did not allow Logan's claim to be heard by the Board because UNICOR was a non-appropriated fund instrumentality for which the government had not waived its sovereign immunity from lawsuit. Concluding that the Board's jurisdiction was broader than that of the Court in this instance, the Board refused to throw the case out. Although neither the Board nor the CFC could handle the case under the CDA, the Board could handle the case under the jurisdiction given it by its charter. [59]

Disputes beyond a BCA's jurisdiction

Certain types of implied and express contracts: A BCA does not have jurisdiction over all contract controversies. Some contract-related disputes are beyond its reach.

Several kinds of implied contracts are not within the board's jurisdiction: implied contracts to treat a bidder honestly and fairly and implied contracts to keep a second-tier subcontractor's drawings confidential—neither are contracts for the procurement of goods or services. Also, breaches of an unsolicited proposal and a confidentiality agreement promising to not disclose trade secrets submitted in that proposal **could** be within the BCA's jurisdiction if the unsolicited proposal or confidentiality agreements are later incorporated into a contract subject to the CDA.[60]

Wesleyan Company, Inc., asked the government to evaluate several unsolicited proposals containing proprietary information. The documents had standard language limiting the government's use of the proprietary information. Wesleyan also signed a memorandum of understanding (MOU) that said the government "has accepted the above proposal for the purpose of evaluating it and advising of any possible Army interest." The Army was interested and bought a number of Wesleyan's products. Wesleyan later believed the government had broken its (alleged) promise to protect government use of proprietary data and filed a claim for breach of contract that a BCA refused to hear. On appeal, the CAFC held that the BCA had some jurisdiction—jurisdiction limited to what the CDA authorized. Since neither the unsolicited proposal nor the MOU was a contract for "the procurement of goods and services," the BCA had no jurisdiction over an alleged breach of them. But to the extent that either of these documents had been incorporated into any of the Army's purchase orders—clearly "procurements" under the CDA— the BCA had jurisdiction over any alleged breach of these incorporated agreements. The appeals court sent the case back to the board to resolve how much, if any, of the promises in the unsolicited proposal and MOU had been incorporated into the purchased orders.[61]

Torts: BCAs are designed to handle contract issues. It is possible, however, that issues involving torts, such as intentional or negligent wrongdoing, can result from contract performance. The line has been drawn: BCAs cannot deal with torts that are independent of the contract for which no violation of a contract duty can be shown.

Torts independent of a contract duty

The FDA installed a security camera in space it leased from a building owner. When the government left, it left the camera behind but came back several months later and removed it. The building owner filed a claim against the government for the tort of conversion, for removing the security camera he thought was now his because the government had left it behind. The board dismissed the claim because it was independent of the lease contract. "We do not have jurisdiction to consider claims that sound in tort, unless there is a direct connection between the Government's alleged tortious conduct and the Government's express or implied contractual obligations. . . . Mr. McCloskey has not pointed us to anything expressed in or implied by the contract that makes GSA responsible for the actions of someone, whether the FDA or its contractor or a professional criminal, who entered the building illegally after the lease expired and removed property that belonged to Mr. McCloskey. We conclude, therefore, that the conversion alleged by Mr. McCloskey is not directly associated with any contractual term. Because GSA's liability for the alleged tortious conversion of Mr. McCloskey's property does not depend upon any contractual promise that GSA made to Mr. McCloskey, we lack jurisdiction to consider the claim for the cost of replacing the security system.[62]

But torts that are tied to a contract can come before the BCAs.

The Army Air Force Exchange Service (AAFES) had a contract with Home Entertainment, Inc., at Fort Clayton. Pipes in the ceiling broke and allegedly caused flooding and damage to the space and to Home Entertainment's property. It filed a claim for damages with the AAFES and then later the ASBCA, arguing that AAFES had breached its contractual duty to repair and maintain AAFES-furnished premises. The board concluded that it had jurisdiction of this tortious breach of contract. A BCA **could** hear a case involving a contractor's "loss derived from negligent performance of a contractual duty to use ordinary care in removing machinery from contractor's premises" which was "in no sense a tort independent of the contract." A BCA **could not** hear a case involving an express or implied Government duty "to protect private vehicle of contractor's employee from a Government helicopter not involved in the contract."[63]

Law applied

Each board applies federal law in the form of other precedents of that board and the law established by its boss, the Court of Appeals for the Federal Circuit. The boards are not bound by the precedents of other boards. Nor are they bound by the precedents of the U.S. Court of Federal Claims. But boards do look to other boards and to the CFC for guidance.

Relief

Although money may be the root of all evil, it's not always the goal of all lawsuits. On occasion, plaintiffs ask judges for something other than money.

Outside the government contracting world, a court can give a plaintiff three different kinds of nonmonetary help: an injunction, a declaratory judgment, and specific performance of a contract.

An *injunction* stops things.

Declaratory judgments declare the rights of the parties, such as whose interpretation of a contract is correct.

And *specific performance of the contract* requires a reluctant contracting party to perform the contract the parties had previously contracted for. For example, if they are home sellers with a contract that the home buyer no longer wants to go through with, the home sellers could ask the court to order the buyer to specifically perform the sales contract that both the buyer and seller have signed.

So plaintiffs in general have four remedies: money and the three nonmonetary forms of relief— injunctions, declaratory judgments, and specific performance of a contract.

That's the situation outside the world of government contracts. Life would have been easy if Congress had allowed the government contracting world to have monetary relief as well as those three nonmonetary remedies. But that's not the case.

Of these four remedies, which remedies has Congress given government contractors? In the CDA, Congress gave government contractors only two remedies: the right to get money and the right to get declaratory judgments. The CDA does not allow the government and a contractor to get injunctions against each other, although the government can stop a contract by terminating it. Nor does it let the parties demand specific performance of the contract, although the government can issue a cure notice demanding that the contract be performed, with the threat of a default hanging over the contractor's head if it is not.

BCA standing

Standing is generally not an issue in claims before the boards. As long as the claim is in the name of the contractor, and the contractor is still a going company, the company has standing to bring the claim.

One recurring standing problem is a claim involving subcontractors.

Subcontractors are the orphans of government contracting. Legally, a subcontractor has no contract with the government. And because a sub has no contract, it has no privity of contract with the government. And because it has no privity of contract, it has no standing. So **generally** a sub cannot sue the government to get paid.

This legal rule can be unfair. A subcontractor who sells something to the government through a prime contractor can be left out in the cold if the prime contractor does not pay the subcontractor. If a prime contractor, for example, is paid by the government but then goes bankrupt before paying the subcontractor, the subcontractor does not get paid. The subcontractor ends up giving but getting nothing in return.

But as always, there are exceptions. In the past, judges have developed a number of exceptions that let a subcontractor sue the government and get paid. One is pretty common and the others are rare.

Prime sponsoring a sub's claim

The most common way is sponsorship. A subcontractor's no standing problem can be fixed by having the prime sponsor the subcontractor's claim. Because in that situation the contractor technically, but not practically, is filing the claim, the standing requirement has been satisfied.

Sub as government purchasing agent

One rare way a sub can get standing is for the sub to prove it is the *government's purchasing agent*. To win on this theory, a subcontractor has to prove three things: "(1) the prime contractor was acting as a purchasing agent for the government; (2) the agency relationship between the government and the prime was established by clear contractual consent; and (3) the contract stated that the government would be directly liable to the vendors for the purchase price."[64]

Direct appeal

Another rare example of a subcontractor's being able to sue is a direct appeal, where both the prime contract and the subcontract allow a subcontractor to file a claim directly with the government. One way this rarity happens is when the prime assigns the subcontract to the government, letting the prime off the hook and putting the sub on the hook.

For 25 years the Department of Energy (DOE) had a contract with RMI Titanium Company (RMI) to produce uranium. When Westinghouse Environmental Management Company (WEMCO) took over as contractor at RMI's Ashtabula site, DOE had RMI and WEMCO enter into a subcontract that left RMI in the same role as before. But this subcontract was assigned back to DOE. "The assignment expressly relieved WEMCO of all responsibility under the subcontract and, pursuant to the assignment provisions of the subcontract, once the subcontract was assigned, RMI was to 'look solely to the DOE' for performance of WMCO's obligations." The RMI/WEMCO subcontract contained a "Disputes" clause which provided that "all disputes *arising under or related to* this contract" were to be resolved by submitting them to the designated DOE contracting officer, whose decision would be "final and conclusive and not subject to review by any forum, tribunal or Government agency" except for "an appeal to the DOE Board of Contract Appeals (EBCA)." The court concluded that RMI, although a sub, could sue DOE. [65]

Third-party beneficiary

A third rare example of a subcontractor's being able to sue the government is as a third-party beneficiary. If a contract between two parties is really for the benefit of someone else, a third-party beneficiary, the third-party should be allowed to sue under the contract. The classic example is where the government agreed to write one check payable to a broke prime and a skittish solvent subcontractor. The government agreed to make a check payable to both the prime and the sub but did not follow the agreement, paying only the government instead. The CAFC concluded that the sub could sue the government.[66]

One subcontractor tried to use all three of these rare arguments and, as expected, lost on all of them.

Network Resource Services (NRS) had a contract to provide the Army with computer equipment. NRS made a subcontract with Alpine Computers for that equipment. Alpine gave the government the equipment. But although the government paid NRS, NRS did not pay Alpine. So Alpine tried to sue the government. It lost all around.

NRS was not a government purchasing agent. The prime contract did not make NRS the government's "purchasing agent," nor did it make NRS an agent of the government. And in fact, NRS, and not the government, actually ordered the equipment. Finally, the prime contract did not say the government would pay any subcontractors.

Alpine's claim is not a direct appeal in the prime's name. The Army and Alpine did not enter into a direct contractual relationship, and NRS's prime contract did not clearly authorize a direct appeal by any subcontractor.

Alpine was not a third-party beneficiary of the NRS-Army contract because "there is no prime contract provision or modification providing for government payment to the prime and a subcontractor jointly."[67]

Sovereign immunity

Sovereign immunity issues that the BCAs face were discussed above in "Jurisdiction." Because the CDA gave a contractor the right to sue the government, the CDA is a waiver of sovereign immunity.

CFC–DISTRICT COURT OVERLAP: DOES THE ISSUE INVOLVE A FEDERAL CONTRACT OR A FEDERAL REGULATION?

Like schoolchildren, lawyers have to find the right cubby to put things in. In giving the various federal courts their jurisdiction, Congress has defined all the cubbies lawyers have to deal with. For example, as we saw above, Congress passed the CDA, which gives the CFC jurisdiction over contract claims. So contract claims against federal agencies go into the CFC cubby. On the other hand, Congress gave local federal district courts jurisdiction over general agency actions like an agency's not issuing an environmental impact statement. It also gave these local Federal courts jurisdiction over taxpayer arguments that an agency acted arbitrarily and capriciously. The end result is, theoretically, that everything is nicely and neatly divided into one cubby or another. Either one court has jurisdiction or the other one does.

But, on occasion, separating a CFC contract issue from a local federal court non-contract issue is difficult. A claim can involve how a federal regulation gets interpreted. Is the claim a contract issue for the CFC or a federal law or regulation issue for a federal district court?

Contractor Not Challenging Federal Regulation

The Office of Personnel Management (OPM) had a contract with Texas Health Choice, L.C. The contract, which was expressly governed by the CDA, required the parties to annually negotiate expected compensation rates and benefits that would be adjusted to actual rates at the end of the contract. After OPM withheld over $600,000 from Texas Health at the end of the contract to reconcile accounts pursuant to a federal regulation, Texas Health went to its local federal district court arguing that the regulation the reconciliation was based on was arbitrary. The CAFC concluded that the CFC and not the local federal district court had jurisdiction over the issue.

> "Texas Health's claim is related to the contract. . . . That Texas Health's complaint, literally read, sought only to invalidate the Final Year Regulation, as opposed to recover the $622,246 reconciliation amount, is of no consequence to the question of jurisdiction because the complaint relates to a dispute implicating a contract with the Government. Indeed, Texas Health's complaint expressly mentions its contract with the Government and the deemed denial of its claim before the contracting officer."[68]

The case was a claim that belonged before the CFC and not the local federal court.

Contractor Challenging Federal Regulation

A Housing and Urban Development (HUD) regulation described how a developer was to be paid for providing low-income housing. The language in the regulation was also included in a contract between a developer and HUD. When the developer did not agree with how much HUD was paying him, he sued HUD in federal district court, asking for a declaratory judgment as to how the regulation should be interpreted. HUD argued that the developer really wanted money damages so the case should be heard by the CFC. The CAFC concluded that a federal district court, and not the CFC, was the right court. The contractor wanted money "to which it alleges it is entitled pursuant to federal statute and regulations; it does not seek money as compensation for a loss suffered. It wants to compel HUD to perform the calculation of contract rents in accordance with 24 C.F.R. § 882.408 and other applicable regulations."[69]

The case was not a claim for the CFC but a regulation interpretation issue for the local federal court.

Endnotes

1. *Ginsberg v. Austin*, 968 F.2d 1198, 1200 (Fed.Cir.1992).

2. *First Hartford Corp. v. United States*, 194 F.3d 1279, 1294 (Fed.Cir.1999).

3. J. Grossbaum. Procedural Fairness in Public Contracts: The Procurement Regulations, 57 Va.L.Rev. 171, 227-28 (1971) *quoted in Peoples Gas, Light, and Coke Co. v. U.S. Postal Service*, 658 F.2d 1182, 1188 (7th Cir. 1981).

4. *Wilner v. U.S.*, 24 F.3d 1397, 1407 (Fed.Cir.1994).

5. The History of the U. S. Court of Federal Claims, available at http://www.uscfc.uscourts. gov/USCFChistory.htm.

6. 28 U.S.C. § 1491(b).

7. *Id.*

8. *LABAT-Anderson Inc., v. The United States*, 65 Fed.Cl. 570 (2005).

9. *Information Technology & Applications Corp. v. The United States,* 316 F.3d 1312, 1319 (Fed. Cir.2003).

10. *Id.*

11. *Id.*

12. *Systems Plus, Inc. v. The United States,* 69 Fed.Cl. 757, 769 (2006).

13. *American Federation of Government Employees, AFL-CIO v. The United States*, 258 F.3d 1294, 1302 (Fed.Cir.2001).

14. *Rex Service Corporation v. The United States, and Associated Aircraft Manufacturing & Sales Inc.*, 448 F.3d 1305 (2006).

15. *Anderson Columbia Envtl., Inc. v. The United States*, 42 Fed.Cl. 880 (1999).

16. *Anderson Columbia Envtl., Inc. v. The United States*, 42 Fed.Cl. 880 (1999).

17. *Banknote Corp. of America, Inc. v. The United States*, 365 F.3d 1345, ftnt. 3, 1352 (Fed. Cir.2004).

18. *Fire-Trol Holdings, LLC v. The United States,* 62 Fed.Cl. 440, 444 (.Cl.,2004).

19. 31 U.S.C. § 3551(1).

20. *Starfleet Marine Transportation Inc.*, B-290,181, July 5, 2002, 2002 CPD ¶ 113.

21. *Ocuto Blacktop and Paving Co. Inc.*, B-284165, March 1, 2000, 2000 CPD ¶ 32.

22. *United Information Systems Inc.*, B-282,895; B-282,896, June 22, 1999, 99-1 CPD ¶ 115.

23. *United States v. Johnson Controls, Inc.*, 713 F. 2d 1541, 1551-52 (Fed. Cir.1983).

24. *STR, L.L.C.*, B-297,421, Dec. 22, 2005, 2006 CPD ¶ 11.

25. *STR L.L.C.*, B-297,421, Dec. 22, 2005, 2006 CPD P 11.

26. *Id.*

27. *Fisher-Cal Industries, Inc.*, B-285150.2, July 6, 2000, 2000 CPD ¶ 115.

28. *Lawrence C. Drake*, B-298143, April 7, 2006, 2006 CPD ¶ 60.

29. See *Blue Cross and Blue Shield of Va.*, B-222485, July 11, 1986, 86-2 CPD ¶ 61.

30. *Virginia Electric and Power Company; Baltimore Gas & Electric Company*, B-285209; B-285209.2, August 2, 2000, 2000 CPD ¶ 134.

31. Bid Protest Regulations, 4 CFR 21.0(a).

32. *Four Winds Servs., Inc.*, B-280714, Aug. 28, 1998, 98-2 CPD ¶ 57.

33. *Gold Cross Safety Corporation*, B-296,099, Jun. 13, 2005, 2005 CPD ¶ 118.

34. *American Government Marketing, Inc.*, B-294,895, Nov. 22, 2004, 2005 CPD ¶ 109.

35. *Armed Forces Merchandise Outlet, Inc.*, B-294,281, Oct. 12, 2004, 2004 CPD ¶ 218.

36. *McDonald Construction Services, Inc.*, B-285980, Oct. 25, 2000, 2000 CPD ¶ 183.

37. *Crane & Co.*, B-297,398, Jan. 18, 2006, 2006 CPD ¶ 22.

38. *Language Services Associates, Inc.*, B-297,392, Jan. 17, 2006, 2006 CPD ¶20.

39. *Sytronics, Inc.*, B-297,346, Dec. 29, 2005, 2006 CPD ¶ 15.

40. *Wilner v. The United States*, 24 F.3d 1397, 1407 (Fed.Cir.1994).

41. 28 U.S.C. § 1491(a)(1).

42. *Frank E. Fisher v. The United States*, 402 F.3d 1167 (Fed.Cir.2004).

43. *AINS, Inc. v. The United States*, 365 F.3d 1333, 1339 (Fed.Cir. 2004).

44. *Id.*

45. *AINS v. The United States*, 365 F.3d 1333 (Fed.Cir.2004).

46. *AINS, Inc. v. The United States*, 365 F.3d 1333, 1340 (Fed.Cir.2004).

47. *Federal Group, Inc. v. The United States*, 67 Fed.Cl. 87 (2005).

48. *Logan Machinists, Inc.,* DOTCAB No. 4184, Mar. 1, 2005.

49. *Trauma Service Group v. The United States*, 104 F.3d 1321, 1324 (Fed.Cir.1997) (quoting *Hercules, Inc. v. United States*, 516 U.S. 417, 423, 116 S.Ct. 981, 134 L.Ed.2d 47 (1996)).

50 *DynCorp Information Systems, LLC v. The United States.* , 58 Fed.Cl. 446 (2003).

51. 28 U.S.C. § 1491(a)(2).

52. *Alliant Techsystems, Inc. v. The United States*, 178 F.3d 1260, 1270 (Fed.Cir.1999).

53. *Alliant,* 178 F.3d at 1271.

54. *Id.*

55. *CW Government Travel Inc. v. The United States,* 63 Fed.Cl. 369 (2004).

56. *United Intern. Investigative Services v. The United States*, 26 Cl.Ct. 892, 899 (1992).

57. *Bruce Zoeller v. The United States*, 65 Fed.Cl. 449 (2005).

58. 41 U.S.C.A. § 602.

59. *Logan Machinists Inc.,* DOTCAB No. 4184, March 1, 2005.

60. *Wesleyan Co.*, 454 F.3d 1375 (Fed.Cir.2006).

61. *Id.*

62. *Thomas D. McCloskey v. GSA*, GSBCA No. 15901, August 14, 2002, 02-2 BCA ¶ 32006.

63. *Home Entertainment, Inc.,* ASBCA No. 50791, 99-2, BCA ¶ 30,550.

64. *United States v Johnson Controls,* 713 F.2d 1541, 1551 (Fed.Cir. 1983).

65. *RMI Titanium Co. v. Westinghouse Elec. Corp.,* 78 F.3d 1125 (6th Cir.1996).

66 *D&H Distributing,* 102 F.3d 542, 546-47 (Fed.Cir.1996).

67. *Alpine Computers, Inc.,* ASBCA No. 54659, 05-2 BCA ¶ 32,997.

68. *Texas Health Choice, L.C. v. Office of Personnel Management,* 400 F.3d 895, 900 (Fed. Cir.2005).

69. *Katz v. Cisneros,* 16 F.3d 1204, 1208 -1209 (Fed.Cir.1994).

Chapter 10
Protests

CONTENTS

*P*rotest is a word that strikes terror into the hearts of any 1102. A protest is a fight over something the government did—or did not do—in the solicitation process.

In everyday language, people tend to mix up protests and claims. But in procurement they are distinctly different. A protest is made by a loser (an unsuccessful offeror) trying to get the contract. A claim, on the other hand, is made by someone who already has a contract trying to get something under the contract from the contracting officer. (The government can file claims against the contractor, of course, but that is rare.)

This chapter will deal solely with protests. Claims are addressed in the next chapter.

Of the three forums for protest, this chapter will deal with only two of them—the Government Accountability Office (GAO) and the Court of Federal Claims (CFC).

A third alternative is a protest to the agency. This alternative is usually used by disappointed vendors who want to get something off their chests. An agency-level protest has a number of disadvantages: there is no discovery available, costs like attorneys fees are not available, and filing one could jeopardize remedies available before GAO and the CFC.

But the biggest drawback with an agency-level protest is a structural/institutional one: Because an agency-level protest may be a protest to the same person who just recently awarded a contract to someone else, the chances are slim that this same decision-maker will suddenly reverse courses, change his mind, and sustain the protest.

In many ways, therefore, an agency-level protest is, unfortunately, a waste of time. And because there are no reported decisions on agency-level protest, this chapter will not deal with them. Instead, we will focus on protests before GAO and the CFC. This chapter deals with the *what, when,* and *how* of the protests before GAO and the CFC. The *who, where,* and *why* (relief) of protests were dealt with in Chapter 9. This chapter also covers a related protest issue: whether the protested contract can be started or whether its start must await resolution of the protest.

The protest process really has two distinct battles: the fight over the protest itself and the fight over the "automatic stay" that automatically prevents the government and the winning contractor from working on the protested and stayed contract until the protest of the losing vendor has been resolved. So the chapter ends with a discussion of the automatic stay available to a protester and how the government can override it.

THE PROTEST

What Can Be Protested?

Any part of the solicitation process can be protested, including

1. The solicitation package itself (Request for Quotations, Request for Proposals, Invitation for Bid); anything included in the solicitation package, such as basic questions like whether the government should use an IFB or an RFP; the evaluation factors to be used in the best value procurement
2. The way the government evaluated offers or bids
3. The way the government carried out discussions in a negotiated procurement
4. The government's determination of responsibility of the winner
5. Picking the winner

When you look at the authority of GAO and the CFC to deal with protests, their authority is essentially the same.

The CFC looks at

> "whether the decision was based on a consideration of the relevant factors, whether the agency articulated a satisfactory explanation for its actions, and whether there has been a clear error of judgment. This includes seeing whether the government 'articulated a rational connection between the facts found and the choice made.' In other words, the reviewing court must determine whether 'the procurement official's decision lacked a rational basis.'"[1]

GAO looks at

> "whether the decision was reasonable, consistent with the stated evaluation criteria, complied with applicable laws and regulations and was adequately documented."[2]

Based on what Congress has told GAO and the CFC to look for, four issues generally get protested. The four reasons are covered below.

The Reasonableness of the Decision

A contract award must be reasonable. But the trouble with a vague test like "reasonableness" is that what's reasonable to you might not be reasonable to me—reasonably.

But some things are clearly unreasonable to all of us. Mechanical decision-making is one.

Opti-Lite submitted a bid that was scored third in technical and first in price because it had the lowest price. Classic Optical Laboratories Inc. submitted the top-rated technical proposal and the second lowest price. When the scores were added, Classic scored 180 and Opti-Lite scored 170. The award memorandum that the contracting officer prepared concluded that Classic should get the contract because it had the highest combined total score. GAO sustained the protest because the VA awarded the contract solely on the basis of a mechanical comparison of the offers. The contracting officer found the higher-rated but more expensive proposal by Classic to be more advantageous based solely on the total point score.[3]

Did the Contracting Officer Use the Stated Evaluation Factors?

A contract award must follow the stated evaluation factors.

A Corps of Engineers solicitation promised to use four technical evaluation factors (project management plan, experience, past performance, and betterments, i.e., amenities. The project management plan factor, the most important factor, was twice as important as any of the other technical evaluation factors. The remaining three factors were equal to each other in importance. In the narrative describing why the winner won, the source selection authority (SSA) described the evaluation factors as being equal to each other in importance in one part of the narrative but later described one factor as the "second most important factor" and another factor as "the fourth, and least most important factor . . . ." GAO found the award to be unreasonable "because the SSA in making his cost/technical tradeoff determination accorded the betterments factor less weight than identified by the RFP."[4]

Did the Contracting Officer Follow All the Laws and Regulations?

It seems too obvious to state. The government has to follow procurement laws.

Under the Competition in Contracting Act, cost or price must **always** be an award factor. And it must be more than just a nominal award factor. A Commerce Department awarded IDIQ contracts focusing almost primarily on technical award factors and not price. GAO sustained a protest. "In our view, the record in this case, particularly the source selection statement, demonstrates that the agency has failed to comply with the regulatory and statutory requirement that contracting agencies give cost or price meaningful consideration in source selections. Contrary to Commerce's apparent belief, there is no exception to the requirement set forth in CICA that cost or price to the government be considered in selecting proposals for award because the selected awardees will be provided the opportunity to compete for task orders under the awarded contract."[5]

Did the Contracting Officer Adequately Document the Decision?

FAR 15.308 gives good guidance on how a contracting officer should document the award decision:

". . . The source selection decision shall be documented, and the documentation shall include the rationale for any business judgments and tradeoffs made or relied on by the SSA, including benefits associated with additional costs."

This paperwork is needed so GAO can evaluate the quality of a contract award decision:

> "In order for us to review an agency's evaluation judgment, the agency must have adequate documentation to support its judgment. Where an agency fails to document or retain evaluation materials, it bears the risk that there may not be adequate supporting rationale in the record for us to conclude that the agency had a reasonable basis for the source selection decision."[6]

Adequate documentation of trade-offs

The paperwork has to show that the contracting officer thought the decision through and used good judgment because

> ". . . the propriety of a cost/technical tradeoff turns not on the difference in technical score, per se, but on whether the contracting agency's judgment concerning the significance of that difference was reasonable in light of the solicitation's evaluation scheme."[7]

One of the recurring problems with a contracting officer's paperwork is the documentation of a best value award. Particularly troublesome is when the government is paying more for a better product or is paying less for a not-as-good product.

Whether the contracting officer is trying to justify why a higher-rated, higher-priced offer or a lower-rated, lower-priced offer won, the contracting officer has to discuss the pros and cons of **all** proposals.

 "Cheaper" can still be chosen even if the contracting officer made technical factors significantly more important than price. But cheaper has to be justified.

> "Where cost is secondary to technical considerations under a solicitation's evaluation scheme, as here, the selection of a lower-priced proposal over a proposal with a higher technical rating requires an adequate justification, i.e., one showing the agency reasonably concluded that notwithstanding the point or adjectival differential between the two proposals, they were essentially equal in technical merit, or that the differential in the evaluation ratings between the

proposals was not worth the cost premium associated with selection of the higher technically rated proposal."[8]

The U.S. Army Corps of Engineers solicitation made "technical evaluation factors, when combined, significantly more important than cost or price." Beneco had the highest-rated proposal but was the ninth lowest in price. Its technical score was 36 percent higher and its price 27 percent higher that the lowest-priced proposal. But all the government documentation said was, "While Beneco is likely to be able to perform the tasks described in the contract in a manner more technically advantageous to the Government; it is noted that, based upon the benefits and advantages of the higher-rated technical proposal . . . payment of the significant additional price for Beneco . . . is neither justified, nor in the best interest of the Government." But the government gave no other reasons for its conclusions. It did no comparative analysis of the strengths and weaknesses of the proposals. GAO said the paperwork was inadequate. "All the paperwork showed was simply that the agency was unwilling to pay a 27 percent price premium to obtain a proposal with a 36 percent higher technical score, without any discussion of the proposals' relative strengths and weaknesses."[9]

Inadequate documentation but other proof

Although FAR 15.308 demands documentation, FAR does not say when that documentation has to be prepared—at the time of award or in the middle of a protest. Because a lawsuit, like a protest, has a way of skewing opinions, forums reviewing the rationale for an agency contract award decision prefer to review the reasons given by the contracting officer at the time the contract award was made. Statements made later, during the protest process, lack credibility. So post-award, mid-protest government documentation of the award is suspect.

Under limited circumstances, however, GAO allows preparation of "adequate documentation" in the middle of the protest. Where the post-award documentation is believable and consistent with the contemporaneous evaluation documentation, GAO may find it adequate.

One case shows that sometimes the contracting officer can win a protest the hard way. One way is to skimp on the paperwork but find a justification for the award elsewhere. The contracting officer will get a protest, but can win it.

A Source Selection Evaluation Board (SSEB) concluded that Highwoods' proposal was technically superior to Simborg's. Significantly, the contracting officer, who would decide the winner, was on the SSEB. Based on the SSEB's recommendation and her own evaluation conclusions, the contracting officer selected Highwoods for award. Her award decision, however, was not described or detailed in writing at the time she made the decision. Why the award was made was described by the contracting officer only after award and then as part of a protest. GAO denied a lack-of-documentation protest. "While we generally accord greater weight to contemporaneous evidence, we will consider post-protest explanations that provide a rationale for contemporaneous conclusions, so long as those explanations are credible and consistent with contemporaneous record." That happened here, according to GAO. The contracting officer's post-award decision "shows that she considered the scores and the SSEB findings, and is consistent with the narrative summaries documenting her own evaluation (as one of the evaluators) of the strengths and weaknesses in the offerors' proposals under each technical factor." Since the pre-award evaluation was consistent with the post-award documentation, GAO found the post-award documentation acceptable.[10]

Unlike the GAO process, some judges on the CFC are reluctant to allow contracting officers to give additional rationale for the award decision once the protest process has started. At the CFC, the standard is somewhat more strict, although this more strict standard varies from judge to judge. A CFC judge may refuse to allow additional statements from both sides to be considered during the protest process, especially if the judge had enough information simply from the information before the contracting officer at the time the contract award was made.

A protester argued that the contracting officer's decision document proved the government did not properly evaluate prices. The contracting officer naturally wanted to say she had done so. She prepared an additional explanation, which the government asked the court to consider. The protester responded with additional information itself, expert opinion countering the contracting officer's supplemental statement. The court didn't want to hear anything other than what was already before it and excluded not only the government statement but also the protester's response to it. A court can consider supplementation of the administrative record if the existing record has gaps in it. But if the judge can adequately review what the agency did from the information that was before the agency at the time the decision was made, there's no need for further, litigation-driven rationalizations. Here, the court concluded that what was before the agency was good enough for the judge. The government's price analysis was properly explained at the time the decision was made and thus there was no need for the additional statements of the contracting officer.[11]

In addition to these elements of the solicitation process, some parts of the contract administration process can be protested. One typical example of this is when the government modifies the contract and a competitor believes that the modification should have been put out for bids from other vendors, rather than given sole source to the incumbent contractor.

Some things cannot be protested to GAO. For example, if Congress has made another agency responsible for certain actions, GAO won't handle protests of them. These include

Disputes by state licensing agencies under the Randolph-Sheppard Act[12]

Determinations by the Small Business Administration under the certificate of competency program[13]

Protests of awards under the Javits-Wagner-O'Day Act[14]

One of the most unlikely losing arguments a protester can make is that the winner's price was too low. It's unlikely, because with agencies strapped for cash, it would seem they should favor the vendor with the lowest price—no matter how low the price. For the same reason, it would also seem strange that an agency would disqualify a vendor for having too low a price. And perhaps strangest of all, an agency generally **cannot** disqualify a vendor with a price that is too low. The general rule is that a price too low is **not** a good reason to disqualify a vendor in a fixed-price solicitation. Unless an agency states in the solicitation that it will consider an offeror's price an indication of how well the offeror understands what the government wants, or unless an agency wants to avoid the risk of poor performance under contract with low profit, a too-low price is irrelevant.

An Air Force solicitation was issued as a Small Business Historically Underutilized Business Zone (HUBZone) set-aside. The solicitation expressly and incorrectly warned vendors that "any offer could be rejected if it is unreasonable as to price." The proposal of J.A. Farrington Janitorial Services (JAF) lost because its proposal was too low, indicating to the Air Force that the vendor did not understand what the Air Force wanted. GAO sustained Farrington's protest. Agencies should have a different focus on price reasonableness depending on whether the contract will be a fixed-price contract or a cost reimbursement contract. When awarding a fixed-price contract, the price reasonableness issue deals with only whether the proposed price is **too high**. That's because a fixed-price contract "places the risk and responsibility for contract costs and resulting profit or loss on the contractor." So the price is the vendor's problem.

A cost reimbursement contract, however, is different. If a vendor's proposal for a cost reimbursement contract has a price that is too low, the government runs the risk of not having the contract completed successfully. If the agency wants to be able to throw out a vendor for having a price that is too low, the solicitation must say that the agency will do a price realism analysis, in GAO's words, "for such purposes as measuring an offeror's understanding of the solicitation requirements, or to avoid the risk of poor performance from a contractor who was forced to provide goods or services at little or no profit." Also, a "too low price" decision actually involves responsibility:

> "Where there is no relevant evaluation criterion pertaining to realism or understanding, a determination that an offeror's price in a fixed-price contract is too low generally concerns the offeror's responsibility, i.e., the offeror's ability and capacity to successfully perform the contract at its offered price."[15]

When Can Something Be Protested?

The rule for timely filing of a protest depends on what is being protested. There are really only two choices: a protest of something in the solicitation package and a protest of everything else.

The Solicitation Package

If a protester does not like something in the solicitation package (e.g., the RFP evaluation factors), he must protest prior to the time that the offers or bids are to be received.

Initial offers were due at GSA by 4:45. An offeror submitted its offer to GSA before 4:45. But the offeror's protest of the GSA solicitation package did not get to GAO until 4:48. GAO concluded that the protest was too late.[16]

Everything Else

If the protest doesn't deal with the solicitation package, the protest is a protest of "everything else." This catchall category includes such things as a protest of being thrown out of the competitive range; a protest of not being found responsible; a protest over whether the agency had meaningful discussions with an unsuccessful vendor; and, more generally, a protest that the winner should not have won.

Protests of everything else must be made within ten days.

> "A protest based on other than alleged improprieties in a solicitation must be filed not later than ten calendar days after the protester knew, or should have known, of the basis for protest, with an exception for protests that challenge a procurement conducted on the basis of competitive proposals under which a debriefing is requested and, when requested, is required. . . . In such cases, protests must be filed not later than ten days after the date on which the debriefing is held."[17]

So this everything-else category has a ten-day deadline, but the real issue is "ten days from when?"

Ten days from

   1. Knowing the basis of a protest

When a vendor knew the basis of the protest should be a fact not open to dispute.

   2. When a vendor "should have known" the basis of a protest

When a vendor should have known the basis of a protest is more difficult to identify.

Significantly, a protestor's clock doesn't start if the vendor is merely suspicious of government conduct that could be protested.

A real estate developer, MP, learned it had lost a government project on February 2. On February 4, in a conversation with its construction company, MP learned that the winning developer had contacted the construction contractor wanting that contractor to prepare plans and build the government building. Because these plans were supposed to have been submitted as part of the offer, MP suspected that the winning developer had won without submitting plans with its offer as required. MP confirmed that suspicion on February 11 when the government told MP that the winner had not submitted plans with its offer. MP filed its protest on February 19. The government argued that the protest was too late, that the losing developer should have filed the protest within ten days of February 4, the day it had the conversation with the construction company.

GAO concluded that MP's protest was on time. Although the conversation MP had with the construction contractor might have led MP to conclude that the winner had not submitted the required plans with its proposal, "that suspicion alone was not adequate to trigger the running of the ten day period for filing a protest. . . . MP could not have discerned from the conversation what information the winner had included with its proposal, the form of that information, or the level of detail describing the proposed new building for the agency to evaluate (e.g., architectural drawings, sketches, schematic plans, landscape, or elevation plans)." It was only after the government confirmed the absence of plans with the winner's offer that the protest clock started.[18]

3. A required debriefing

One exception to the "ten-day knew or should have known" rule involves a required debriefing. Where there has been a required debriefing of a procurement using competitive procedures, the protest deadline is ten days from the required debriefing.

First, what are *debriefings*?

They are meetings held by the government to explain to a losing vendor why the vendor lost the negotiated contract. (FAR 15.505 deals with pre-award debriefings; FAR 15.506 deals with post-award debriefings.) A debriefing may be in writing or in person. Normally, a debriefing lasts an hour or so, but it can go longer if a complex solicitation is involved.

Second, what is a *required debriefing*?

A required debriefing is one for which a protester has followed, for example, FAR 15.506, which makes a protester get into the government's hands 3 days from learning that the protester lost, a written request for a debriefing. If a protester follows this tight timetable, it gets a required debriefing.

Third, what is a *procurement using competitive procedures*?

Generally, it's a solicitation using FAR Part 15 negotiation procedures. Surprisingly, a competitive solicitation under the Federal Supply Schedule was not a procurement entitled to the "ten days from debriefing" exception.

The Navy issued a request for quotations for information technology (IT) help-desk support services to 12 vendors on the General Services Administration's Federal Supply Schedule (FSS). The solicitation package sure looked like a "competitive procurement." It had a statement of work, instructions to vendors regarding the submission of quotations, a description of four evaluation factors for award, and a "best value" basis of award.

MIL protested to GAO well **within** ten days of a debriefing, but well **after** ten days from learning it had lost. GAO said that MIL had filed its protest too late. This FSS competition was not a procurement based on competitive proposals. "The term 'competitive proposals' is not defined by our Bid Protest Regulations, nor is it defined by statute or regulation. However, we have previously determined that the use of negotiated procedures in accordance with Federal Acquisition Regulation (FAR) Part 15 and as evidenced by the issuance of a request for proposals, constitutes a procurement conducted on the basis of competitive proposals . . . ."

Here, the procurement was not conducted pursuant to the negotiated procedures of FAR Part 15, nor did it involve the issuance of a request for proposals. Rather, the procurement was conducted under the FSS program, pursuant to the procedures set forth in FAR Subpart 8.4 and using a request for quotations.[19]

There is also an exception to **all** the GAO deadlines:

GAO rules say GAO can hear a late protest "for good cause shown" or where GAO "determines that a protest raises issues significant to the procurement system."[20]

But these exceptions are rarely used.

> "Under this exception, our Office may consider an untimely protest that raises issues significant to the procurement system that have not been considered previously; however, in order to prevent the timeliness rules from becoming meaningless, this exception is strictly construed and seldom used."[21]

In some cases, the CFC has followed the GAO rule requiring protests of the solicitation package to be made before the deadline for submission of offers.

But not in all cases.

> ". . . [T]his court, with all due respect, fails to see how a GAO rule that self-limits that agency's advisory role constitutes a limit, either legally or prudentially, on this court's exercise of jurisdiction. In this regard, 28 U.S.C. § 1491(b)(1) (2000) explicitly provides that this court shall have bid protest jurisdiction 'without regard to whether suit is instituted before or after the contract is awarded.' In this court's view, while delay in bringing a protest undoubtedly may be considered in the multi-factored analysis of whether injunctive relief is warranted, absent the application of equitable doctrines such as laches, such delay does not constitute an independent legal ground for rejecting a request for injunctive relief. Indeed, were this court to rule otherwise, it seemingly would have to apply the entire GAO rule, which includes exceptions to the timeliness requirement for 'good cause shown' or if a protest raises 'issues of significance.' 4 CFR 21.2(c). This court cannot imagine that Congress intended this court's bid protest jurisdiction (or the prudential exercise thereof) to rise or fall on such squishy considerations."[22]

Another CFC judge concluded that GAO's timeliness rule "is not binding on this court."[23]

How Is Something Protested?

GAO protests

It does not take much to file a protest at GAO. Its fax machines are running 24/7, and it accepts protests by e-mail.

The GAO regulations describe what a protest has to include:

> (b) Protests must be in writing and addressed as follows: General Counsel, General Accounting Office, 441 G Street, NW., Washington, DC 20548, Attention: Procurement Law Control Group.

> (c) A protest filed with GAO shall:

>> (1) Include the name, street address, electronic mail address, and telephone and facsimile numbers of the protester,

>> (2) Be signed by the protester or its representative,

>> (3) Identify the contracting agency and the solicitation and/or contract number,

>> (4) Set forth a detailed statement of the legal and factual grounds of protest including copies of relevant documents,

>> (5) Set forth all information establishing that the protester is an interested party for the purpose of filing a protest,

>> (6) Set forth all information establishing the timeliness of the protest,

>> (7) Specifically request a ruling by the Comptroller General of the United States, and

>> (8) State the form of relief requested.[24]

CFC protests

It takes much more effort and a lot more money to file a protest at the CFC. Its rules make a protester file a formal complaint, typically drafted by a lawyer.

Here's one reason why. Unlike GAO rules that spell out exactly what a protest should include, the CFC says simply:

> "A civil action is commenced by filing a complaint with the court."[25]

This is why a lawyer can be especially helpful at the CFC.

GAO and the CFC, looking at the same case, can reach opposite conclusions. In one procurement, a vendor's protest to GAO was not successful but a protest to the CFC by that same vendor was successful.

An Army solicitation for a small business set-aside omitted a necessary clause. GAO and the CFC took opposite approaches to dealing with a protest over the missing clause. GAO said that protest was too late since offers had already been submitted. But to the CFC, it wasn't too late. First, the GAO rules didn't apply to the court. More important, the court noted that GAO's "offer deadline" rule was not binding even on GAO since GAO's own rules allow late protests "for good cause shown" and where the late protest "raises issues significant to the procurement system." The CFC heard the protest of that issue.

The solicitation also required that the cargo ships have "self-sustaining refrigerated cargo containers." Refrigeration available only in port would not be acceptable. Both also reached opposite conclusions about whether the winner had promised to have such containers. GAO said the contracting officer's decision that the winner promised to provide self-refrigerated cargo containers was reasonable. First, the winner took no exception to the requirement and "there is nothing in the record here that provides any basis to question the reasonableness of the agency's determination of the awardee's intention and capability to meet the self-sustaining requirement." But the CFC seriously disagreed with GAO and the contracting officer's "reasonable" conclusion. The contracting officer's "reasonable" conclusion was made when he looked at a picture of what the winner had proposed and concluded, from that picture, that the containers would have self-sustaining refrigeration. But paperwork the winner submitted with the proposal showed that it was not complying. Its contingency plan for loss of power at sea was to have the ship head for port. Its plan didn't mention the solution required by the solicitation: self-sustaining generators when power is lost on the high seas.[26]

THE AUTOMATIC STAY

The protest process has two distinct battles: the fight over the protest itself, which we have discussed, and the fight over the automatic stay that automatically prevents the government and the winning contractor from working on the protested and stayed contract until the protest has been resolved.

This second fight started in 1984, when Congress gave potential contractors and government agencies something important to each. To potential contractors, Congress gave the right to automatically stop the performance of a protested contract until the protest was settled. All a protester had to do was file a protest early in the contracting process. Automatically, the government had to stop work on that contract until the protest was over. And to government agencies, Congress gave an "almost automatic" override of the automatic stay given to contractors. It did so by giving the government a number of huge loopholes that would let it go ahead with a protested procurement—let it override the automatic stay—if necessary.

The exact loophole the government could use to override the automatic stay depended on where the protest had been filed (agency or GAO) and how early in the process it had been filed (before award or after). If a protest was filed before the agency awarded the contract, the winning contractor could keep working if someone above the contracting officer found that continued performance was "in the best interest of the government" or that there were "urgent and compelling reasons" for continuing performance.

These same two loopholes are available to override a stay imposed in a post-award protest to an agency. But to get the stay in the first place, a protester must file the protest really early in the contract performance process.

If the protest is before the GAO, the government has a harder time overriding the stay. The override decision has to be made by someone way above the contracting officer—usually, the agency's head of contract activity.

Before award, there is only one loophole: urgent and compelling circumstances. If the protest to GAO is filed after award, there are two loopholes: best interest, as mentioned above, and urgent and compelling reasons. Although these similar loopholes are huge, some things don't get through them. Two rules arise from override decisions.

First, if the work could have continued under an incumbent contract, the government's "urgent and compelling" argument could be in trouble.

The government said it had to override the stay to continue providing health benefits since the automatic stay would delay streamlining of the health administration process by four months. The court didn't agree. The government had not considered that it could play catch-up if delayed by a protest. Second, the government claimed there was no easy way to extend the existing contracts to cover any delay that might be caused by a protest, "potentially leaving the beneficiaries without services." But the court noted that the contracts being protested included FAR 52.217-8, which authorizes extensions of the existing contracts of up to 6 months to deal with delays occasioned by bid protests. Third, the government argued that the new contracts would be better for the healthcare beneficiaries. The court agreed but said, in effect, so what. The override refers to the best interests of the United States, not those of the agency or the agency's contracting officials. To the court, the best interests of the United States "necessarily include weighing the benefits Congress obviously felt were furthered by bolstering the bid protest process and in turn, promoting competition contracting."[27]

In another case, the court would not let HUD override a stay of a contract for services to sell HUD properties. The judge said, "Normally the fact that a new contract is better than an old contract would not constitute a valid basis for an override decision. . . ." Here, a new contract was not essential because the incumbent contract still had several months left on it. Also, the new contract covered two whole states but the override was based on only the Chicago HUD program. In addition, only ten properties would be involved. Finally, the incumbent could do the new work under its original contract or under a contract modified under the Changes clause. Because the incumbent could do this work, any need for the new contract to help "several properties in Chicago cannot rationally form the basis for an urgent and compelling circumstance and best interests of the United States determination to authorize performance of the new contract which covers all of Illinois and Indiana."[28]

National defense, however, can easily justify overriding a stay and letting contract performance continue.

Cell phone calls depend on the electromagnetic spectrum, a range of frequencies that the whole world has to fight over because there's only so much within the range. Which country gets which frequencies allocated to it depends on international conferences. In 2007 the Department of Defense will attend a major conference that DoD believes is critical to keeping the frequencies it has.

To prepare for this important conference, DoD awarded a contract for spectrum management engineering services. After one unsuccessful offeror protested and got the automatic stay, the government overrode the stay using both loopholes: best interest of the United States and urgent and compelling reasons. The protester challenged the validity of the override but lost. One reason was that important preliminary international meetings would be held during the override period. More important, these preliminary meetings dealt with issues that DoD had classified, well before the protest, as "high" concern rather than "moderate" or "low" concern. The court thought that DoD could best represent the government at the 2007 major conference if it was well represented at these preliminary meetings. The court found that there was a time-critical need for performing the protested services during the override period. Also, the protested work involved "new work," so there was no incumbent contractor that could be used during the override period. And the court did not agree with the protester that the government "by some mixing and matching of the pre-existing contracts" could find the people to do the work during the override.[29]

Endnotes

1. *Beta Analytics International v. The United States,* 67 Fed.Cl. 384, 394-95 (2005).

2. *ProTech Corporation,* B-294818, Dec. 30, 2004, 2005 CPD ¶ 73.

3. *Opti-Lite Optical,* B-281693, Mar. 22, 1999, 99-1 CPD ¶ 61.

4   *ProTech Corporation, supra.*

5. *The MIL Corporation,* B-294836, Dec. 30, 2004, 2005 CPD ¶ 29.

6. *Keeton Corrections, Inc.,* B-293348, 2005 CPD ¶ 44.

7. *Preferred Sys. Solutions, Inc.,* B-292322, Aug. 25, 2003, 2003 CPD ¶ 166.

8. *Id.*

9. *Beneco Enterprises, Inc.* B-283.154, Oct. 13, 1999, 2000 CPD ¶ 69.

10. *Simborg Development, Inc.*, B-283538, Dec. 7, 1999, 2000 CPD ¶ 12.

11. *Al Ghanim Combined Group v. The United States*, 56 Fed.Cl. 502 (2003).

12. *Mississippi State Dep't of Rehab. Servs.*, B-250783.8, Sept. 7, 1994, 94-2 CPD ¶ 99.

13. *High Point Sec., Inc.—Recon. and Protest*, B-255747.2, B-255747.3, Feb. 22, 1994, 94-1 CPD ¶ 169.

14. *ARA Envtl. Servs., Inc.*, B-254321, Aug. 23, 1993, 93-2 CPD ¶ 113.

15. *J.A. Farrington Janitorial Services*, B-296875, Oct. 18, 2005, 2005 CPD ¶ 187.

16. *120 Church St.*, B-232139, B-232139.3, Mar. 7, 1989, 89-1 CPD ¶246.

17. *New SI, LLC*, B-295209, Nov. 22, 2004, 2005 CPD ¶ 71.

18. *Marshall-Putnam Soil and Water Conservation District*, B-289949, B-289949.2, May 29, 2002, 2002 CPD ¶ 90.

19. *The MIL Corporation*, B- 297,508, B- 297508.2, Jan. 26, 2006, 2006 CPD ¶ 34.

20. 4 CFR 21.2.

21. *HMX, Inc.* B- 291,102, Nov. 4, 2002, 2003 CPD ¶ 52.

22. *Software Testing Solutions, Inc. v. U.S.*, 58 Fed.Cl. 533, 536-37 (2003).

23. *Transatlantic Lines LLC v. U.S.* 68 Fed.Cl. 48, 52 (2005).

24. 4 CFR 21.1.

25. Rule 3, Rules of the U.S. Court of Federal Claims.

26. The GAO decision is *Transatlantic Lines, LLC*, B-296, 245, B-296245.2, July 14, 2005, 2005 CPD ¶ 147. The CFC decision is *Transatlantic Lines LLC v. The United States*, 68 Fed.Cl. 48 (2005).

27. *PGBA, LLC v. The United States*, 57 Fed.Cl. 655 (2003), *aff'd PGBA, LLC v. U.S.*, 389 F.3d 1219 (Fed.Cir.2004).

28. *Chapman Law Firm v. The United States*, 62 Fed.Cl.464 (2004).

29. *Alion Science and Technology Corp. v. The United States*, 69 Fed.Cl. 14 (2005).

Chapter 11

The Claims Process

CONTENTS

We know from previous chapters that there are two kinds of fights that the government and vendors can get into: protests and claims. Protests are fights by unsuccessful vendors trying to get the contract. Claims are typically fights by contractors trying to get out from under a termination for default or contractors trying to get the contracting officer to do something like pay more money or interpret ambiguous contract wording. Claims can come from the government as well, such as a contracting officer's demand for liquidated damages. Because government claims are relatively rare, in this chapter we will discuss claims by assuming they are contractor claims.

Although this chapter talks about the fights the contracting officer and the contractor get into, it's important to mention arbitration. The Disputes Clause, FAR 52.233-1 at clause (g), allows the contractor and the government to agree to alternative dispute resolution (ADR). ADR can be very effective in quickly resolving disputes between the contractor and the government.

What is ADR? It's many things, so it cannot be neatly described in 25 words or less. Basically, it is an attempt to keep the dispute out of the courtroom and put it into the conference room. In the non-government contracting world, ADR includes alternatives like Judge Joe Brown. In the government contracting world, ADR could be binding arbitration by a judge from the CFC or a board; mini-trials where each side gets the chance to informally present its case to the judge, at which time an advisory or binding decision is made by the judge; or simply using a judge to discuss with the parties the strengths and weaknesses of their case. The Court of Federal Claims (CFC) and boards use various forms of ADR.

When filing claims, contractors have a choice of going to the Court of Federal Claims (CFC) or a board of contract appeals (BCA). Both forums have become quite good at handling government contract issues. But each retains its independence. The court is not bound by precedents from the boards; nor are boards bound by court precedents.

(continued on next page)

(continued from previous page)

A government employee working as a credit union examiner for the National Credit Union Administration sued the government in the Court of Federal Claims (CFC) for overtime pay. The court concluded that he was not entitled to overtime pay for several reasons, including the fact that the claims were too late, that he was exempt from overtime, and that he had never gotten the okay for overtime from his boss. After losing, he came back to the CFC asking it to reconsider its decision, citing precedent decisions from the General Services Board of Contract Appeals (GSBCA). In refusing to reconsider the case, the court explained the role that board precedents play in resolving issues before the court. "Although opinions of the GSBCA are persuasive authority, they do not bind this court." It also cited court precedents calling the Government Accountability Office and the Armed Services Board of Contract Appeals decisions persuasive but not controlling and "not accorded *stare decisis* effect." The court went on to describe the reason for its independence: "It is the duty of this court to apply the statutes and regulations to the facts of the case. This court is not bound by GSBCA's approach to the evaluation of personal convenience travel expense claims. Even if the GSBCA takes an inconsistent approach to personal convenience travel expense claims, that circumstance would have no bearing on the decisions of this court."

Corrigan v. The United States, 70 Fed. Cl. 665 (2006).

One way of looking at claims is with a *who*, *what*, *when*, *where*, *why*, and *how* approach. In Chapter 9, we discussed three aspects of claims before the CFC and the agency BCAs: the *where* in terms of jurisdiction; the *who* in terms of contractors finding standing; and the *why* in terms of relief available there. In this chapter, we look at the *what*, *when*, and *how* of claims.

In doing so, we look at claims from the perspective of a contractor filing claims against the government. This ignores—but only for purposes of simplicity—the fact that the contracting officer can file government claims against the contractor. But since contractor claims are much more common than government claims, we will focus on these more common types of claims—contractor claims.

WHAT IS A "CLAIM"?

Why All the Fuss Over Whether Something Is a Claim?

A *claim* is a term of art. It means something very precise, very specific, in government contracting. Before something is a claim, the government doesn't have a deadline to answer. And before something is a claim, a contractor doesn't get interest if its claim turns out to be successful. So the fuss over a claim has to do with deadlines and interest. A claim must be responded to by the government within 60 days, and a claim earns a contractor interest.

With time and money at stake, you'd think Congress would have made it easy for the government and contractors to easily spot a claim. But that didn't happen. As we will see, only a few formalities are required to make a contractor's letter a claim.

Complicating things further, the courts and the boards have followed Congress's laid-back approach to claims by reinforcing the principle that a formal claim has only the barest of essentials.

> "No particular language is required to create a claim as long as the contractor submits to the contracting officer a 'clear and unequivocal statement' providing adequate notice of the basis and amount of the claim."[1]

Interest is paid on claim amounts not yet paid.

The government entered into a lease for space occupied by the Environment Protection Agency. The monthly rent was approximately $66,000. When the government did not move out on time, the landlord immediately filed a claim for the past-due rent, at that time just $66,000 for one month. In 2005 the CFC concluded that several months' back rent was due, a total of over $264,000. The successful landlord got interest under the Contract Disputes Act. That law says successful claims are entitled to interest on the amount of the award. And interest starts to run on the date

(continued on next page)

(continued from previous page)

the claim is received by the contracting officer. "This date is fixed by statute, and applies to the total costs embodied in the claim to the Contracting Officer, even if some of the costs have not yet been incurred by the contractor. Although this statutory imperative may lead to incongruous results, as in this case, where interest begins to run on rent that is ultimately found owing even before some of that rent is actually due, the statutory scheme is intended to promote prompt submission and resolution of claims. It is not the role of this court to tinker with the rule."

Modeer v. The United States, 68 Fed. Cl. 131 (2005).

But this creates a terrible problem: if "no particular language" creates a claim that starts the contracting officer's deadlines clock and the contractor's interest clock, how does anybody know when those clocks start?

The best way to know whether something is a claim is to look at the process from start to finish and distinguish a request for equitable adjustment (REA) from a claim.

REA and Claim Distinguished

It's important to distinguish an REA from a claim.

An REA from a contractor does not earn interest. Nor does it start a contracting officer's clock. Although a contracting officer must respond to an REA, there is no formal claims clock running. So to understand claims, you have to understand the overall process. It often starts with a phone call.

1. **The contractor's phone call**. The equitable adjustment process often begins with a phone call from the contractor to the contracting officer letting the contracting officer know that there's a problem with the contract. This phone call, we will see, cannot be a claim. But it's a helpful part of the process because the phone call gives the contracting officer notice that something needs attention.

2. **The contractor's follow-up letter.** A letter from the contractor usually follows up this phone call. The wise contracting officer will attempt to control the equitable adjustment process as much as possible by asking the contractor to send him a letter about the issue raised in the phone call, describing it in as much detail as possible, and asking for an estimate of how much contractor would need to fix the problem. The contractor's letter is typically labeled a *request for an equitable adjustment,* or REA. The contractor could make this letter a formal claim but typically does not for good reasons. If a contractor makes the letter a claim, it starts the litigious claims process, sends the wrong message to the contracting officer, and forces the contracting officer to get the agency's lawyers involved. So making this letter a claim, though legally possible, gets the equitable adjustment process off to a bad start. Usually, the contractor's letter is an REA.

3. **The contracting officer's investigation.** Since the contracting officer now is on notice that there's a problem with the contract, the contracting officer looks into it, often by consulting with the contracting officer's technical representative.

4. **Negotiations between the parties.** If the contracting officer believes that there must be a change in the project as a result of the contractor's call and letter, the contracting officer can try to negotiate a resolution of the problem. Sometimes the parties will negotiate the amount of money needed to resolve the issue. If the contractor is satisfied with the contracting officer's response at this time, both parties modify the contract and no formal claim ever arises. The REA process ends and the claims process never begins.

5. **The formal claim.** If a contractor is not satisfied with the contracting officer's resolution of the problem, the contractor now is at the claim stage. Typically, the contractor writes another letter to the contracting officer, describing the problem again, as well as the contractor's proposed resolution, certifying the claim if it's over $100,000, and demanding a final decision of the contracting officer on the claim. Now the claims process has begun. Interest on the claim is running, and the contracting officer's 60-day clock is also running.

Definition of a Claim

FAR defines a *claim*:

> "'Claim' means a written demand or written assertion by one of the contracting parties seeking, as a matter of right, the payment of money in a sum certain, the adjustment or interpretation of contract terms, or other relief arising under or relating to the contract. However, a written demand or written assertion by the contractor seeking the payment of money exceeding $100,000 is not a claim under the Contract Disputes Act of 1978 until certified as required by the Act. A voucher, invoice, or other routine request for payment that is not in dispute when submitted is not a claim. The submission may be converted to a claim, by written notice to the contracting officer as provided in 33.206(a), if it is disputed either as to liability or amount or is not acted upon in a reasonable time."[2]

HOW IS A CLAIM RAISED AND RESOLVED?

The *how* of a claim has two perspectives: the perspective of a contractor filing one and the perspective of a contracting officer resolving one.

How Does a Contractor File a Claim?

How a contractor files a claim depends on what the contractor is asking for—money, a contract interpretation, or "other relief."

Claims for Money

A claim for money has three or, if over $100,000, four simple elements.

a. A sum certain. To make a claim for money, a contractor must demand a specific dollar amount from the government. There can be no claim if a contractor simply tells the contracting officer vague things like "the contractor demands fair compensation for this" or makes other demands that lack a specified dollar amount.

Congress demanded that a contractor give a "sum certain" for several good reasons. It did not want a contracting officer to settle claims based on estimates.

> "The legislative history shows the purpose to be so that government representatives can readily examine and evaluate contractor claims. Otherwise, there's no sound basis for evaluation, negotiation or legal claim settlement."[3]

Another rationale is that the certification of claims over $100,000 is designed to encourage contractors to submit claims with good numbers in them. The use of estimates or other fuzzy language in place of a sum certain would make the certification meaningless.

But Congress's approach sometimes presents problems. One of the problems with determining a sum certain at the beginning of a claim is that further review of a claim might well lead to an increase in the claimed amount. So contractors are sometimes hesitant to give an unequivocal dollar amount as part of the claim. Instead, they use words that give them room to increase the claimed amount. One way they do so is to use phrases like *at least* or *well over* a specific dollar amount. But these fuzzy words don't create a valid claim.

Eaton Contract Services filed a claim against the U.S. Army Corps of Engineers for consequential damages "well over $2 million." The ASBCA denied the claim, concluding that the language used by the contractor on the consequential damage element, "well over $2 million," did not set a sum certain as required by Congress. The Board gave a couple of examples of language considered equivocal and not stating a sum certain. For example, claims for "in excess of" a particular amount did not satisfy the sum certain requirement. Nor did the phrase "an unspecified amount anticipated to be in excess of" a particular dollar amount establish a claim.[4]

---

b. Specific demand for a contracting officer's final decision. The contractor must demand—expressly or implicitly—a final decision of the contracting officer.

c. State the basis of the claim. The contractor must tell the contracting officer the rationale for filing the claim. For example, it could be having to do extra work without additional pay, encountering a differing site condition without getting any additional money, being delayed by the government, or having the government make the contractor responsible for warranty work when the damage is not the contractor's fault.

The claim may include documentation that helps the contractor's case. Typically, this would include invoices or canceled checks showing that the contractor actually spent the money that the contractor is now requesting from the government.

d. Certification. If the money demanded is for more than $100,000, the contractor must certify the claim. The exact magic words a contractor must use are stated in the Disputes clause in the contract.

Claims for Interpretation of Contract Terms

When the contract tells a contractor nothing more than that it must "stock the restroom," does that mean one-ply or two-ply toilet paper? In an actual case, all the building maintenance contract said about bathroom supplies was that the contractor had to "stock the restroom." The government wanted the best—two-ply paper. The contractor client wanted to give the government the cheapest—one-ply paper. A claim over contract interpretation was needed to resolve this "constitutional" issue.

Every contract is full of similar language problems that must be solved. Anytime the contractor says the contract means one thing and the government says it means another, there is the possibility of a claim over contract interpretation.

And although these issues will involve money down the road, they don't involve money right now. So a claim for money is not yet appropriate. Alternatively, the contractor could provide the two-ply and file a claim for the additional cost. The immediate issue, however, is "what does it mean?" That makes it a claim involving the interpretation of contract terms.

The contractor can file a claim that forces the government to give a formal answer to any contract interpretation issue. And it's much easier than money claims. There is no need to provide backup or invoices as in a money claim. Nor is there any need to certify the claim.

How does a contractor file a legally sufficient claim over a contract interpretation issue? It's simple. The contractor sends the government a letter describing the controversy: what the contractor thinks the contractor language means, what the government has told the contractor that it thinks it means (if it has done so). The contractor ends by demanding a formal decision of the contracting officer on the issue.

In some cases, a valid claim for a contract interpretation can be indirect and can be found by combining several letters.

Clearwater Constructors Inc. had a contract with the U.S. Army Corps of Engineers to build a hangar at Grand Forks Air Force Base in North Dakota. The hangar work was subcontracted to Fleming Steel Company. The parties argued over whether the contract required explosion-proof doors. After the government said it did, Clearwater disagreed, sending the government a letter saying that the government's requiring explosion-proof doors was "a change in scope and should be covered by a contract modification." Attached to the contractor's letter was a letter from Fleming arguing that the hangar doors at issue were not in hazardous area and therefore did not have to be explosion-proof. The court concluded that the two letters Clearwater had sent to the government (its letter to the contracting officer accompanied by Fleming's letter to Clearwater) established this necessary element. Fleming's letter to Clearwater had said the doors did not have to be explosion-proof. Its letter also told Clearwater that it wanted to be reimbursed for the explosion-proof doors. Clearwater's letter to the contracting officer said that the change in scope should be covered by a contract modification. "In sum, Fleming and Clearwater clearly offered a precise and well explained rationale, founded both upon the facts of this matter and the language of the contract and contract modifications, setting forth the reasons for its interpretation of the contract. . . ."[5]

Claims for "Other Relief"

What is this catchall "other relief"? Typically, it is a claim involving a termination for default. When a contractor asks the government to reconsider its termination because there was an excusable delay such as the government's slowing the project down, that's a claim for "other relief." Also, asking the government to reduce or eliminate the assessment of liquidated damages could be "other relief." Or it could be a request that the contracting officer change the past performance evaluation it gave a contractor at the end of a contract.

A claim for "other relief" can be made simply by sending the government a letter describing what happened to the contractor and why the contractor wants relief. As in a claim for contract interpretation, a claim for other relief does not need any certifications.

The U.S. Army Corps of Engineers did not evaluate the performance of Record Steel and Construction, Inc., as well as the contractor wanted it to. So the contractor filed a claim requesting that the Army's evaluation of its performance be corrected. The CFC said the contractor's request was a claim. The contractor's letter asking for reevaluation of its performance was a claim. "By doing so, Record Steel was seeking relief relating to the contract pursuant to a claim of right. Specifically, under the FAR, a contracting agency is required to prepare performance evaluations for each construction contract of at least $500,000." Here, the agency did a performance evaluation and sent it to the contractor. In its response, the contractor disagreed with the evaluation and asked for some changes. The government refused to make those changes. The government's denial "meant that the agency had issued its final agency action. . . . Record Steel had sought reconsideration of the Corps's evaluation of performance under the contract, and the contracting officers representative had denied reconsideration, rendering the evaluation a final action."[6]

It's interesting to note that the ASBCA reached the opposite conclusion.[7]

What clause a contractor uses has $$$ consequences.

Every claim involves at least two clauses—the Disputes clause and another one. That "other one" can be very important because in government contracting, some types of harm can be covered by more than one clause.

Reducing the work under a contract. This reduction in work, often referred to as de-scoping or deductive change, can be done as a deductive change order under the Changes clause or as a partial termination for convenience under the Termination for Convenience clause. Typically, minor (10 percent) reductions can be done under the Changes clause. Changes any larger must be done under the Termination for Convenience clause. The difference is that, under a termination for convenience settlement, a contractor gets settlement costs, like the costs of having an accountant tally up the damages, or legal fees, under the Termination for Convenience clause but not under the Changes clause.

Delay. This is even more complex. A contractor can get delay damages under the Suspension of Work clause, the Changes clause, and the Differing Site Condition clause. One big difference is that under the Suspension of Work clause, there is no profit. Thus, a contractor might try to stay away from making the claim under that clause. Under the Differing Site Condition clause, any delay waiting for the government to decide how to fix the condition gets compensated under the Suspension of Work clause (no profit). But if the delay is due to a defective specification, the delay gets paid for under the Changes clause, which includes profit.

How the Contracting Officer Handles the Claim

When a claim demands that the contracting officer issue the contracting officer's final decision, that decision must be the decision of the contracting officer and not someone else in the government.

Content of the Contracting Officer's Final Decision

FAR 33.211(a)(4) gives a good description of what a contracting officer's final decision should look like. The contracting officer has to:

> Prepare a written decision that shall include a—
>
> (i) Description of the claim or dispute;
>
> (ii) Reference to the pertinent contract terms;
>
> (iii) Statement of the factual areas of agreement and disagreement;
>
> (iv) Statement of the contracting officer's decision, with supporting rationale; . . .

That same section provides boilerplate advising the contractor of appeal rights.

One problem with the contracting officer's final decision is that on occasion a contracting officer refuses to issue one. One good reason for not issuing a final decision is that the contractor has not formally filed a claim that would be entitled to such a decision.

One bad reason for failing to issue a contracting officer's final decision is that a contracting officer wants to keep a contractor from going to court or a board. Apparently, some contracting officers believe that if they simply don't issue a final decision, the contractor can't go over their heads to the CFC or BCA.

Congress anticipated this problem and provided for "a deemed denial." If a contracting officer doesn't honor the 60-day deadline, a contractor can deem its claim denied and go to the court or board anyway. If a contractor does not get an answer by the deadline, the silence of a contracting officer is considered a denial.

Quality of the Contracting Officer's Final Decision

A contracting officer's final decision must be the personal and independent decision of the contracting officer. It must consider the views of agency experts, but it still has to be a decision that is truly the contracting officer's and not the decision of some other person in the agency.

In numerous cases, particularly those involving highly technical issues, a contracting officer has an expert prepare a report. When the report is finished, the contracting officer often issues a contracting officer's final decision adopting the expert's report in its entirely. Relying on an expert's report does not necessarily rob the contracting officer's decision of independence.

> A construction contractor argued that the contracting officer's final decision was invalid because it was a "wholesale adoption of a litigation expert's report" and not the "personal and independent decision" of the contracting officer as required by FAR and applicable case law principles. The board refused to draw such an automatic conclusion as it set out the requirements of a valid contracting officer's final decision. "It is well established that the contractor is entitled to a decision that has been independently rendered by the contracting officer. A decision issued by a contracting officer acting solely pursuant to the dictates of other, higher-level, personnel in the Government is not valid. At the same time, the regulations and case law anticipate that the contracting officer, particularly in complex matters, will seek and consider advice of counsel and experts as an integral part of the process of formulating a final decision. The contracting officer is not required to be isolated from the advice and guidance of others."[8]

Congressional Reference Cases before the CFC

A contractor can also ask Congress to refer the claim to the CFC because the CFC also has jurisdiction over cases specifically referred to it by Congress. These so-called "congressional reference" cases require the court to review the cases and report back to Congress with recommendations for how they should be resolved. They are cases the court gets not because a plaintiff files the case before the court but because Congress asks the court to look at the case and report back. Specifically, the court is to tell Congress whether what the taxpayer is asking for is "a legal or equitable claim against the United States, or a gratuity." In other words, does the taxpayer have a legitimate gripe or is a taxpayer looking for something for nothing, a gratuity?

> In 1949 the Veterans Administration awarded a contract to JL Simmons Company Inc. for a construction project. The government

specifications were defective, and Simmons filed a claim for damages. When the case was finally resolved in 1969, Simmons was awarded damages but no interest. (It wasn't until 1978 that contractors could get interest on their claims.) And since the case was heard in the 1950s and 1960s, due process was different: Contractors didn't have the right to cross-examine government witnesses at a claims hearing. All the contractor could do was submit written views on the government's evidence. To win a congressional reference case, the contractor here had to prove that, decades ago, the lack of interest was the results of "wrongful or negligent conduct by the government." It also had to prove that the absence of cross-examination was "a travesty of justice." The contractor could not prove these. Although the one-sided proceeding before the board "undoubtedly seems out of step under today's standards, those procedures were consistent with the approach used by many agencies at the time." Nor could Simmons prove that this "travesty of justice" caused it to incur most of the interest requested. That was not true. The reason the Simmons case had dragged out through the 1950s and 1960s was that Congress and the Supreme Court were grappling with the issue of how government contract claims should be handled. So the court could find no wrongful conduct by the government and concluded that any damage award like interest would be a gratuity.[9]

WHEN MUST A CLAIM BE FILED?

Claims have two statutes of limitations or deadlines: a deadline to file claims with the contracting officer in the first place and then a deadline to appeal a contracting officer's final decision to the appropriate BCA or the CFC.

Statute of Limitations for Filing Claims with the Contracting Officer

A claim by a contractor has to be filed "within 6 years after the accrual of the claim."[10]

Accrual is the key word here. Unfortunately, Congress did not give us a definition of *accrual*. So FAR wrote one:

> "'Accrual of a claim' means the date when all events, that fix the alleged liability of either the Government or the contractor and permit assertion of the claim, were known or should have been

known. For liability to be fixed, some injury must have occurred. However, monetary damages need not have been incurred."[11]

Because this 6-year limitation applies only to contracts entered into on or after October 1, 1995,[12] there have not yet been many decisions interpreting it.

One thing is clear—when the statute of limitations starts on breach of contract claims:

> "In breach of contract actions, accrual generally occurs at the time of breach."[13]

As always, there are exceptions.

A construction company sued the government for breach of contract because the government did not tell the contractor about asbestos. Asbestos injuries typically take years to show up in workers. The CFC concluded that since any worker injuries would show up later, years after the government's alleged breach of contract, the contractor would have an opportunity to file claims for those injuries in the future. "Although a claim for breach of contract ordinarily accrues, and the statute of limitations begins to run, at the time of the breach, this is not always the case. . . . a claim does not accrue until the claimant has suffered damages. . . . the Federal Acquisition Regulations ('FAR') provide that a claim does not accrue until all events that fix the liability of the government occur. For liability to be fixed, some injury must have occurred. Accordingly, the statute of limitations for the plaintiff's claims based on exposure to asbestos and lead and for cleanup costs and penalties will not begin to run until damages or injuries arise."[14]

There is a rare exception to the strict application of the 6-year limit: equitable tolling. This principle holds that a statute of limitations is tolled or suspended where it would be unjust to rigorously apply a statute of limitations. The CAFC discussed this exception and noted that this principle applies

> "where the claimant has actively pursued his judicial remedies by filing a defective pleading during the statutory period, or where the complainant had been induced or tricked by his adversary's misconduct into allowing the filing deadline to pass. We have generally

been much less forgiving in receiving late filings where the claimant failed to exercise due diligence in preserving his legal rights."

Bonneville appealed a contracting officer's final decision to the GSBCA. But after the Board let Bonneville withdraw its appeal, and Bonneville went to the CFC, the CFC concluded that it had no jurisdiction because Bonneville had already elected to go to the Board. Bonneville then went back to the Board, which concluded that Bonneville's return to the Board was long after the 90-day deadline for appeals to the Board and that Bonneville had missed the statute of limitations. The appeals court agreed. Bonneville's situation "falls far short of the situations in which equitable tolling has been applied." Here the deadline was not missed for minor technical or inadvertent mistakes, nor did Bonneville tell the Board that if the court's suit was dismissed, it would seek to reinstate its appeal to the Board. Nor was there any claim that government officials had advised Bonneville to withdraw from the Board. "What the record suggests is that Bonneville dismissed its suit because it had decided that it wished to pursue the alternative remedy of litigation in court rather than before the board." Bonneville's actions were comparable to "a garden variety claim of excusable neglect" that could not be cured by applying equitable tolling.[15]

Statute of Limitations for Appealing a Contracting Officer's Final Decision

A contracting officer's final decision may be appealed to a BCA within 90 days of receipt by the contractor or to the CFC within 1 year of receipt.

But the statute of limitations does not run unless the government can prove that the contractor actually got the contracting officer's final decision.

A contractor does not officially receive a contracting officer's final decision until there is an "objective indicia" of its receipt. If a contracting officer's final decision is faxed, the government should confirm receipt with a follow-up phone call.

In November 2001, a contracting officer sent Riley & Ephriam Construction Company, Inc., (R&E) a contracting officer's final decision denying R&E an equitable adjustment. The decision was mailed to

R&E's P.O. box, as well as faxed to R&E's attorney. But R&E received neither. Its attorney never received the fax. And the mailed document, sent "return receipt requested," was never picked up at the post office and was eventually returned to the contracting officer, return receipt unsigned. The contracting officer tried again later and succeeded, at least with a fax that the attorney received on January 30, 2002.

More than a year after the contracting officer sent the decision but less than a year after the attorney received the decision, R&E filed suit in the U.S. Court of Federal Claims. After the court said the appeal was too late, the contractor appealed to the CAFC, which reversed the lower court's conclusion. It concluded that R&E's clock started with the re-sent fax of January 2002. FAR makes the government give the contractor a copy of a final decision by "certified mail, return receipt requested, or by any other method that provides evidence of receipt." Significantly, there must be "objective indicia of receipt by the contractor." Here, the government's fax and mail efforts resulted in no such "objective indicia." R&E's lawyer never got the contracting officer's fax: "the government cannot produce a fax confirmation sheet for the November 27, 2001, fax to R&E's attorney. Moreover, we cannot infer receipt from evidence of transmission" that the government had. "Proof of message exit from a transmitting machine cannot serve as a proxy for proof of actual receipt of the sent message by a remote receiving terminal." The appeals court wanted "confirmation" of the fax and offered a simple solution: make a phone call. "All the government has to do is make a simple telephone call to the contractor or its authorized representative to affirm actual receipt of the fax. This simple step would give the government the assurance of actual receipt that the regulation requires it to have." Nor was there any proof that the mailed final decision had been received by the contractor. The unsigned return receipt showed that the contractor had not received the final decision.[16]

APPEAL TO THE CFC OR BCA

If a contractor is not happy with the contracting officer's final decision, the contractor has a choice: It can appeal to the CFC or to a BCA.

But it cannot appeal to both, as shown by "the election doctrine" described below.

And when a contractor does bring an appeal of the contracting officer's decision, it's a whole new ballgame on appeal. On appeal, the case is tried *de novo*. This means that the contracting officer's decision is by no means binding when it is appealed.

The significant downside of this for a contractor is that appealing a contracting officer's decision can be risky. If the contracting officer has, in effect, given the contractor at least half a loaf of bread, an appeal of that decision could end up with the contractor's having no bread at all. Because the case is *de novo*, the contractor has no guarantee that appealing the contracting officer's final decision has no downside—that is, there is no guarantee that an appeal can result in only a win or at least no loss. As we will see, a contractor can come away from an appeal of the contracting officer's decision to a court or board with much less money or with no money at all.

Election Doctrine

Contractors wanting to appeal a contracting officer's final decision have a choice of two options. They can appeal to a BCA or file suit in the CFC. They can't do both, no matter how unfortunate that might be.

Recall the earlier example of Bonneville Associates. Bonneville appealed a contracting officer's final decision to the General Services Board of Contract Appeals. But before the Board could act on the case, Bonneville asked the Board to dismiss the case without prejudice, which the Board did. Bonneville then went to the CFC, which dismissed the suit on the basis that Bonneville had previously elected to appeal to the Board. The CAFC upheld this decision. Bonneville then went back to the Board. But the Board concluded that it, too, had no jurisdiction. Because the Board's earlier dismissal without prejudice was treated as if Bonneville had never been before the Board in the first place, Bonneville's return to the Board was deemed a new appeal filed years after the 90-day time limit imposed on such appeals. Dissenting from the Board's opinion, Chairman Daniels opined, "It must have been a decision like this one that caused Dickens' Mr. Bumble to say, 'If the law supposes that, the law is an ass.'" The CAFC upheld the board's decision. Having tried to go down both roads, Bonneville ended up going down neither.[17]

But a contractor cannot elect a claim forum that has no jurisdiction. If the forum has no jurisdiction, there has been no election, so the contractor can appeal to the other forum.

Edward Grinnell had a contract with the U.S. Postal Service. While he was performing the contract, he got a contracting officer's final decision denying him access to the Postal Service's facilities. The final decision, however, did not state (as required by law) the appeal rights he had. Regardless, he appealed to the Postal Service Board of Contract Appeals but did so after the 90-day deadline for appeals to a BCA had passed. He thought he might have a shot at the Board's hearing his appeal even though it was late because precedent gave some deadline flexibility when the contracting officer's final decision had omitted the appeal rights. But he was not sure, so to cover his bets he also appealed to the CFC, this time within the 1-year deadline for CFC appeals.

The government asked the CFC to throw his CFC case out because Grinnell had already "elected" to go to the BCA. The court refused, concluding that no election had been made because it was not clear that the Board had jurisdiction of his late appeal: "An election does not become binding until the selected forum determines that it has jurisdiction over the appeal. The mere filing . . . of an appeal with the appropriate board of contract appeals was not a binding election . . . and did not bar the subsequent filing of a claim with the Claims Court *if* it was determined by the board that the contractor's appeal to the board was untimely. Accordingly, under this doctrine, 'a contractor's choice to pursue an appeal in a forum lacking jurisdiction is *not* a binding election.'" In this case, there could be no binding election until the BCA decided whether it had jurisdiction over Grinnell's appeal: "In light of the fact that the BCA has not yet rendered a decision on the timeliness of Plaintiff's appeal, the court finds that Plaintiff has not made a binding election."[18]

De novo

The CDA says that "any action under [the CDA] . . . shall proceed *de novo* in accordance with the rules of the appropriate court."[19] This means that the parties start with a clean slate.[20]

The practical aspect of this is that the contractor has to decide whether to take what the contracting officer has given and run with it or gamble and go to the board or the court for more. It is a gamble because going for more jeopardizes what the contracting officer has already given. For example, if the contracting officer awards the contractor $20,000 but the contractor thinks it should get $40,000, the contractor could appeal the contracting officer's decision and try to get the extra $20,000 from the board or the court. But the contractor could fail to get the extra $20,000, and worse than that, the board could order the contractor to return to the government the original $20,000 the contracting officer has already awarded. The contracting officer's giving the contractor some money does not guarantee the contractor that it will get at least that much by appealing to a board or court.

APPEAL TO THE CAFC

The final stage of the process is that a decision by the CFC or a board can be appealed to the Court of Appeals for the Federal Circuit.

At this stage, the appeal is not *de novo*. The appeals court usually will not second-guess what the board or the court has done. All the appeals court looks for is whether the court or board had "substantial evidence" for its decision.

The only time that the appeals court totally second-guesses the court or board is on contract interpretation issues. Regardless of what the forum below concluded, the appeals court can reach its own conclusion and have the final word on what contract terms mean.

Endnotes

1. *Cubic Copr. v. United States,* 20 Cl.Ct. 610, 616 (1990).

2. FAR 2.101.

3. *Eaton Contract Services, Inc.,* ASBCA No. 52,888, 02-2 BCA ¶ 32023.

4. *Id.*

5. *Clearwater Constructors Inc. v. The United States,* 71 Fed.Cl. 25 (2003).

6. *Record Steel and Construction Inc. v. The United States,* 62 Fed. Cl.508 (2004).

7. *TLT Construction Corp.,* ASBCA No. 53,769, 02-BCA ¶ 31,969.

8. *Washington Development Group v. GSA,* GSBCA no. 15137, 03-2 BCA ¶ 32,319.

9. *J. L. Simmons Company Inc., v. The United States,* 60 Fed.Cl. 388 (2004).

10. 41 U.S.C. § 605(a).

11. FAR 33.201.

12. 41 U. S.C. § 251 note.

13. *Arakaki v. The United States*, 62 Fed. Cl. 244, 254 (2004).

14. *SAB Const., Inc. v. The United States*, 66 Fed.Cl. 77, 88 (2005).

15. *Bonneville Associates v. GSA*, 165 F.3d 1360 (Fed.Cir.1999).

16. *Riley and Ephriam Construction Co. Inc. v. The United States*, 408 F.3d 1369 (Fed. Cir.2005).

17. *Bonneville Assocs. v. The United States*, 43 F.3d 649 (Fed.Cir.1994); Bonneville Assocs., Ltd. P'ship v. Barram, 165 F.3d 1360, 1362 (Fed.Cir.1999).

18. *Edward Grinnell v. The United States*, 71 Fed.Cl. 202 (2006).

19. 41 U.S.C. § 609(a)(3).

20. *Wilner v. The United States*, 24 F.3d 1397, 1401-02 (Fed. Cir. 1994).

Chapter 12

Costs of Litigation

CONTENTS

The cost of lawyers and other litigation costs are both a known and unknown element in any lawsuit. They are known costs because everybody knows that a lawsuit costs money. They're an unknown element because exactly how much the legal costs will be is often unknown to contractors and certainly unknown to contracting officers, who think the salaries of their legal staffs are free to the agency.

Known or unknown, litigation expenses costs can be high. So naturally this issue comes up: "Who's going to pay attorneys' fees?"

The British do it one way: The loser pays. For many reasons, including the belief that the British system discourages the underdog from suing a wealthy big business, the American system is different. The American way is that each side pays its own costs. But in American courts, there are a few exceptions to the American way.

One exception involves frivolous lawsuits. If a judge considers a lawsuit frivolous, the judge can make the frivolous plaintiff pay the defendant's attorneys' fees.

Two other exceptions apply to government contract lawsuits. These exceptions are based on the Equal Access to Justice Act (EAJA) and the Competition in Contracting Act (CICA). In looking at these laws, it's important to keep this distinction in mind: EAJA applies to claims before the courts and boards of contract appeals, and to protests before the Court of Federal Claims (CFC). We'll look at EAJA in Section A.

Protests to the Government Accountability Office (GAO) are covered by a different law, CICA. When Congress passed CICA in 1984, it allowed GAO to recommend that an agency pay attorneys' fees in protests. When an agency would have to pay attorneys' fees and how much an agency would have to pay are different from EAJA, as we will see in Section B.

EAJA

In 1981 Congress passed the Equal Access to Justice Act (EAJA). This law allowed a judge to require the government to pay attorneys' fees under certain circumstances. Previously, the government had been immune from paying attorneys' fees because of sovereign immunity; Congress had not previously consented to the federal government's being sued for attorneys' fees and having to pay them. EAJA changed that.

One of the driving forces behind EAJA was a belief in Congress that government lawyers on salary could take advantage of small businesses and individuals by forcing them to spend large amounts of money to sue the government or to defend against a government lawsuit when the government did not have a good legal argument. On the other hand, Congress did not want to prevent the government from defending close cases or from making novel legal arguments.

Nor did Congress want litigants against the government to recoup huge amounts of tax dollars for their attorneys' fees.

These beliefs led to the three requirements of EAJA: an **eligible party** who is a **prevailing party** in a lawsuit against the government must recover attorneys' fees not to exceed $125 an hour unless the government has a legal position that is "**substantially justified**." In this section we look at the three elements of EAJA: an eligible party, a prevailing party, and a substantially justified legal position.

Prevailing Party

Winning the case is one requirement Congress put on vendors trying to recover attorneys' fees. When Congress passed the EAJA, allowing winning vendors to recover their attorneys' fees, it required a winning party to prove that it was a "prevailing party."

But there are many ways of winning a case—some obvious, some subtle. The decisions show three ways for a vendor to be a prevailing party.

A Win on the Merits

The most obvious way for a contractor to win is for a judge to look at the merits of the case and rule in favor of the contractor.

Court-Ordered Consent Decrees

Another way a winning vendor can become a "prevailing party" is for both sides to agree to a settlement agreement and have a court issue an order dealing with the settlement. These court-ordered consent decrees change the legal relationship between the parties and thus are considered a "win" that makes the vendor a prevailing party.

An Equivalent of One of the Above

The two above "obvious" victories are not the only ways to become a prevailing party. A third way is to get a court to impose "the equivalent" of a judgment on the merits or a consent decree.

Typically, the equivalent argument comes up when the government "voluntarily" gives the vendor some or all of the relief for which the vendor had asked the court. If the government voluntarily gives in and does what the plaintiff asked the court to do, has the lawsuit had any impact? If the lawsuit brought about no change in the legal relationship between the parties, how can a protester claim to be a prevailing party?

Not a prevailing party: No change in the legal relationship

Rice Services Ltd. lost a Navy contract and asked the Court of Federal Claims to stop performance on it, award a new one, and stop the Navy from exercising any options with the new vendor. But before the court had made any ruling on the merits of the protest, the Navy itself fixed Rice's problem, opened up discussions with Rice and the other offerors, and awarded a new contract. Without ruling on the merits of the protest, the court issued an order concluding that it no longer had to rule on the protest because the Navy had solved the problem all by itself without any court involvement. Rice's attempt to get attorneys' fees was denied. The CAFC concluded that Rice was not a prevailing party. To be the "equivalent" to a merits ruling or a consent decree, a court order must "materially change" the legal relationship of the parties. Here, "the Navy acted unilaterally in reevaluating the bids before the lower court made any rulings. In addition, all the offerors, including Rice, responded to the Navy's reevaluation before the lower court had done anything. And finally, the lower court's order itself said the Navy had voluntarily fixed the problem."[1]

Prevailing party: Change in the legal relationship

When the IRS issued a solicitation for debt collection services, it limited the solicitation to vendors that were currently doing debt collection for IRS. A vendor not currently working for the IRS protested to the CFC. After a hearing, the court issued an order advising the parties that it intended to enjoin the solicitation. But before the order was issued, the government cancelled the solicitation, so the court eventually dismissed the case. The court concluded that the protester was a prevailing party. The court said its order had "had sufficient judicial imprimatur to materially alter the legal relationship between Universal and the Government. . . . The matter had been fully briefed, and the court and the parties agreed that no hearing was necessary . . . this court's conclusions exhibited an essence of finality and were made late in the process. Moreover, we stated a legal conclusion: 'excluding vendors on the Schedule that do not have current task orders irrespective of their experience or ability is arbitrary and capricious in the circumstances presented.' Had defendant not performed the curative act right away, we were prepared to issue an opinion granting injunctive relief to plaintiff."[2]

Eligible Party

To be an eligible party, a prevailing party has to fall into one of the following categories:

> (i) an individual whose net worth did not exceed $2,000,000 at the time the civil action was filed, or (ii) any owner of an unincorporated business, or any partnership, corporation, association, unit of local government, or organization, the net worth of which did not exceed $7,000,000 at the time the civil action was filed, and which had not more than 500 employees at the time the civil action was filed.[3]

Substantially Justified Position

EAJA makes the government pay if its litigation position on the facts and the law is not "substantially justified."

"'Substantially justified' does not mean 'justified to a high degree,' but rather 'justified in substance or in the main'—that is, justified to a degree that could satisfy a reasonable person. . . . The Government's position must have a reasonable basis both in law and fact."[4]

When the federal government lost a case because it relied on information—wrong information—from a local government, the government was substantially justified.

GSA typically promises to pay any real estate tax increase imposed by a local jurisdiction on landlords renting space to the government. After GSA signed a lease with Airport Building Associates (ABA) in fall 1997, the lessor asked GSA for the tax increase over taxes ABA had paid in 1999. GSA checked with the local tax assessors, who told GSA in effect that the lessor should start getting tax increases at the earliest only for taxes paid in 2000. Relying on the word and expertise of the local tax officials, GSA refused to pay ABA for any increase in taxes paid in 1999.

But it turned out that the local tax collectors were wrong. Their opinion was based on the mistaken belief that only one property was involved when in fact several properties were involved. So GSA lost to ABA on the tax increase issue at the Board. ABA came back to the Board for attorneys' fees. Now ABA lost. Even though GSA had lost the earlier case, it had a decent argument. The Board said, "We cannot fault the Government for relying on the information provided by the County Assessor's Office. Any reasonable person would have done the same. Neither are we surprised that the Government, relying on the information it so diligently garnered at the outset of this dispute and during discovery, brought a motion for summary relief. In a well-reasoned and documented opposition to the motion, counsel for ABA convinced us that the motion should be denied. . . . We saw nothing unjustified on the part of GSA in standing firm on its position." The Board refused to award ABA its attorneys' fees.[5]

But the government's position is not substantially justified when the government has bad facts and a contracting officer makes mistakes.

After 25 years of being in a rented office building, the government moved out. According to the landlord, A&B Limited Partnership, the government left the building in shambles. And to prove its point, the landlord had pictures of the building's condition. A&B also gave GSA a seven-page letter describing the damaged condition of the building and asked for $239,000 to repair the building. GSA didn't agree with the landlord. GSA thought it owed A&B only $16,032. Unfortunately for GSA, it did not have much information on the condition of the building when GSA left it. The contracting officer did not inspect the building after the government moved out. The GSA property manager's inspection was labeled by the board to be "cursory," lasting only a half-hour, and he had made no notes of his inspection. These were Government Mistake No. 1: little effort and little documentation.

Adding to the lack of government effort and documentation was the government's belief of what was permissible "fair wear and tear" by the government employees after 25 years of being there. For example, the government thought that leaving wires dangling from the ceiling and putting holes in walls and concrete floors could be considered normal wear and tear. Relying on these bad facts, bad law, and little effort, the government fought the case and lost. The landlord came back for attorneys' fees and won. The board said that the government's argument "was based on assumptions of agency employees which were without any justification whatsoever. The employees' views as to the agency's liability were predicated on cursory investigation, extravagant ideas of the critical question of what constitutes normal wear and tear, and admittedly erroneous arithmetic." The Board awarded the landlord over $31,000 for attorneys' fees and costs of the litigation.[6]

Amount

The EAJA sets the hourly rate at $125. But that rate can be increased by cost of living or special circumstances.

After winning a protest against HUD, the protester, Chapman, came back to the court trying to get more than $28,000 in attorneys' fees it had spent in winning the case. Specifically, it wanted $18,522.46 in fees for Chapman's lawyer on the case (74 hours billed at $250.00 per hour) and $8,325.00 for its in-house counsel (37 hours billed at $225.00 per hour).

The EAJA limits attorneys' fees to $125 per hour but lets a court increase that rate based on ". . . the cost of living or a special factor, such as the limited availability of qualified attorneys for the proceedings involved. . . ." Chapman asked the court to allow payment of its asked-for rates based on both exceptions but ended up with a partial increase based on one of them, the COLA. Using the Department of Labor's Consumer Price Index March 1996 as the baseline, the court increased the statutory $125 per hour to $152.46. This totaled $15,108.78 for the lawyers' time. All the court had to say about the second adjustment factor was nice words for the lawyers—but no money. "The attorney work product in this litigation was excellent, but bid protest litigation does not require the distinctive knowledge or specialized skill required for further enhancement of the statutory EAJA rate. Legal competence in administrative law is generally sufficient for bid protest litigation and this does not qualify for rate enhancement."[7]

CICA

GAO can recommend that an agency give a protester attorneys' fees and protest costs.

> (d) If GAO determines that a solicitation, proposed award, or award does not comply with statute or regulation, it may recommend that the contracting agency pay the protester the costs of:
>
>> (1) Filing and pursuing the protest, including attorneys' fees and consultant and expert witness fees; and
>>
>> (2) Bid and proposal preparation.
>
> (e) If the contracting agency decides to take corrective action in response to a protest, GAO may recommend that the

agency pay the protester the reasonable costs of filing and pursuing the protest, including attorneys' fees and consultant and expert witness fees.[8]

When a protester wins at GAO, one remedy is to put the solicitation process back on track and put the protester back into the solicitation. This is a victory of sorts for the protester. Usually that victory is enough.

But sometimes a protester gets a double dip. Not only does the agency take "corrective" action, like fixing the solicitation the way the protester wanted in the first place, but the agency also has to pay the protester's costs.

Under 4 CFR 21.8(e), quoted above, GAO may recommend that the agency pay costs when an agency unduly delays taking corrective action in the face of a clearly meritorious protest. GAO's rule

> "is intended to prevent inordinate delay in investigating the merits of a protest and taking corrective action once an error is evident, so that a protester will not incur unnecessary effort and expense in pursuing its remedies before GAO."[9]

Congress did not want agencies needlessly running up the money protesters would pay to protest an agency decision. So it let GAO recommend that an agency pay a protester's costs if the agency "unduly delays taking corrective action in the face of a clearly meritorious protest." What do these three critical phrases mean?

Undue Delay

What is *undue delay*? There is **no** undue delay, generally, if an agency admits defeat before it submits its report on the protest to GAO.[10] There **is** undue delay if an agency waits more than 2 months to fix things, according to GAO.

> "The record here shows that the agency filed three requests for dismissal, two of them after we had already informed the Air Force that we were treating BFI's challenge to the estimates as timely. Despite the acknowledged validity of the protester's questions and the agency's own professed concerns about the estimates, the agency made no reasonable factual investigation of the basis for the estimates for more than 2 months after the filing of the protest. That investigation occurred only in response to our questions, which

essentially repeated those asked by the protester in its response to the agency's third motion to dismiss."[11]

In another case, GAO found this:

> "In resolving requests for declaration of entitlement to costs following corrective action by contracting agency, the General Accounting Office does not deem 38 working days taken by the agency before taking corrective action to be an undue delay where four separate protests were filed simultaneously against the agency; the protests involved complex and detailed evaluation issues; the agency had to review and organize numerous documents to respond to the protester's document production requests; four separate good faith dismissal requests by the agency had to be resolved; and the agency diligently and quickly responded to all requests by our Office to expedite the discovery and protest process."[12]

Corrective Action

But delay in an agency's studying a protest isn't enough. The critical error an agency must make is delay in taking corrective action on a valid protest. A recent GAO decision gives one answer: When an agency simply lets the protested contract die, making the protest a moot issue, an agency is not taking corrective action that may let a protester get protest costs.

REMSA, Inc., protested the use of an option to a contract issued by the National Oceanic and Atmospheric Administration (NOAA) for fishery observer services. As the protester, REMSA, and the agency argued over whether the option was beyond the scope of a competitor's contract and whether the government should have competed its needs and not used an option, the contracting officer found himself with not enough time to thoroughly review the option, so he let the contract expire and never exercised the option. But he didn't tell his lawyers right away, so the agency and the protester continued the protest fight for another 28 days after the contract expired. Since there was no contract and therefore no option, the protest was dismissed by GAO as academic.

REMSA came back to GAO for protest costs because the agency had not taken "corrective action." GAO granted that the parties had continued to fight needlessly for weeks after the contract had expired. But the agency did not take any corrective action in the face of the protest. It simply let the protested contract die, and it did so without regard to the protest: "The administrative contracting officer states that as a result of an administrative lapse by the procuring activity, a request to exercise options under either contract was not submitted to him until April 30, the day on which the contract expired. The contracting officer explains that he did not have sufficient time to obtain the necessary contractor consent and legal review prior to the time the contracts expired and, therefore, he allowed the contracts to expire."[13]

Clearly Meritorious Protest

Losing a protest does not automatically mean the agency pays protest costs. The government is entitled to make losing arguments as long as those arguments are good ones. The government will pay only where the protest is clearly meritorious. "A protest is clearly meritorious when a reasonable agency inquiry into the protest allegations would show facts disclosing the absence of a defensible legal position. For protest to be clearly meritorious, the issue involved must not be a close question. Rather, the record must establish that the agency prejudicially violated a procurement statute or regulation."[14]

In one case, GAO found a protest to be clearly meritorious.

"The solicitation the Army used required vendors for bus services to have a sufficient number of buses currently available. The Army, however, awarded the contract to a company even though the equipment was on order. 'In the case at hand, the record clearly shows that the agency's determination that the winner's proposal was overall technically acceptable—and that it met the solicitation's requirements concerning the equipment factor—was inconsistent with the stated evaluation factors.' The competitor's successful protest clearly raised the issue of whether the winner had the buses currently available. The company clearly argued that the winner 'did not, and does not yet, possess such buses.'"[15]

Amount

One remedy GAO can give a successful protester is paying the protester's "reasonable" costs of successfully protesting. If the successful protester is a large business, the hourly rate is capped at $150. But if the protester is a small business, $475 an hour for a protest lawyer is reasonable.

In CourtSmart's attorneys' fees claim for $213,434, three items became important: the hourly rate for the lawyers, the hourly rate for a paralegal, and the cost of the time spent by CourtSmart to simply get all these protest costs back. Lawyer's hourly rate: GAO will pay attorneys' fees if they are "reasonable" considering "the customary fee charged for similar work in the community, as well as the experience, reputation and ability of the practitioner. . . . In doing so, where relevant and appropriate, we will consider the fee rates found allowable by our Office in similarly complex proceedings." CourtSmart asked for an hourly rate of $475. CourtSmart gave GAO an article in a legal newspaper surveying 19 firms in the Washington, D.C. area showing that hourly rates for partners ranged from $185 to $750. "The highest rates for partners for all but two of these firms were in excess of $500." GAO concluded that the $475 rate was reasonable.[16]

Endnotes

1. *Rice Services, Ltd. v. The United States*, 405 F.3d 1017 (2005).

2. *Universal Fidelity LP v. The United States*, 70 Fed.Cl. 310 (2006).

3. 28 U.S.C.A. § 2412.

4. *Pierce v. Underwood*, 487 U.S. 552, 565, 108 S.Ct. 2541, 2550, 101 L.Ed.2d 490 (1988).

5. *Airport Building Associates v. GSA*, GSBCA No. 16429-C(15535), 04-2 BCA ¶ 32,773.

6. *A&B Limited Partnership v. GSA*, No. 16322-C (15208), 04-2 BCA ¶ 32,641.

7. *The Chapman Law Firm v. The United States*, 66 Fed.Cl. 422 (2005).

8. 4 CFR 21.8.

9. *Williamson County Ambulance Service, Inc. Costs*, B-293811.4, Sep. 16, 2004.

10. *The Sandi-Sterling Consortium–Costs*, B-296246.2, Sep. 20, 2005, 2005 CPD ¶ 173.

11. *Browning-Ferris Industries of Hawaii, Inc.–Costs*, B-278,051, B-278051.2, April 29, 1998.

12. *Carlson Wagonlit Travel--Request for Declaration of Entitlement to Costs*, B-266,337, B-266,338, B-266,346, B-266337.3, B-266338.3, B-266346.3, July 3, 1996, 96-2 CPD ¶ 99.

13. *REMSA, Inc.–Costs*, B-293771.2, Sep. 3, 2004.

14. *Shindong–A Express Tour Company, Ltd.–Costs*, B-292459.3, March 25, 2004.

14. *CourtSmart Digital Systems, Inc.–Costs*, B-292995.7, March 18, 2005.

Index